GREAT LIVES OBSERVED

Gerald Emanuel Stearn, *General Editor*

EACH VOLUME IN THE SERIES VIEWS THE CHARACTER AND ACHIEVEMENT OF A GREAT WORLD FIGURE IN THREE PERSPECTIVES—THROUGH HIS OWN WORDS, THROUGH THE OPINIONS OF HIS CONTEMPORARIES, AND THROUGH RETROSPECTIVE JUDGMENTS—THUS COMBINING THE INTIMACY OF AUTOBIOGRAPHY, THE IMMEDIACY OF EYEWITNESS OBSERVATION, AND THE OBJECTIVITY OF MODERN SCHOLARSHIP.

MILTON CANTOR, *editor of this volume in the Great Lives Observed series, is Associate Professor of History at the University of Massachusetts. He has written numerous other books on the men and problems of American History.*

GREAT LIVES OBSERVED

HAMILTON

Edited by MILTON CANTOR

*Hamilton is really a Colossus to the anti-republican party.
Without numbers, he is an host within himself.*

—THOMAS JEFFERSON

A SPECTRUM BOOK

PRENTICE-HALL, INC., ENGLEWOOD CLIFFS, N.J.

To my children, David, Elisabeth,
and Daniel—the renewers of optimism

Current printing (last number): 10   9   8   7   6   5   4   3   2   1

C–13-372292-9

P–13-372284-8

Library of Congress Catalog Card Number: 72-133054

Printed in the United States of America

PRENTICE-HALL INTERNATIONAL, INC. (*London*)
PRENTICE-HALL OF AUSTRALIA, PTY. LTD. (*Sydney*)
PRENTICE-HALL OF CANADA, LTD. (*Toronto*)
PRENTICE-HALL OF INDIA PRIVATE LIMITED (*New Delhi*)
PRENTICE-HALL OF JAPAN, INC. (*Tokyo*)

Contents

PART THREE
HAMILTON IN HISTORY

Introduction

The overthrow of British colonial rule was the signal for the realignment of conflicting forces in American life. The Revolution had temporarily ended the great debate over the *question* of union (now the *nature* of the union became *the* issue), over how much power to give to the Empire's parts and how much to the whole, how much to local and how much to central authority. Armed conflict had evoked deep feelings of nationalism and gave a sense of purpose to a heretofore divided and fractious people. For a few frenetic years, localism yielded to solidarity, petty particularism to national need. But the Revolution also severed traditional ties between colonies and motherland, and, if it made a greater degree of nationalization seem essential for the conduct of hostilities, it also gave effective power to the state governments, making them the ultimate locus of sovereignty. Even before the Revolution ended, many prominent Americans—lawyers like John Jay, merchants like Pelatiah Webster, poets like Timothy Dwight, schoolmasters like Noah Webster, statesmen like George Washington—had concluded that the need to strengthen the central government was paramount; otherwise, it was believed, financial chaos and mob rule would bring down the struggling young republic.

No man was more conscious of the successive national crises, none more aware of the weaknesses of government under the Articles of Confederation, than Alexander Hamilton. For a decade, he had watched the storm clouds of disunion gathering as one disaster piled on another, and exerted himself to prevent what seemed almost inevitable—the dissolution of the fabric of government. The Articles, approved by Congress on November 15, 1777 (though not ratified by all the states until 1781), had been designed to guarantee that sovereign power would continue to reside in the states. In effect, they created a quasi-federal system and thereby reheated the debate that had first fired colonists and vexed Whitehall: namely, how to distribute power so as to reconcile liberty and order.

Specifically and immediately, the states failed to meet wartime requisitions set by the second Continental Congress; they refused to pay their financial levies in full or on time; they responded indifferently or erratically to congressional efforts to impose taxes; they refused to accept any imposts, any uniform regulation of commerce over which they lacked full control. After a brief moratorium during the opening years of Revolution, local fears and local suspicions again were on the ascendancy. Each state claimed it contributed more to the revolutionary cause than the

1

others; each was jealous of its neighbor. Together, they blocked all efforts to establish effective government. Congress, consequently, lacked power to make operative tax laws or to levy uniform duties or to retaliate against the commercial depredations of foreign powers; that is, it lacked the *sine qua non* of efficient government—the power to govern.

Nationalists were not alone responsible for the movement toward stronger central authority. Even the most sincere and energetic advocates of states rights were apprehensive over the erosion of effective national government; even they conceded that the Articles were imperfect and that, at a minimum, substantial changes were essential if the republic were to survive. But it remained for Alexander Hamilton to seize the initiative. Taking advantage of the 1786 Annapolis Convention—that gathering of delegates from five states which sought to reduce interstate trade rivalry —he urged a Constitutional Convention upon his listeners. In this year of political-financial crisis, of Shay's Rebellion in Massachusetts and creditor-debtor unrest everywhere, his proposal found a receptive audience.

What manner of man was he, this young New Yorker who, throughout the 1780s, had ceaselessly championed a unitary and coercive central government? His birth and boyhood in the West Indies, on Nevis in the British Leeward Islands, are vague and shadowy. His mother was of French Huguenot extraction who had left her husband after five years of marriage and, following a succession of lovers, met and lived for fifteen years with young James Hamilton, an indigent Scottish merchant. There is no record of marriage and we may assume that their offspring were illegitimate. Alexander Hamilton himself was born in 1755 (though evidence exists fixing his birth a year or two earlier). He left the islands in late 1772 (or early 1773), for Boston and then Elizabethtown, New Jersey, where he lived for a year. Ebullient, energetic and ambitious, Hamilton was not long for the provinces. He went on to New York City and, in 1773, to Kings College, then dominated by an Episcopal-Tory-lawyer circle that graduated most of the city's leading attorneys, as it would young Hamilton. He arrived in New York, as he had in Boston, without family or money, but he had the afflatus of youth, a sense of unique worth which denied the finality of failure; and he made friends quickly, mostly Episcopalians of some influence. Eventually this city would shower him with such rewards and such hatred as few men have acquired.

Hamilton was nothing yet, at least nothing fully formed or clear. Sentiment was only just hardening into conviction, knowledge into philosophy, autistic dreams into hard realities. Small wonder, then, that he behaved like someone from a remote island enclave. Witness, for instance, the marked Presbyterian zeal which he brought in his baggage and which, according to his college friend, Robert Troup, found him "praying upon his knees both night and morning." Eventually, he would discard such deep convictions and fall back upon a polite belief in religion, an absence of which, for him, encouraged social dislocation.

Turning to politics, the raw West Indian showed an early impulse toward empire, toward England and the authority of law and order, rather than toward revolution. Nor would his spirit ever wholly reject this incubus. But New York was a window on a larger world—in more ways than one for someone who was not doctrinaire. And the 1773 Tea Party prompted him to write an essay defending the Bostonians; they had no alternatives to their actions. Hamilton, to be sure, did not seek independence; he wrote this tract in the hope it could be avoided; that he wrote it is in itself significant, for it suggests that virile fraternity of ideas and actions which would mark his entire life.

Not easily relinquishing a belief in a constitutional relationship between England and the colonies, Hamilton nonetheless was among those college-student volunteers who drilled every morning in St. George's churchyard in the Spring of 1775. On August 23rd, the twenty-year-old militiaman came under fire for the first time. A year later, as an artillery captain, he was at work on the defenses of Manhattan Island. He would serve with distinction in the New York and New Jersey campaigns, join Washington's New York staff as a lieutenant colonel in 1777, cross the Delaware, freeze at Valley Forge, storm the last redoubt at Yorktown.

Like many colonists, Hamilton justified his actions as a defense of the traditional legal order against Parliamentary encroachments. Great Britain simply could not tax her colonies at will and without their consent, and the English argument of "virtual representation" was inapplicable to subjects across the seas. Westminster, in so taxing, violated the immutable "laws" of God and nature as well as the English constitution. This constitution, he declared, was only a variant of the laws of nature —which he defined as the accumulated wisdom of the English common law, a law evolving from unchanging dicta laid down by a divine hand— and neither crown nor Parliament could violate such law without "overleaping" their foundations.

Armed with both God and nature, Hamilton possessed an invincible sense of rectitude and self-confidence. No closet philosopher, he joined these radical theorems to practice, becoming one of Washington's "beardless boys" and thereby stepping from the comparative shadows onto military stage center. Preoccupied by the endless problems that beset the army after 1777, he nonetheless found time to woo and win Elizabeth Schuyler in 1780 and was welcomed into one of New York's leading families. By deft and urbane financial counselling, for his father-in-law and for Robert Morris, the Philadelphia financier, Hamilton won a reputation as a fiscal specialist. Nor did he ignore the local political scene. He even had opportunity to read carefully and critically the 1777 New York constitution. Its Senate, he cautioned, "will be liable to degenerate into a body purely aristocratical."

Hamilton's concern in 1777 was not protection of property so much as the "substantial happiness" of the people. He warned that the elitist charge of "unstable democracy" was an epithet frequently used by politicians (though no one would be more ready than Hamilton to invoke it in later years). In other words, Hamilton cannot be reduced to a flat-line drawing of a conservative. But he was staunchly so on the matter of mob action—the violence of the "unthinking multitude"—and it was a lifelong contention that democracy was the worst (and republicanism the best) of governments. Like most enlightened men of the eighteenth century, he recognized that human nature was not perfect, that "men are ambitious, vindictive and rapacious," and he sought a polity which would hedge in these qualities.

Even before 1780, inflation and lowering troop morale—with mutinies in Pennsylvania and New York—had begun to curb Hamilton's radical sympathies. That he was the son-in-law of Philip Schuyler, the Albany Federalist, contributed to this. For now Hamilton was on intimate terms with New York's great families, a member of the "Livingston Party," that remarkable group of conservatives who, toward the end of the war, served the cause of nationalism. Disillusioned by parlous political and economic conditions, he increasingly placed his trust in strong central government which seemed best suited to the need for sound fiscal planning and for preservation of the union—in peace as well as in wartime. In support of these ends, in a remarkable letter to Robert Morris, he urged the creation of a great moneyed corporation. Further serving the twin causes of sound finance and unitary central government, Hamilton, as "The Continentalist," exploded into print with a series of six essays for the *New York Packet* in 1781.

By the early 1780s, then, Hamilton was already on the way to becoming the most influential constitutionalist of his age. But he remained the man of action, and resented Washington's reluctance to give him an independent command. He became New York's receiver of taxes, serving as Morris' agent, until the state legislature saved him from this vexatious and unpopular job by electing him to Congress in 1782. At a time when creditors and soldiers were unpaid, when most states had enacted tariff acts and obstructed national revenue measures, Hamilton worked with Madison in the hopeless effort to give greater powers to Congress. But he recognized that even added commercial and financial authority was not enough; Congress's weaknesses were too fundamental to be cured by eliminating a single sore on the body politic. Indeed, he had already proposed a convention of the states which, he hoped, would grant greater income and power to the national legislature. Nonetheless, he continued to support every proposal to strengthen the Articles; admittedly inadequate, they remained the solvent holding the states together.

Quitting Congress in despair, Hamilton returned home in 1783 and was soon involved in litigation, *Rutgers v. Waddington,* a case which gave him a greater degree of notoriety than ever before. For Hamilton's rousing defense of his client, Tory merchant Benjamin Waddington, and of

Loyalist property rights generally, brought down popular wrath around him. In the course of his defense Hamilton also made a plea for nationalism and for judicial review of state legislation. As "Phocion," Hamilton also contributed to the hot debate over Tory rights. In the form of two pamphleteering letters, he made the chief newspaper defense of a policy of moderation toward former Tories, a stand which earned him public condemnation. But these letters helped block efforts to drive the Loyalists out of New York.

By the time of the *Rutgers* case, as Hamilton had predicted, government authority had eroded sharply, the Confederation was bankrupt, interest on the domestic debt was in default, congressional requisitions were ignored, the states owed sizable sums to their militia, to their citizens who furnished military supplies, and to holders of state paper issued during the war. Convinced that something had to be done, that the general government must be sovereign and coercive—otherwise there could be neither survival nor prosperity—Hamilton bent his great talents to these ends. He was increasingly in the limelight, at the center of plans for redirecting and refining national powers. Small wonder, then, that he saw the enormous possibilities inherent in the Annapolis Convention, an assembly convened in September 1786 to consider a uniform system of commercial regulation. — Hamilton was one of New York's three delegates to Annapolis. While not officially a member of the committee authorized to draft the convention's report, he in effect composed it. This report, displaying his characteristic audacity, proposed another convention—to meet in Philadelphia and to consider all the problems, financial, political as well as commercial, confronting the new nation. As a state legislator, Hamilton was in a position to do even more for the nationalist cause; and he took a leading role in persuading New York to send delegates to Philadelphia.

Hamilton went himself. Considering his seven-year advocacy of centrist rule, he eminently deserved to go. Yet he was hardly conspicuous, notwithstanding his reputation as the boldest and most dashing spokesman for nationalism. There was, to be sure, a brilliant five-hour oration; but it was delivered to a silent assembly, provoked no discussion, and won no converts—and, in sum, he played a minor role. Small wonder, since his views were atypical. Even the most extreme nationalist solution, the Virginia Plan, we may be sure was inadequate as far as Hamilton was concerned, while the constitution as finally approved he pronounced "a frail and worthless fabric." But the alternative was "anarchy and convulsion"; and so he made a positive contribution in the struggle over ratification.

Indeed, at the critically important New York State ratifying convention, meeting in Poughkeepsie in June 1788, Hamilton fought with fervor, gallantry, and astonishing tact, for a constitution which was not of his choosing. He boldly rallied the nationalist forces; he delayed action in the hope that New Hampshire and Virginia would ratify and that this news would influence the decision of his fellow New Yorkers; and, ably seconded by John Jay and Chancellor Livingston among others, he effectively countered the Clintonians who would press for "conditional" ratification. If he was at his parliamentary best as politician, rhetorician, tactician, he was at his most brilliant as a political theorist. For, together with Jay and Madison, Hamilton wrote the *Federalist* papers; indeed, he contributed the lion's share. These papers were designed to clarify the need for energetic central government and to influence New York voters in favor of the Constitution. They have survived such ephemeral motives, however, and rightly remain among the classics of political thought, possibly the most distinguished American contribution to the science of government.

Hamilton was by now a leader of the Society of the Cincinnati, director of the Bank of New York, speculator in northern and western New York lands, and inevitably associated with the State's aristocrats, with landholders and bankers, with military establishment and strong government. But it was Hamilton's gifts, not his associations, that carried him to national prominence; it was his ability to plan *and* execute, think *and* act, master the large *and* the detailed. He was an adroit organizer, a gifted orator, a leader of men, a writer of the first rank. These qualities helped bring New York to ratification. And they brought him to national prominence.

Hamilton bursts fully upon the scene in Washington's first Administration, becoming its directing intelligence. As the new Secretary of the Treasury, he was in a commanding position: he presided over the largest department; he had constant access to the chief executive; and he was responsible for handling the most critical problem of Washington's initial term in office; namely, to bring the new nation to its feet financially and to establish the proper relationship between the national economy and the government.

Hamilton, we have seen, had long believed that government must play an active and decisive role in economic affairs. It must shape an expanding self-sufficiency. It must encourage an economy balanced among agriculture, manufacturing and trade. It must create positive conditions for economic growth. It must, to accomplish these goals, enlist the support of the propertied and encourage their loyalty. Hamilton, then, sought to win the allegiance of business and financial circles, to bind these groups to the national interest, to make government and business partners. Hamilton's great Reports were designed to speed this happy development. That they were specific proposals, unlike the vague intentions of other leading public figures, gave their author a great advantage.

But these proposals would provide the burgeoning anti-Federalist press with a field day. Philip Freneau of the *National Gazette* led the opposition pack. His savage and highly personal invective—to which Hamilton replied, giving as much as he took—was hardly the New Yorker's only source of discomfort. The federalists were in deep trouble, their Southern wing crumbling under Republican attack. Jefferson's *cri de coeur* that Hamiltonian fiscal policy demeaned the husbandman and would destroy the American farm was proving very persuasive below the Potomac. Nor were Hamilton's affairs in order elsewhere. Even New York presented grave difficulties which, like the newspaper war, were partly of his own making. Hamilton had, in 1789, given his support to Rufus King for the United States Senate rather than to James Duane, the Livingston candidate, a tactical mistake which destroyed Federalist unity, something Governor George Clinton had unsuccessfully sought for some years. Meanwhile, Representative William Giles, a Jeffersonian planter-politician from Virginia, initiated the first of two congressional investigations (early in 1793, with the second about a year later) of the Treasury Department, seeking proof of financial irregularities.

Hamilton's sea of troubles was further stirred up by ongoing political squalls in New York and political-economic storms in Pennsylvania. New York's developments brought on the inevitable clash between two natural rivals. Hamilton and Burr had known one another since 1776. Marriage to Betsy Schuyler had vaulted Hamilton into a position of leadership among the State's Federalists—at a time when Burr was still satisfied with being a practicing attorney. Although they were courtroom adversaries, their relations seemed amicable enough, and they even worked together in 1789, supporting Judge Robert Yates, the moderate Republican, in an unsuccessful attempt to stop Clinton's campaign to be returned to the governor's office. But once Burr ventured into political waters, and he had by 1790, it was obvious that he could never aspire to more than second-in-command among New York's Federalists. Hence, while not a Jeffersonian, he was sufficiently equivocal about party loyalty to accept the offer of Governor Clinton, who was not one to nurse grudges, to be state attorney general.

Having been cheated of their senatorial seat earlier, the Livingstons, meanwhile, were in alliance with Clinton's forces. They put up Burr for Philip Schuyler's office, and the Hamilton-Schuyler forces suffered a stinging defeat. It led to an open declaration of factional war in the state and eventually in the nation; ultimately, it would bring death to Hamilton and disgrace to Burr.

Displaying his characteristic political infidelity, Burr expressed a willingness to run against Clinton for the highest State office in 1792. New York's Federalists were pleased by this development and urged Hamilton to support him, even sending General Schuyler to plead their case. But Hamilton, his hatred of Burr now public knowledge, refused to go along. He considered his New York rival totally "unprincipled, both as a public and private man." Even Clinton, egregious as he was, was preferable to this "embryo Caesar" whose "aim it is to mount at all costs to the full honors of the state." For Burr these were the first of a long train of disappointments; he would neither forget nor forgive.

Thwarting Burr was hardly Hamilton's only problem at this time. The excise tax, ironically first proposed by Madison and strongly recommended in the Treasurer's first Report, had provoked local resistance in Western Pennsylvania, where whisky was a means of exchange as well as a source of liquid refreshment, and a tax on it was resisted by the tough Ulster breed which inhabited the back country. These farmers proclaimed their right to distill without interference from federal revenue agents, a challenge welcomed by Hamilton—as a test of the government's right to collect this tax; that is, to do the unpopular but necessary thing. He drew up a report alleging that judicial processes had collapsed in the area and that force was essential; and 15,000 militiamen from four states were called out in August 1794. Temperamentally unsuited to a desk job and still seeking military glory and national union, Hamilton rode with Washington to Western militia headquarters at Carlisle. He made some bullying arrests of alleged insurgents and hoped, as he wrote to the President, "there will be found characters fit for examples." But the "rebellion" itself, much to his discomfort, melted away. Evidence linking it with prominent Pennsylvania Republicans, Albert Gallatin chief among them, was not forthcoming.

Party developments were accelerated by foreign crises after 1792, and administration concern shifted from domestic to oversea issues. Hamilton had taken over the Treasury Department at about the time that the Bastille fell before Parisian mobs. To many Americans, especially to Republicans, the French Revolution appeared to be a replica of their own and loyalty to both seemed the touchstone of patriotism. Worsening relations with Great Britain in 1794–1795 simply confirmed the Jeffersonians in their course. But Hamilton, who continually intruded into foreign affairs, did not share these feelings of kinship kindled by the French Revolution. To the contrary, he was from the first alarmed by French messianic rhetoric, fearful of its contagious potential for mob outbursts in the name of liberty. Regicide, the rise of the Jacobins, and the Terror confirmed these fears. The revolutionary spirit, he believed, could produce hostility to England and even, so he thought after February 1793—when British ambassador Hammond brought him the distressing news of a French declaration of war against England—drive the United States into an alliance with France.

For Hamilton, then, the arrival of Edmund Genet, the dashing young French ambassador, was a godsend. Genet had instructions to promote the use of American manpower and port facilities in his government's cause, which Hamilton shrewdly realized could be popularized as an illegal activity toward the end of American involvement in overseas conflict. In a series of newspaper articles—"No Jacobin" (in the *Daily Advertiser*)—

he charged Genet's conduct with being a violation of United States sovereignty. This conduct did indeed greatly embarrass Jefferson and facilitate Hamilton's task of mobilizing public opinion in favor of England or, at a minimum, of a neutral position.

Hamilton was presented with another opportunity to make foreign policy after Jefferson had resigned (and while Edmund Randolph was in office), when John Jay was sent to London in the hope of negotiating a treaty which would settle outstanding issues between the United States and Great Britain. Hamilton had fathered the initial proceedings, arranged Jay's appointment, composed his instructions, watched over developments with a fiercely proprietary spirit. He had a hard-headed grasp of existing diplomatic realities and acquiesced in the balance-of-power game. Consequently, he accepted British domination as a fact of life and readily believed that the island kingdom would again defeat her Continental rival. His aims for the United States were limited: neutrality, as he again and again stressed in his "No Jacobin" articles ("as strict a neutrality as may not be . . . contrary to public engagements") as well as the freest possible trade and foreign capital, both of which were desperately needed for national development.

These twin needs of neutral rights and national development required, so Hamilton believed, English friendship and conciliation. In so thinking, he was not viewing national policy from a pro-English perspective; he simply was opting for a foreign policy based upon national self-interest. Hence Jay's Treaty, however disappointing—and Hamilton was critical of it, especially articles twelve and thirteen—should be ratified (he wrote in a memorandum to Washington: "Remarks on the treaty of amity, commerce and navigation, made between the United States and Great Britain") since it closed the "controverted points between the two countries." In the storm which broke over the Treaty, Hamilton, as "Camillus," defended it against predictable attack—from the Republicans and from all nationalists who interpreted it as a surrender of American national interests.

The dispute over Jay's Treaty revealed deep factional rifts in Washington's second administration. It widened the division first opened by Hamilton's fiscal policies, the French Revolution, and the Anglo-French conflict, and helped to crystallize political parties by 1796. Hamilton was now in retirement. He had resigned in 1794, when the fabled years had passed, when only the drudgery of balancing the budget remained, and when he could quit "with honor." To be sure, the role of sage was not congenial to him and, being a leader among leaders, he was inevitably drawn into the political maneuverings of 1796.

That the Party did not split in two or, minimally, that Hamilton and Adams did not move to an open break, was due to a sudden deterioration of relations with France. Napoleon, having embarked on a supreme effort to crush England, invoked a "continental system" which was almost as menacing to American shipping as was English maritime practices. Always sensitive to military requirements, Hamilton urged that the armed forces be strengthened and that, rather than a beefed-up militia, a 25,000-man provisional army be created. As "Titus Manlius," he pushed this proposal in the daily press, alerting readers to the moral dangers posed by France. But Hamilton was not unequivocally belligerent—even after the Directory rejected Charles Pinckney, America's newly appointed minister. He also pressed for renewed negotiations. He did, to be sure, urge his friends in the cabinet, especially Oliver Wolcott, to consider war measures, but he proposed a three-man commission as well and even nominated Jefferson and Madison to it. Both of them declined appointments, but three commissioners did go abroad. They soon reported the bribe demand of three French agents—designated as XYZ—and their news electrified the nation.

— Though in retirement, Hamilton was inextricably enmeshed in national and international affairs, especially in the successive foreign policy crises of the late 1790s. Always prepared to act as an honest broker or to serve his country militarily, he even found leisure time to support the Alien and Sedition Acts, those measures inspired by Francophobia and by Federalist desire to ride down the opposition, and to condemn the Virginia and Kentucky Resolutions which would, according to Hamilton, destroy the Constitution and the national government.

— Hamilton officially returned to the political wars in the spring 1800 elections for New York State legislators, and to a fight to the finish with Aaron Burr. Since state lawmakers chose electors for the forthcoming national election, the balloting would determine how critically important New York cast its vote. Burr, meanwhile, had been mending his political fences, having been trounced in the 1799 elections. A consummate machine politician, possibly the first of the breed, he gave the city's voters, Hamilton included, an example of the practical politician in action. For example, he used his Bank of Manhattan to swing the affluent to his political standard in exchange for bank favors. He kept an open house for two months. He indexed practically every city voter—his temperament, habits, opinions, exertions necessary to get him to the polls and to the Republican column. The campaign, in sum, was a total effort for Burr—in sharp contrast to that of New York's Federalists who seemed lethargic throughout—and he scored a personal triumph, guaranteeing that the state would vote Republican in the electoral college. Hamilton, in a letter to Jay, advanced a desperate plan which would strip the legislature of its right to choose presidential electors (by convening the lame-duck Federalist-controlled assembly and passing a law placing the election of electors in the hands of the voters themselves). This proposal, rejected by Jay, was possibly the most conspicuous blot on Hamiltons' record, undertaken in the belief that any means might be used, including fraud and hyprocrisy, to save the country from Jefferson.

Hamilton was equally concerned with blocking Adams, and the Party caucus, at his instigation, renominated the chief executive and C. C. Pinckney, pledging to support both equally as in 1796; and, once again, the strategy dictated that New England's Federalists would vote equally for both candidates while South Carolina, balloting last, would deny some votes to Adams and thereby give the presidency to Pinckney, its favorite son. But the election results again backfired and created a further crisis for Hamilton. Jefferson and Burr were tied at seventy-three votes apiece; and Hamilton, having to chose between the two, had no choice: better his historic foe from Monticello than the scheming New Yorker. He warned his fellow Federalists anew about the latter's Caesarism, portraying Burr as totally depraved, an infamous wretch, "the Cataline of America" who must be blocked from the White House at all costs.

Hamilton's prayers and commands to Party members were successful, but it was his last victory. Indeed he was ringing his own death knell in political as well as personal terms. Over the next few years, he was a man in search of an issue, one that might reinvigorate Federalism. He raised the cry of a Republican "reign of terror" when Jefferson removed a few Federalist officeholders, but aroused no one. He charged the president with courting popularity when Jefferson repealed the excise tax, again to no effect. He protested in vain when Republicans pressed the Repealing Act which would have eliminated positions created by the 1801 Judiciary Act currently held by Federalist judges. Bruised and exhausted by such encounters, Hamilton temporarily retired from the political scene. The decision was understandable. After all, his was a voice crying in the wilderness. Republican successes mounted; the economy flourished; and even his most faithful supporters in the business community responded to his prophecies of doom with insouciant disregard.

Hamilton's futility and despair over the ways of the world peaked when his eldest son was killed in a senseless duel, stemming from an argument that involved his own alleged indiscretions. His jeremiads seemed to be in striking contrast to the realities of social and economic stability. But he was not totally removed from life around him. He raised sufficient funds to finance a daily newspaper, the New York *Evening Post,* in the hope that its thrusts and ripostes on current affairs might revive his comatose and shattered votaries. He even defended Harry Croswell, the Federalist editor of the Hudson, New York *Wasp.* Croswell had been charged with seditiously libelling Jefferson, and Hamilton delivered a memorable and incandescent defense of freedom of the press. The last important speech of his career, Hamilton's summation helped to liberalize the law of libel and recalled his finest hours.

All this time—over a four-year span—Burr's hatred rankled. It was refreshed and deepened when Hamilton blocked his attempt to win the state gubernatorial nomination. Burr's ambitions in 1804 must be seen as an aspect of the political strategy of those Federalists who, prompted by the imminent purchase of Louisiana as well as by increasing Southern and Democratic domination of government, sought New England's separation from the Union. Their scheme for a Northern confederacy depended upon electing Burr to the governorship and then making him and New York the centerpiece in their secessionist design. New York, it was believed, was the key to success and must be brought into the fold. Hamilton himself had been approached by Timothy Pickering with a proposal to lead the military forces of this projected Northern tier of states but always the nationalist and always fearful of social dislocation and its attendant chaos, he firmly refused. Still New York's participation seemed necessary and New England Federalists turned to Burr who had been discarded by the Republicans after 1800 and who was willing to play Pickering's game. Speaking at a Federalist party caucus in Albany in 1804, Hamilton pleaded for a repudiation of Burr: no "union of honest men" could find him acceptable. Many state party leaders thereupon threw their strength to the regular Republican candidate, Judge Morgan Lewis. Burr carried New York City but suffered a crushing statewide defeat. His political plans were now irretrievably wrecked. Hamilton again! Hamilton must have seemed ubiquitous: he was always there to block him; he had destroyed his presidential ambitions and now his hopes for high state office; he had brought him to the point of no political return.

Understandably, then, Burr nursed an open and festering wound, and the deep conviction that Hamilton himself had to be destroyed. And a correspondence of nine days, marked by increasingly bitter invective and rapidly deteriorating negotiations, led to the duel which, Hamilton knew from the opening letter, had been fated. Hamilton brought on the immediate incident by his terse and uncompromising replies; he would not conciliate, he would not equivocate, he would not retract one word, or seek a way out. Hamilton hated dueling, his son's death reinforcing his own sentiments. But he was a man of honor and as such had no options. He accepted the challenge, rowed across the Hudson River at 7:00 A.M. on the morning of July 12, 1804, and, refusing to fire at Burr, went to his death on the duelling grounds of Weehawken Heights on July 12, 1804.

The spelling and punctuation in the documents that have been selected follow the original. Therefore, what may appear to the contemporary reader to be errors of spelling or grammar, or gaucheries of style, is conventional usage to the eighteenth and nineteenth centuries.

Chronology of the Life of Hamilton

1755	(January 11; or 1757). Born on Nevis, son of James Hamilton.
1772	Left St. Croix to attend school in the American colonies.
1772–76	Studied at King's College, New York City.
1776	(March 14). Appointed captain of a New York artillery company.
1777–81	(March 1). Appointed aide-de-camp to General George Washington and resigned on February 16, 1781.
1780	(December 14). Married Elizabeth Schuyler.
1781	(July). Commanded a battalion of light infantry.
1782	(July 2). Appointed Continental Receiver of Taxes. Admitted to the bar of New York City. (July 22). New York legislature appointed him a delegate to the Continental Congress.
1782–83	Member of the Continental Congress.
1783–87	Practiced law in New York City. (1784). Assisted in founding the Bank of New York. (1785). Assisted in founding the New York Society for Promoting the Manumission of Slaves. (September 11–14, 1786). Served as a delegate to the Annapolis Convention. (January 12–April 21, 1787). Member of the New York State Assembly. Attended the federal Constitutional Convention in Philadelphia.
1789	(September 11). Appointed as the first Secretary of the Treasury.
1795	(January 31). Resigned from the Cabinet.
1798–1800	(July 19). Appointed as Inspector General of the Army.
1804	(July 11). Duel with Aaron Burr and died on July 12.

PART ONE

HAMILTON LOOKS AT THE WORLD

This section presents extracts from two of Hamilton's principal articles dealing with the major events of his time.

1

On Revolution

Two early pamphlets indicate that Hamilton had already overcome the provincialism of his island background. They suggest his youthful attraction to nationalism as well as to ordeal by polemic. They also tell us that this nineteen-year-old rustic had suddenly emerged, like Pallas Athene from the brow of Zeus, as a highly effective pamphleteer. The first of these tracts was published one month after Free Thoughts, on the Proceedings of the Continental Congress. . . . By a Farmer, *believed to be authored by Reverend Samuel Seabury, then an effective Westchester Episcopal minister. Without even a college degree and with a precociousness that leaves the reader gasping, Hamilton composed a reply which belligerently defended the Continental Congress and the concept of colonial union. He pictured the ruin beckoning America's farmers if they submitted to Parliament; he arraigned the policy of internal taxation, such as the tea tax; and he urged support of the Continental Association—with its non-importation, non-exportation, and non-consumption of British goods. It was essential, he argued, that New York join this Association. The times were so critical that local and sectional jealousies were luxuries which Americans could not afford.*

Seabury's answer began with an ad hominem *attack on the Whig view of empire and included highly critical commentary on Hamilton's* Full Vindication. *The youthful New Yorker's swift and penetrating rejoinder rebutted scurrility with scurrility, but added something more; namely, that trinity of articles which comprised the colonial creed: reliance upon the English constitution, the colonial charters, and the Lockean compact of civil society. He rejected Seabury's claim that the Association would leave Americans naked to their enemies. To the contrary, he replied. Predicting material prosperity for the struggling young republic, he declared that God and nature had ordained self-sufficiency—in the form of inter-colonial trade—as the path to well-being and happiness. Hamilton's unique and prescient vision, now stated for the first time, adumbrates the future Report on Manufactures as well as the future economic well-being of the United States.*

Hamilton, finally, emerges here as a brilliant polemicist. He does not invent anything new, to be sure, but he does contribute as much as any colonist to the great and growing debate about colonial rights. He was not proposing civil war within the empire; rather his whole purpose was to avoid a resort to the sword. Indeed, he emphasizes "the powerful bands of self-interest" and the "perpetual and mutually beneficial union." But he falls short of embracing imperial federation, and he had already begun an inch-by-inch retreat into the fortress of political and economic nationalism.

A FULL VINDICATION OF THE MEASURES OF CONGRESS [1]

And first, let me ask these restless spirits, whence arises that violent antipathy they seem to entertain, not only to the natural rights of mankind; but to common sense and common modesty. That they are enemies to the natural rights of mankind is manifest, because they wish to see one part of their species enslaved by another. That they have an invincible aversion to common sense is apparent in many respects: They endeavour to persuade us, that the absolute sovereignty of parliament does not imply our absolute slavery; that it is a Christian duty to submit to be plundered of all we have, merely because some of our fellow-subjects are wicked enough to require it of us, that slavery, so far from being a great evil, is a great blessing; and even, that our contest with Britain is founded entirely upon the petty duty of 3 pence per pound on East India tea; whereas the whole world knows, it is built upon this interesting question, whether the inhabitants of Great-Britain have a right to dispose of the lives and properties of the inhabitants of America, or not? And lastly, that these men have discarded all pretension to common modesty, is clear from hence, first, because they, in the plainest terms, call an august body of men, famed for their patriotism and abilities, fools or knaves, and of course the people whom they represented cannot be exempt from the same opprobrious appellations; and secondly, because they set themselves up as standards of wisdom and probity, by contradicting and censuring the public voice in favour of those men.

A little consideration will convince us, that the congress instead of

[1] "A Full Vindication of the Measures of Congress . . . ," New York [December 15, 1774]. From *The Papers of Alexander Hamilton* (New York, 1961), vol. 1.

having "ignorantly misunderstood, carelessly neglected, or basely betrayed the interests of the colonies," have, on the contrary, devised and recommended the only effectual means to secure the freedom, and establish the future prosperity of America upon a solid basis. If we are not free and happy hereafter, it must proceed from the want of integrity and resolution, in executing what they have concerted; not from the temerity or impolicy of their determinations.

Before I proceed to confirm this assertion by the most obvious arguments, I will premise a few brief remarks. The only distinction between freedom and slavery consists in this: In the former state, a man is governed by the laws to which he has given his consent, either in person, or by his representative: In the latter, he is governed by the will of another. In the one case his life and property are his own, in the other, they depend upon the pleasure of a master. It is easy to discern which of these two states is preferable. No man in his senses can hesitate in choosing to be free, rather than a slave.

That Americans are intitled to freedom, is incontestible upon every rational principle. All men have one common original: they participate in one common nature, and consequently have one common right. No reason can be assigned why one man should exercise any power, or preeminence over his fellow creatures more than another; unless they have voluntarily vested him with it. Since then, Americans have not by any act of their's impowered the British Parliament to make laws for them, it follows they can have no just authority to do it.

Besides the clear voice of natural justice in this respect, the fundamental principles of the English constitution are in our favour. It has been repeatedly demonstrated, that the idea of legislation, or taxation, when the subject is not represented, is inconsistent with *that*. Nor is this all, our charters, the express conditions on which our progenitors relinquished their native countries, and came to settle in this, preclude every claim of ruling and taxing us without our assent.

Every subterfuge that sophistry has been able to invent, to evade or obscure this truth, has been refuted by the most conclusive reasonings; so that we may pronounce it a matter of undeniable certainty, that the pretensions of Parliament are contradictory to the law of nature, subversive of the British constitution, and destructive of the faith of the most solemn compacts.

What then is the subject of our controversy with the mother country? It is this, whether we shall preserve that security to our lives and properties, which the law of nature, the genius of the British constitution, and our charters afford us; or whether we shall resign them into the hands of the British House of Commons, which is no more privileged to dispose of them than the Grand Mogul? What can actuate those men, who labour to delude any of us into an opinion, that the object of contention between the parent state and the colonies is only three pence duty upon tea? or that the commotions in America originate in a plan, formed by some turbulent men to erect it into a republican government? The parliament claims a right to tax us in all cases whatsoever: Its late acts are in virtue of that claim. How ridiculous then is it to affirm, that we are quarrelling for the trifling sum of three pence a pound on tea; when it is evidently the principle against which we contend. . . .

The only scheme of opposition, suggested by those, who have been, and are averse from a non-importation and non-exportation agreement, is, by REMONSTRANCE and PETITION. The authors and abettors of this scheme, have never been able to *invent* a single argument to prove the likelihood of its succeeding. On the other hand, there are many standing facts, and valid considerations against it.

In the infancy of the present dispute, we had recourse to this method only. We addressed the throne in the most loyal and respectful manner, in a legislative capacity; but what was the consequence? Our address was treated with contempt and neglect. The first American congress did the same, and met with similar treatment. The total repeal of the stamp act, and the partial repeal of the revenue acts took place, not because the complaints of America were deemed just and reasonable; but because these acts were found to militate against the commercial interests of Great Britain: This was the declared motive of the repeal. . . .

There is less reason now than ever to expect deliverance, in this way, from the hand of oppression. The system of slavery, fabricated against America, cannot at this time be considered as the effect of inconsideration and rashness. It is the offspring of mature deliberation. It has been fostered by time, and strengthened by every artifice human subtilty is capable of. After the claims of parliament had lain dormant for awhile, they are again resumed and prosecuted with more than common ardour. The Premier has advanced too far to recede with safety: He is deeply interested to execute his purpose, if possible: we know he has declared, that he will never desist, till he has brought America to his feet; and we may conclude, nothing but necessity will induce him to abandon his aims. . . .

There is no law, either of nature, or of the civil society in which we live, that obliges us to purchase, and make use of the products and manufactures of a different land, or people. It is indeed a dictate of humanity to contribute to the support and happiness of our fellow creatures and more especially those who are allied to us by the ties of blood, interest, and mutual protection; but humanity does not require us to sacrifice our own security and welfare to the convenience, or advantage of others. Self preservation is the first principle of our nature. When our lives and properties are at stake, it would be foolish and unnatural to refrain from such measures as might preserve them, because they would be detrimental to others. . . .

No person, that has enjoyed the sweets of liberty, can be insensible of its infinite value, or can reflect on its reverse, without horror and detestation. No person, that is not lost to every generous feeling of humanity, or that is not stupidly blind to his own interest, could bear to offer himself and posterity as victims at the shrine of despotism, in preference to enduring the short lived inconveniencies that may result from an abridgment, or even entire suspension of commerce.

Were not the disadvantages of slavery too obvious to stand in need of it, I might enumerate and describe the tedious train of calamities, inseparable from it. I might shew that it is fatal to religion and morality; that it tends to debase the mind, and corrupt its noblest springs of action. I might shew, that it relaxes the sinews of industry, clips the wings of commerce, and introduces misery and indigence in every shape. . . .

Should Americans submit to become the vassals of their fellow-subjects in Great Britain, their yoke will be peculiarly grievous and intolerable. A vast majority of mankind is intirely biassed by motives of self-interest. Most men are glad to remove any burthens off themselves, and place them upon the necks of their neighbours. We cannot therefore doubt, but that the British Parliament, with a view to the ease and advantage of itself, and its constituents, would oppress and grind the Americans as much as possible. . . .

These are not imaginary mischiefs. The colonies contain above three millions of people. Commerce flourshes with the most rapid progress throughout them. This commerce Great-Britain has hitherto regulated to her own advantage. Can we think the annihilation of so exuberant a source of wealth, a matter of trifling import. On the contrary, must it not be productive of the most disastrous effects? It is evident it must. It is equally evident, that the conquest of so numerous a people, armed in the animating cause of liberty could not be accomplished without an inconceivable expence of blood and treasure.

We cannot therefore suspect Great-Britain to be capable of such frantic extravagance as to hazard these dreadful consequences; without which she must necessarily desist from her unjust pretensions, and leave us in the undisturbed possession of our privileges. . . .

The FARMER, I am inclined to hope, builds too much upon the present disunion of Canada, Georgia, the Floridas, the Mississippi, and Nova Scotia from other colonies. A little time, I trust, will awaken them from their slumber, and bring them to a proper sense of their indiscretion. I please myself with the flattering prospect, that they will, ere long, unite in one indissoluble chain with the rest of the colonies. I cannot believe they will persist in such a conduct as must exclude them from the secure enjoyment of those heaven-descended immunities we are contending for.

THE FARMER REFUTED [2]

The first thing that presents itself is a wish, that "*I* had, explicitly, declared to the public my ideas of the *natural rights* of mankind. Man, in a state of nature (you say) may be considered, as perfectly free from all restraints of *law* and *government,* and, then, the weak must submit to the strong."

I shall, henceforth, begin to make some allowance for that enmity, you have discovered to the *natural rights* of mankind. . . .

Upon this [natural] law, depend the natural rights of mankind, the supreme being gave existence to man, together with the means of preserving and beatifying that existence. He endowed him with rational faculties, by the help of which, to discern and pursue such things, as were consistent with his duty and interest, and invested him with an inviolable right to personal liberty, and personal safety.

Hence, in a state of nature, no man had any *moral* power to deprive another of his life, limbs, property or liberty; nor the least authority to command, or exact obedience from him; except that which arose from the ties of consanguinity.

Hence also, the origin of all civil government, justly established, must be a voluntary compact, between the rulers and the ruled; and must be liable to such limitations, as are necessary for the security of the *absolute rights* of the latter; for what original title can any man or set of men have, to govern others, except their own consent? To usurp dominion over a people, in their own despite, or to grasp at a more extensive power than they are willing to entrust, is to violate that law of nature, which gives every man a right to his personal liberty; and can, therefore, confer no obligation to obedience.

"The principal aim of society is to protect individuals, in the enjoyment of those absolute rights, which were vested in them by the immutable laws of nature; but which could not be preserved, in peace, without that mutual assistance, and intercourse, which is gained by the institution of friendly and social communities. Hence it follows, that the first and primary end of human laws, is to maintain and regulate these *absolute rights* of individuals." BLACKSTONE.

If we examine the pretensions of parliament, by this criterion, which is evidently, a good one, we shall, presently detect their injustice. First, they are subversive of our natural liberty, because an authority is assumed over us, which we by no means assent to. And secondly, they divest us of that moral security, for our lives and properties, which we are intitled to, and which it is the primary end of society to bestow. For such security

[2] "The Farmer Refuted . . . ," New York [February 23, 1775]. From *The Papers of Alexander Hamilton* (New York, 1961), vol. 1.

can never exist, while we have no part in making the laws, that are to bind us; and while it may be the interest of our uncontroled legislators to oppress us as much as possible. . . .

The idea of colony does not involve the idea of slavery. There is a wide difference, between the dependence of a free people, and the submission of slaves. The former I allow, the latter I reject with disdain. Nor does the notion of a colony imply any subordination to our fellow subjects, in the parent state, while there is one common sovereign established. . . .

Admitting, that the King of Great Britain was enthroned by virtue of an act of parliament, and that he is King of America, because he is King of Great-Britain, yet the act of parliament is not the *efficient cause* of his being the King of America: It is only the *occasion* of it. He is King of America, by virtue of a compact between us and the Kings of Great-Britain. . . .

To disclaim, the authority of a British Parliament over us, does by no means imply the dereliction of our allegiance to British Monarchs. Our compact takes no cognizance of the manner of their accession to the throne. It is sufficient for us, that they are Kings of England.

The most valid reasons can be assigned for our allegiance to the King of Great-Britain; but not one of the least force or plausibility for our subjection to parliamentary decrees.

We hold our lands in America by virtue of charters from British Monarchs; and are under no obligations to the lords or commons for them: Our title is similar and equal to that, by which they possess their lands; and the King is the legal fountain of both: this is one grand source of our obligation to allegiance.

Another, and the principal source is, that protection which we have hitherto enjoyed from the Kings of Great-Britain. Nothing is more common than to hear the votaries of parliament urge the protection we have received from the mother country, as an argument for submission to its claims. But they entertain erroneous conceptions of the matter; the King himself, being the supreme executive magistrate, is regarded by the constitution, as the supreme protector of the empire. For this purpose, he is the generalissimo, or first in military command; in him is vested the power of making war and peace, of raising armies, equipping fleets and directing all their motions. He it is that has defended us from our enemies, and to him alone, we are obliged to render allegiance and submission.

The law of nature and the British constitution both confine allegiance to the person of the King; and found it upon the principle of protection. . . .

The right of parliament to legislate for us cannot be accounted for upon any reasonable grounds. The constitution of Great Britain is very properly called a limited monarchy, the people having reserved to themselves a share in the legislature, as a check upon the regal authority, to prevent its degenerating into despotism and tyranny. The very aim and intention of the democratical part, or the house of commons, is to secure the rights of the people. Its very being depends upon those rights. Its whole power is derived from them, and must be terminated by them.

It is the unalienable birth-right of every Englishman, who can be considered as *a free agent* to participate in framing the laws which are to bind him, either as to his life or property. But, as many inconveniences would result from the exercise of this right, in person, it is appointed by the constitution, that he shall delegate it to another. Hence he is to give his vote in the election of some person he chuses to confide in as his representative. This right no power on earth can divest him of. It was enjoyed by his ancestors time immemorial; recognized and established by Magna Charta, and is essential to the existence of the constitution. Abolish this privilege, and the house of commons is annihilated.

But what was the use and design of this privilege? To secure his life and property from the attacks of exorbitant power. And in what manner is this done? By giving him the election of those, who are to have the disposal and regulation of them, and whose interest is in every respect connected with his.

The representative in this case is bound by every possible tie to consult the advantage of his constituent. Gratitude for the high and honourable trust reposed in him demands a return of attention and regard to the advancement of his happiness. Self-interest, that most powerful incentive of human actions, points and attracts towards the same object.

The duration of his trust is not perpetual; but must expire in a few years, and if he is desirous of the future favour of his constituents, he must not abuse the present instance of it; but must pursue the end, for which he enjoys it; otherwise he forfeits it, and defeats his own purpose. Besides, if he consent to any laws hurtful to his constituent, he is bound by the same, and must partake in the disadvantage of them. His friends, relations, children, all whose ease and comfort are dear to him, will be in a like predicament. And should he concur in any flagrant acts of injustice or oppression, he will be within the reach of popular vengeance, and this will restrain him within due bounds.

To crown the whole, at the expiration of a few years, if their representatives have abused their trust, the people have it in their power to change them, and to elect others, who may be more faithful and more attached to their interest. . . .

When we ascribe to the British house of commons a jurisdiction over the colonies, the scene is entirely reversed. All these kinds of security immediately disappear; no ties of gratitude or interest remain. Interest, indeed, may operate to our prejudice. To oppress us may serve as a recommendation to their constituents, as well as an alleviation of their own incumbrances. The British patriots may, in time, be heard to court the gale of popular favour, by boasting their exploits in laying some new impositions on their American vassals, and, by that means, lessening the burthens of their friends and fellow subjects. . . .

The fundamental source of all your errors, sophisms and false reasonings is a total ignorance of the natural rights of mankind. Were you once to become acquainted with these, you could never entertain a thought, that all men are not, by nature, entitled to a parity of privileges. You would be convinced, that natural liberty is a gift of the beneficent Creator to the whole human race, and that civil liberty is founded in that; and cannot be wrested from any people, without the most manifest violation of justice. *Civil liberty, is only natural liberty, modified and secured by the sanctions of civil society.* It is not a thing, in its own nature, precarious and dependent on human will and caprice; but is conformable to the constitution of man, as well as necessary to the *well-being* of society.

Upon this principle, colonists as well as other men, have a right to civil liberty. . . .

The right of colonists, therefore, to exercise a legislative power, is an inherent right. It is founded upon the right of all men to freedom and happiness. For civil liberty cannot possibly have any existence, where the society, for whom laws are made, have no share in making them; and where the interest of their legislators is not inseparably interwoven with theirs. Before you asserted, that the right of legislation was derived "from the indulgence or grant of the parent state," you should have proved two things, that all men have not a natural right to freedom, and that civil liberty is not advantageous to society. . . .

The foundation of the English constitution rests upon this principle, that no laws have any validity, or binding force, without the consent and approbation of the *people,* given in the persons of *their* representatives, periodically elected by *themselves.* This constitutes the democratical part of the government.

It is also, undeniably, certain, that no Englishman, who can be deemed *a free agent* in a *political* view, can be bound by laws, to which he has not consented, either in person, or by *his* representative. Or, in other words, every Englishman (exclusive of the mercantile and trading part of the nation) who possesses a freehold, to the value of forty shillings per annum, has a right to a share in the legislature, which he exercises, by giving his vote in the election of some person, he approves of, as his representative. . . .

It is therefore, evident to a demonstration, that unless every *free agent* in America be permitted to enjoy the same privilege, we are entirely stripped of the benefits of the constitution, and precipitated into an abyss of slavery. For, we are deprived of that immunity, which is the grand pillar and support of freedom. And this cannot be done, without a direct violation of the constitution, which decrees, to every *free agent,* a share in the legislature.

It deserves to be remarked here, that those very persons in Great Britain, who are *in so mean a situation,* as to be excluded from a part in elections, are in more eligible circumstances, than she should be in, who have every necessary qualification.

They compose a part of that society, to whose government they are subject. They are nourished and maintained by it, and partake in every other emolument, for which they are qualified. They have no doubt, most of them, relations and connexions, among those who are privileged to vote, and by that means, are not entirely without influence, in the appointment of their rulers. They are not governed by laws made expressly and exclusively for them; but by the general laws of their country; equally obligatory on the legal electors, and on the law makers themselves. So that they have nearly the same security against oppression, which the body of the people have. . . .

These considerations plainly shew, that the people in America, of all ranks and conditions, opulent as well as indigent (if subjected to the British Parliament) would be upon a less favourable footing, than that part of the people of Britain, who are *in so mean a situation,* that they are supposed to have no will of their own. The injustice of this must be evident to every man of common sense. . . .

There is no need, however, of this plea: The sacred rights of mankind are not to be rummaged for, among old parchments, or musty records. They are written, as with a sun beam, in the whole *volume* of human nature, by the hand of the divinity itself; and can never be erased or obscured by mortal power. . . .

I will now venture to assert, that I have demonstrated, from the voice of nature, the *spirit* of the British constitution, and the charters of the colonies in general, the absolute non-existence of that parliamentary supremacy, for which you contend. I am not apt to be dogmatical, or too confident of my own opinions; but, if I thought it possible, for me to be mistaken, when I maintain, that the parliament of Great-Britain has no sovereign authority over America, I should distrust every principle of my understanding, reject every distinction between truth and falshood, and fall into an universal scepticism. . . .

The regulation of our trade, in the sense it is now admitted, is the only power we can, with justice to ourselves, permit the British parliament to exercise; and it is a privilege of so important a nature, so beneficial and lucrative to Great-Britain, that she ought, in equity, to be contented with it, and not attempt to grasp at any thing more. The Congress, therefore, have made the only concession which the welfare and prosperity of America would warrant, or which Great Britain, in reason could expect. . . .

It is a necessary consequence, and not an assumed point, that the claim of parliament to *bind us by statutes in all cases whatsoever,* is unconstitutional, unjust and tyrannical; and the repeated attempts to carry it into execution, evince a fixed inveterate design to exterminate the liberties of America. . . .

Extraordinary emergencies, require extraordinary expedients. The best mode of opposition was that in which there might be an union of councils. This was necessary to ascertain the boundaries of our rights; and to give weight and dignity to our measures, both in Britain and America. A Congress was accordingly proposed, and universally agreed to.

You, Sir, triumph in the supposed *illegality* of this body; but, granting your supposition were true, it would be a matter of no real importance. When the first principles of civil society are violated, and the rights of a whole people are invaded, the common forms of municipal law are not to be regarded. Men may then betake themselves to the law of nature; and, if they but conform their actions, to that standard, all cavils against them, betray either ignorance or dishonesty. There are some events in society, to which human laws cannot extend; but when applied to them lose all their force and efficacy. In short, when human laws contradict or discountenance the means, which are necessary to preserve the essential rights of any society, they defeat the proper end of all laws, and so become null and void. . . .

It is the common trick of ministerial writers to represent the Congress, as having made some new demands, which were unknown to former times; whereas, in truth, they have, in substance, acknowledged the only dependence on parliament which was ever intended, by their predecessors. Nor [is] it true, that they have claimed an *absolute independency*. It is insulting common sense, to say so when it is notorious, that they have acknowledged the right of parliament to regulate the trade of the colonies. Any further dependence on it, is unnecessary and dangerous. They have professed allegiance to the British King, and have bound themselves, on any emergency, to contribute their proportion of men and money, to the defence and protection of the whole empire. Can this be called *absolute independency?* Is it better for Britain to hazard the total loss [of] these colonies, than to hold them upon these conditions? Is it preferable to make enemies of the people of America, instead of being connected with them, by the equal tie of fellow subjects? Is it not madness, to run the risk of losing the trade of these colonies, from which the mother country, drew "more clear profit, than Spain has drawn from all her mines," because they insist only upon all the essential rights of free men? You may call it effrontery, consummate assurance, or what you please, to say so; but every man, capable of taking a full prospect of all the probable mischiefs, which may result, from an open rupture between Britain and the colonies, will coincide with me, when I affirm, that nothing, but the most *frantic extravagance*, can influence administration to attempt the reduction of America, by force of arms.

It is sufficiently evident, from the respective charters, that the rights, we now claim, are coeval with the original settlement of these colonies. These rights have been, at different times, strenuously asserted, though they have been suffered to be violated, in several instances, through inattention, or, perhaps, an unwillingness to quarrel with the mother country. . . .

A supreme authority, in the Parliament, to make any special laws for this province, consistent with the internal legislature here claimed is impossible; and cannot be supposed, without falling into that solecism, in politics, of *imperium* in *imperio*. . . .

Whatever opinion may be entertained of my sentiments and intentions, I attest that being, whose all-seeing eye penetrates the inmost recesses of the heart, that I am not influenced (in the part I take) by any unworthy motive—that, if I am in an error, it is my judgment, not my heart, that errs. That I earnestly lament the unnatural quarrel, between the parent state and the colonies; and most ardently wish for a speedy reconciliation, a perpetual and *mutually* beneficial union, that I am a warm advocate for limitted monarchy, and an unfeigned well-wisher to the present Royal Family.

But on the other hand, I am inviolably attached to the essential rights of mankind, and the true interests of society. I consider civil liberty, in a genuine unadulterated sense, as the greatest of terrestrial blessings. I am convinced, that the whole human race is intitled to it; and, that it can be wrested from no part of them, without the blackest and most aggravated guilt.

I verily believe also, that the best way to secure a permanent and happy union, between Great-Britain and the colonies, is to permit the latter to be as free, as they desire. To abridge their liberties, or to exercise any power over them, which they are unwilling to submit to, would be a perpetual source of discontent and animosity. A continual jealousy would exist on both sides. This would lead to tyranny, on the one hand, and to sedition and rebellion, on the other. Impositions, not really grievous in themselves, would be thought so; and the murmurs arising from thence, would be considered as the effect of a turbulent ungovernable spirit. These jarring principles would, at length, throw all things into disorder; and be productive of an irreparable breach, and a total disunion.

2

On Political Theory and the Principles of Government

The articles, letters, speeches and opinions which follow again suggest Hamilton's precosity. They recall the ambience of this world of Confederation military and financial reverses. They tell us something about Hamilton as a political scientist, a political thinker of the first order, a powerful and timely writer on government.

In the early 1780s, political reform—even more than monetary—had priority in Hamilton's scheme of things. Congress must have greater powers as well as autonomous and permanent funds. The major administrative departments of government must, for the sake of fiscal and military operations, be the sole responsibility of individual office-holders (rather than, as currently, the responsibility of congressional boards). Hamilton even made so bold as to propose a constitutional convention which would replace the Articles. In this letter to Duane (from Washington's camp at Liberty Pole, New Jersey), Hamilton pressed home the argument that greater powers were necessary for the central government. He also includes premature commentary on the need to give "discretionary powers [to Congress], limited only by the object for which they were given; in the present case the independence and freedom of America." This letter initiated a seven-year period in which Hamilton argued and advocated—in private correspondence, public appeals, speeches in assemblies and maneuvers at conventions—for a national gathering authorized to strengthen congressional powers or, preferably, write a new constitution.

In the first numbers of "The Continentalist," Hamilton hammers home the same theme—greater power to the federal legislature. These papers, a series of six newspaper articles signed "AB," warned of a long war, appealed for a closer union of the states than then existed and again proposed—for the first time publicly—a constitutional convention which would rewrite the fundamental law in order to give Congress the powers necessary to defeat Great Britain and preserve the union. Suggesting the continuity and consistency of Hamilton's political views, these articles present them in succinct as well as convenient form. They are familiar articles of faith; they are interwoven with Hamilton's search for national prosperity and repudiation of Manchester liberalism; and they lead inexorably to the longer, more elaborate, more analytical exegeses of the Federalist Papers. *The major difference between his commentaries of 1781–1782 and 1787 is that the former for the most part urges refinements of ongoing practices and policies; the latter proposes approval of a new compact of government.*

Hamilton played a diffident role at the Constitutional Convention, which was probably wise since his view of the Confederation and the solution for its problems was too extreme, even for those— and they were in the majority—who espoused a nationalist solution. Having moved to the right over a decade, he no longer appeared concerned about safeguards for the libertarian and "natural" rights of man. Nor did he place any specific limits upon the powers of government. His proposals were shaped by the conviction that "the mass of people seldom judge or determine right," that "the imprudence of democracy" must be checked, that the English government was "the best in the world (and he made no secret of his admiration for English laws and institutions), a claim damaging to his reputation in both his time and ours. Specifically, Hamilton urged that the states be reduced to mere administrative units of the general government (with governors appointed by the President and with life tenure, and with veto power over state legislation), and that the President and the Senate be elected for life.

TO JAMES DUANE [1]

[Liberty Pole, New Jersey, September 3, 1780]

Dr. Sir

Agreeably to your request and my promise I sit down to give you my ideas of the defects of our present system, and the changes necessary to save us from ruin. They may perhaps be the reveries of a projector rather than the sober views of a politician. You will judge of them, and make what use you please of them.

The fundamental defect is a want of power in Congress. . . . Congress had never any definitive powers granted them and of course could exercise none—could do nothing more than recommend. The manner in which Congress was appointed would warrant, and the public good required, that they should have considered themselves as vested with full power *to preserve the republic from harm.* They have done many of the highest acts of sovereignty, which were always cheerfully submitted to—the decla-

[1] From *The Papers of Alexander Hamilton,* vol. 1.

ration of independence, the declaration of war, the levying an army, creating a navy, emitting money, making alliances with foreign powers, appointing a dictator &c. &c.—all these implications of a complete sovereignty were never disputed, and ought to have been a standard for the whole conduct of Administration. Undefined powers are discretionary powers, limited only by the object for which they were given—in the present case, the independence and freedom of America. The confederation made no difference; for as it has not been generally adopted, it had no operation. . . .

But the confederation itself is defective and requires to be altered, it is neither fit for war, nor peace. The idea of an uncontrolable sovereignty in each state, over its internal police, will defeat the other powers given to Congress, and make our union feeble and precarious. There are instances without number, where acts necessary for the general good, and which rise out of the powers given to Congress must interfere with the internal police of the states, and there are as many instances in which the particular states by arrangements of internal police can effectually though indirectly counteract the arrangements of Congress. You have already had examples of this for which I refer you to your own memory.

The confederation gives the states individually too much influence in the affairs of the army; they should have nothing to do with it. The entire formation and disposal of our military forces ought to belong to Congress. It is an essential cement of the union; and it ought to be the policy of Congress to des[troy] all ideas of state attachments in the army and make it look up wholly to them. For this purpose all appointments promotions and provisions whatsoever ought to be made by them. It may be apprehended that this may be dangerous to liberty. But nothing appears more evident to me, than that we run much greater risk of having a weak and disunited federal government, than one which will be able to usurp upon the rights of the people. Already some of the lines of the army would obey their states in opposition to Congress notwithstanding the pains we have taken to preserve the unity of the army—if any thing would hinder this it would be the personal influence of the General, a melancholy and mortifying consideration. . . .

The confederation too gives the power of the purse too intirely to the state legislatures. It should provide perpetual funds in the disposal of Congress—by a land tax, poll tax, or the like. All imposts upon commerce ought to be laid by Congress and appropriated to their use, for without certain revenues, a government can have no power; that power, which holds the purse strings absolutely, must rule. This seems to be a medium, which without making Congress altogether independent will tend to give reality to its authority.

Another defect in our system is want of method and energy in the administration. . . .

I shall now propose the remedies, which appear to me applicable to our circumstances, and necessary to extricate our affairs from their present deplorable situation.

The first step must be to give Congress powers competent to the public exigencies. This may happen in two ways, one by resuming and exercising the discretionary powers I suppose to have been originally vested in them for the safety of the states and resting their conduct on the candor of their country men and the necessity of the conjuncture: the other by calling immediately a convention of all the states with full authority to conclude finally upon a general confederation, stating to them beforehand explicit the evils arising from a want of power in Congress, and the impossibily of supporting the contest on its present footing, that the delegates may come possessed of proper sentiments as well as proper authority to give to the meeting. Their commission should include a right of vesting Congress with the whole or a proportion of the unoccupied lands, to be employed for the purpose of raising a revenue, reserving the jurisdiction to the states by whom they are granted. . . .

The confederation in my opinion should give Congress complete sovereignty; except as to that part of internal police, which relates to the rights of property and life among individuals and to raising money by internal taxes. It is necessary, that every thing, belonging to this, should be regulated by the state legislatures. Congress should have complete sovereignty in all that relates to war, peace, trade, finance, and to the management of foreign affairs, the right of declaring war of raising armies, officering, paying them, directing their motions in every respect, of equipping fleets and doing the same with them, of building fortifications arsenals magazines &c. &c., of making peace on such conditions as they think proper, of regulating trade, determining with what countries it shall be carried on, granting indulgencies laying prohibitions on all the articles of export or import, imposing duties granting bounties & premiums for raising exporting importing and applying to their own use the product of these duties, only giving credit to the states on whom they are raised in the general account of revenues and expences, instituting Admiralty courts &c, of coining money, establishing banks on such terms, and with such privileges as they think proper, appropriating funds and doing whatever else relates to the operations of finance, transacting every thing with foreign nations, making alliances offensive and defensive, treaties of commerce, &c. &c.

The confederation should provide certain perpetual revenues, productive and easy of collection, a land tax, poll tax or the like, which together with the duties on trade and the unlocated lands would give Congress a substantial existence, and a stable foundation for their schemes of finance. What more supplies were necessary should be occasionally demanded of the states, in the present mode of quotas.

The second step I would recommend is that Congress should instantly appoint the following great officers of state—A secretary for foreign affairs

—a President of war—A President of Marine—A Financier—A President of trade; instead of this last a board of Trade may be preferable as the regulations of trade are slow and gradual and require prudence and experience (more than other qualities), for which boards are very well adapted. . . .

The advantages of securing the attachment of the army to Congress, and binding them to the service by substantial ties are immense. We should then have discipline, an army in reality, as well as in name. Congress would then have a solid basis of authority and consequence, for to me it is an axiom that in our constitution an army is essential to the American union.

The providing of supplies is the pivot of every thing else (though a well constituted army would not in a small degree conduce to this, by giving consistency and weight to government). There are four ways all which must be united—a foreign loan, heavy pecuniary taxes, a tax in kind, a bank founded on public and private credit. . . .

If a Convention is called the minds of all the states and the people ought to be prepared to receive its determinations by sensible and popular writings, which should conform to the views of Congress. There are epochs in human affairs, when *novelty* even is useful. If a general opinion prevails that the old way is bad, whether true or false, and this obstructs or relaxes the operation of the public service, a change is necessary if it be but for the sake of change. This is exactly the case now. 'Tis an universal sentiment that our present system is a bad one, and that things do not go right on this account. The measure of a Convention would revive the hopes of the people and give a new direction to their passions, which may be improved in carrying points of substantial utility. The Eastern states have already pointed out this mode to Congress; they ought to take the hint and anticipate the others. . . .

I wish too Congress would always consider that a kindness consists as much in the manner as in the thing: the best things done hesitatingly and with an ill grace lose their effect, and produce disgust rather than satisfaction or gratitude. In what Congress have at any time done for the army, they have commonly been too late: They have seemed to yield to importunity rather than to sentiments of justice or to a regard to the accomodation of their troops. An attention to this idea is of more importance than it may be thought. I who have seen all the workings and progress of the present discontents, am convinced, that a want of this has not been among the most inconsiderable causes.

THE CONTINENTALIST NO. 1 [2]

An extreme jealousy of power is the attendant on all popular revolutions, and has seldom been without its evils. It is to this source we are to

[2] [July 12, 1781]. From *The Papers of Alexander Hamilton*, vol. 1.

trace many of the fatal mistakes, which have so deeply endangered the common cause; particularly that defect, which will be the object of these remarks, A WANT OF POWER IN CONGRESS.

The present Congress, respectable for abilities and integrity, by experience convinced of the necessity of a change, are preparing several important articles to be submitted to the respective states, for augmenting the powers of the Confederation. But though there is hardly at this time a man of information in America, who will not acknowledge, as a general proposition, that in its present form, it is unequal, either to a vigorous prosecution of the war, or to the preservation of the union in peace; yet when the principle comes to be applied to practice, there seems not to be the same agreement in the modes of remedying the defect; and it is to be feared, from a disposition which appeared in some of the states on a late occasion, that the salutary intentions of Congress may meet with more delay and opposition, than the critical posture of the states will justify. . . .

Yet whatever may be the advantage on our side, in such a comparison, men who estimate the value of institutions, not from prejudices of the moment, but from experience and reason, must be persuaded, that the same JEALOUSY of POWER has prevented our reaping all the advantages, from the examples of other nations, which we ought to have done, and has rendered our constitutions in many respects feeble and imperfect.

Perhaps the evil is not very great in respect to our constitutions; for notwithstanding their imperfections, they may, for some time, be made to operate in such a manner, as to answer the purposes of the common defence and the maintenance of order; and they seem to have, in themselves, and in the progress of society among us, the seeds of improvement.

But this is not the case with respect to the FOEDERAL GOVERNMENT; if it is too weak at first, it will continually grow weaker. The ambition and local interests of the respective members, will be constantly undermining and usurping upon its prerogatives, till it comes to a dissolution; if a partial combination of some of the more powerful ones does not bring it to a more SPEEDY and VIOLENT END. . . .

THE CONTINENTALIST NO. 2 [3]

In a single state, where the sovereign power is exercised by delegation, whether it be a limitted monarchy or a republic, the danger most commonly is, that the sovereign will become too powerful for his constituents; in fœderal governments, where different states are represented in a general council, the danger is on the other side—that the members

[3] [July 19, 1781]. From *The Papers of Alexander Hamilton*, vol. 1.

will be an overmatch for the common head, or in other words, that it will not have sufficient influence and authority to secure the obedience of the several parts of the confederacy.

In a single state, the sovereign has the whole legislative power as well as the command of the national forces, of course, an immediate controul over the persons and property of the subjects. Every other power is subordinate and dependent. If he undertakes to subvert the constitution, it can only be preserved by a general insurrection of the people. The magistrates of the provinces, counties, or towns, into which the state is divided, having only an executive and police jurisdiction, can take no decisive measures for counteracting the first indications of tyranny; but must content themselves with the ineffectual weapon of petition and remonstrance. They cannot raise money, levy troops, nor form alliances. The leaders of the people must wait till their discontents have ripened into a general revolt, to put them in a situation to confer the powers necessary for their defence. It will always be difficult for this to take place; because the sovereign possessing the appearance and forms of legal authority, having the forces and revenues of the state at his command, and a large party among the people besides, which with those advantages he can hardly fail to acquire, he will too often be able to baffle the first motions of the discontented, and prevent that union and concert essential to the success of their opposition.

The security therefore of the public liberty, must consist in such a distribution of the sovereign power, as will make it morally impossible for one part to gain an ascendency over the others, or for the whole to unite in a scheme of usurpation.

In fœderal governments, each member has a distinct sovereignty, makes and executes laws, imposes taxes, distributes justice, and exercises every other function of government. It has always within itself the means of revenue, and on an emergency can levy forces. If the common sovereign should meditate, or attempt any thing unfavourable to the general liberty, each member, having all the proper organs of power, can prepare for defence with celerity and vigour. Each can immediately sound the alarm to the others, and enter into leagues for mutual protection. If the combination is general, as is to be expected, the usurpers will soon find themselves without the means of recruiting their treasury, or their armies; and for want of continued supplies of men and money, must, in the end fall a sacrifice to the attempt. If the combination is not general, it will imply, that some of the members are interested in that which is the cause of dissatisfaction to others, and this cannot be an attack upon the common liberty, but upon the interests of one part in favour of another part; and it will be a war between the members of the fœderal union with each other, not between them and the fœderal government. . . .

The particular governments will have more empire over the minds of their subjects, than the general one, because their agency will be more direct, more uniform, and more apparent. The people will be habituated to look up to them as the arbiters and guardians of their personal concerns, by which the passions of the vulgar, if not of all men are most strongly affected; and in every difference with the confederated body will side with them against the common sovereign. . . .

THE CONTINENTALIST NO. 3 [4]

[Fishkill, New York, August 9, 1781]
In the midst of a war for our existence as a nation; in the midst of dangers too serious to be trifled with, some of the states have evaded, or refused, compliance with the demands of Congress in points of the greatest moment to the common safety. If they act such a part at this perilous juncture, what are we to expect in a time of peace and security? . . .

Our whole system is in disorder; our currency depreciated, till in many places it will hardly obtain a circulation at all, public credit at its lowest ebb, our army deficient in numbers, and unprovided with every thing, the government, in its present condition, unable to command the means to pay, clothe, or feed their troops, the enemy making an alarming progress in the southern states, lately in complete possession of two of them, though now in part rescued by the genius and exertions of a General without an army, a force under Cornwallis still formidable to Virginia.

We ought to blush to acknowledge, that this is a true picture of our situation, when we reflect, that the enemy's whole force in the United States, including their American levies and the late reinforcement, is little more than fourteen thousand effective men; that our population, by recent examination, has been found to be greater, than at the commencement of the war; that the quantity of our specie has also increased, that the country abounds with all the necessaries of life, and has a sufficiency of foreign commodities, with a considerable and progressive commerce; that we have beyond comparison a better stock of warlike materials, than when we began the contest, and an ally as willing as able to supply our further wants: And that we have, on the spot, five thousand auxiliary troops, paid and subsisted by that ally, to assist in our defence.

Nothing but a GENERAL DISAFFECTION of the PEOPLE, or MISMANAGEMENT in their RULERS, can account for the figure we make, and for the distresses and perplexities we experience, contending against so small a force. . . .

[4] [August 9, 1781]. From *The Papers of Alexander Hamilton,* vol. 1.

THE CONTINENTALIST NO. 4 [5]

The great defect of the confederation is, that it gives the United States no property, or in other words, no revenue, nor the means of acquiring it, inherent in themselves, and independent on the temporary pleasure of the different members; and power without revenue in political society is a name. While Congress continue altogether dependent on the occasional grants of the several States, for the means of defraying the expences of the FOEDERAL GOVERNMENT, it can neither have dignity vigour nor *credit*. CREDIT supposes specific and permanent funds for the punctual payment of interest, with a moral certainty of a final redemption of the principal. . . .

There are some among us ignorant enough to imagine, that the war may be carried on without credit; defraying the expences of the year with what may be raised within the year. But this is for want of a knowledge of our real resources and expenses. . . .

THE CONTINENTALIST NO. 6 [6]

We may preach till we are tired of the theme, the necessity of disinterestedness in republics, without making a single proselyte. The virtuous declaimer will neither persuade himself nor any other person to be content with a double mess of porridge, instead of a reasonable stipend for his services. We might as soon reconcile ourselves to the Spartan community of goods and wives, to their iron coin, their long beards, or their black broth. . . .

The Foederal Government should neither be independent nor too much dependent. It should neither be raised above responsibility or controul, nor should it want the means of maintaining its own weight, authority, dignity and credit. To this end permanent funds are indispensable, but they ought to be of such a nature and so moderate in their amount, as never to be inconvenient. Extraordinary supplies can be the objects of extraordinary grants; and in this salutary medium will consist our true wisdom. . . .

The genius of liberty reprobates every thing arbitrary or discretionary in taxation. It exacts that every man by a definite and general rule should know what proportion of his property the state demands. . . .

The establishment of permanent funds would not only answer the public purposes infinitely better than temporary supplies; but it would be the most effectual way of easing the people. With this basis for procuring credit, the amount of present taxes might be greatly diminished. Large sums of money might be borrowed abroad at a low interest, and

[5] [August 30, 1781]. From *The Papers of Alexander Hamilton,* vol. 1.
[6] [July 4, 1782]. From *The Papers of Alexander Hamilton* (New York, 1962), vol. 3.

introduced into the country to defray the current expences and pay the public debts; which would not only lessen the demand for immediate supplies, but would throw more money into circulation, and furnish the people with greater means of paying the taxes. Though it be a just rule, that we ought not to run in debt to avoid present expence, so far as our faculties extend; yet the propriety of doing it cannot be disputed when it is apparent, that these are incompetent to the public necessities. Efforts beyond our abilities can only tend to individual distress and national disappointment.

The product of the three forgoing articles will be as little as can be required to enable Congress to pay their debts, and restore order into their finances. In addition to these—

The disposal of the unlocated lands will hereafter be a valuable source of revenue, and an immediate one of credit. As it may be liable to the same condition with the duties on trade, that is the product of the sales within each state, to be creditted to that state, and as the rights of jurisdiction are not infringed, it seems to be susceptible of no reasonable objection.

Mines in every country constitute a branch of the revenue. . . . All the precious metals should absolutely be the property of the Fœderal Government, and with respect to the others, it should have a discretionary power of reserving in the nature of a tax, such part as it may judge not inconsistent with the encouragement due to so important an object. This is rather a future than a present resource. . . .

THE CONSTITUTIONAL CONVENTION [7]

MR. HAMILTON, had been hitherto silent on the business before the Convention, partly from respect to others whose superior abilities age & experience rendered him unwilling to bring forward ideas dissimilar to theirs, and partly from his delicate situation with respect to his own State, to whose sentiments as expressed by his Colleagues, he could by no means accede. The crisis however which now marked our affairs, was too serious to permit any scruples whatever to prevail over the duty imposed on every man to contribute his efforts for the public safety & happiness. He was obliged therefore to declare himself unfriendly to both plans. He was particularly opposed to that from N. Jersey, being fully convinced, that no amendment of the Confederation, leaving the States in possession of their Sovereignty could possibly answer the purpose. . . . The States sent us here to provide for the exigences of the Union. To rely on & purpose any plan not adequate to these exigences, merely because it was not clearly within our powers, would be to sacrifice

[7] From James Madison's version of Hamilton's "Speech on a Plan of Government," June 18, 1787. From *The Papers of Alexander Hamilton* (New York, 1962), vol. 4.

the means to the end. It may be said that the *States* can not *ratify* a plan not within the purview of the article of Confederation providing for alterations & amendments. But may not the States themselves in which no constitutional authority equal to this purpose exists in the Legislatures, have had in view a reference to the people at large. In the Senate of N. York, a proviso was moved, that no act of the Convention should be binding untill it should be referred to the people & ratified; and the motion was lost by a single voice only, the reason assigned agst. it being, that it might possibly be found an inconvenient shackle.

The great question is what provision shall we make for the happiness of our Country? He would first make a comparative examination of the two plans—prove that there were essential defects in both—and point out such changes as might render a *national one,* efficacious. The great & essential principles necessary for the support of Government are 1. an active & constant interest in supporting it. This principle does not exist in the States in favor of the federal Govt. They have evidently in a high degree, the esprit de corps. They constantly pursue internal interests adverse to those of the whole. They have their particular debts—their particular plans of finance &c. All these when opposed to, invariably prevail over the requisitions & plans of Congress. 2. The love of power. Men love power. The same remarks are applicable to this principle. The States have constantly shewn a disposition rather to regain the powers delegated by them than to part with more, or to give effect to what they had parted with. The ambition of their demagogues is known to hate the controul of the Genl. Government. It may be remarked too that the Citizens have not that anxiety to prevent a dissolution of the Genl. Govt. as of the particular Govts. A dissolution of the latter would be fatal; of the former would still leave the purposes of Govt. attainable to a considerable degree. Consider what such a State as Virga. will be in a few years, a few compared with the life of nations. How strongly will it feel its importance & self-sufficiency? 3. An habitual attachment of the people. The whole force of this tie is on the side of the State Govt. Its sovereignty is immediately before the eyes of the people: its protection is immediately enjoyed by them. From its hand distributive justice, and all those acts which familiarize & endear Govt. to a people, are dispensed to them. 4. *Force* by which may be understood a *coertion of laws* or *coertion of arms.* Congs. have not the former except in few cases. In particular States, this coercion is nearly sufficient; tho' he held it in most cases, not entirely so. A certain portion of military force is absolutely necessary in large communities. Masss. is now feeling this necessity & making provision for it. But how can this force be exerted on the States collectively. It is impossible. It amounts to a war between the parties. Foreign powers also will not be idle spectators. They will interpose, the confusion will increase, and a dissolution of the Union will ensue. 5. *influence.* he did not mean corruption, but a dispensation of those regu-

lar honors & emoluments, which produce an attachment to the Govt.
Almost all the weight of these is on the side of the States; and must
continue so as long as the States continue to exist. All the passions then
we see, of avarice, ambition, interest, which govern most individuals,
and all public bodies, fall into the current of the States, and do not flow
in the stream of the Genl. Govt. The former therefore will generally be
an overmatch for the Genl. Govt. and render any confederacy, in its
very nature precarious. . . . How then are all these evils to be avoided?
only by such a compleat sovereignty in the general Governmt. as will
turn all the strong principles & passions above mentioned on its side.
Does the scheme of N. Jersey produce this effect? does it afford any substantial remedy whatever? On the contrary it labors under great defects,
and the defect of some of its provisions will destroy the efficacy of others.
It gives a direct revenue to Congs. but this will not be sufficient. The
balance can only be supplied by requisitions: which experience proves
can not be relied on. If States are to deliberate on the mode, they will
also deliberate on the object of the supplies, and will grant or not grant
as they approve or disapprove of it. The delinquency of one will invite
and countenance it in others. Quotas too must in the nature of things
be so unequal as to produce the same evil. . . . Mr. Ps. plan provides
no remedy. If the powers proposed were adequate, the organization of
Congs. is such that they could never be properly & effectually exercised.
The members of Congs. being chosen by the States & subject to recall,
represent all the local prejudices. Should the powers be found effectual,
they will from time to time be heaped on them, till a tyrannic sway
shall be established. The general power whatever be its form if it pre-
serves itself, must swallow up the State powers. Otherwise it will be
swallowed up by them. It is agst. all the principles of a good Government
to vest the requisite powers in such a body as Congs. Two Sovereignties
can not co-exist within the same limits. Giving powers to Congs. must
eventuate in a bad Govt. or in no Govt. The plan of N. Jersey therefore
will not do. What then is to be done? Here he was embarrassed. The
extent of the Country to be governed, discouraged him. The expence of
a general Govt. was also formidable; unless there were such a diminution
of expence on the side of the State Govts. as the case would admit. If
they were extinguished, he was persuaded that great œconomy might be
obtained by substituting a general Govt. He did not mean however to
shock the public opinion by proposing such a measure. On the other
hand he saw no *other* necessity for declining it. They are not necessary
for any of the great purposes of commerce, revenue, or agriculture. Subordinate authorities he was aware would be necessary. There must be
district tribunals: corporations for local purposes. But cui bono, the
vast & expensive apparatus now appertaining to the States. The only
difficulty of a serious nature which occurred to him, was that of drawing
representatives from the extremes to the center of the Community. What

inducements can be offered that will suffice? The moderate wages for the 1st. branch would only be a bait to little demagogues. Three dollars or thereabouts he supposed would be the utmost. The Senate he feared from a similar cause, would be filled by certain undertakers who wish for particular offices under the Govt. This view of the subject almost led him to despair that a Republican Govt. could be established over so great an extent. He was sensible at the same time that it would be unwise to propose one of any other form. In his private opinion he had no scruple in declaring, supported as he was by the opinions of so many of the wise & good, that the British Govt. was the best in the world: and that he doubted much whether any thing short of it would do in America. He hoped Gentlemen of different opinions would bear with him in this, and begged them to recollect the change of opinion on this subject which had taken place and was still going on. It was once thought that the power of Congs. was amply sufficient to secure the end of their institution. The error was now seen by every one. The members most tenacious of republicanism, he observed, were as loud as any in declaiming agst. the vices of democracy. This progress of the public mind led him to anticipate the time, when others as well as himself would join in the praise bestowed by Mr. Neckar on the British Constitution, namely, that it is the only Govt. in the world "which unites public strength with individual security." In every community where industry is encouraged, there will be a division of it into the few & the many. Hence separate interests will arise. There will be debtors & creditors &c. Give all power to the many, they will oppress the few. Give all power to the few, they will oppress the many. Both therefore ought to have power, that each may defend itself agst. the other. To the want of this check we owe our paper money, instalment laws &c. To the proper adjustment of it the British owe the excellence of their Constitution. Their house of Lords is a most noble institution. Having nothing to hope for by a change, and a sufficient interest by means of their property, in being faithful to the national interest, they form a permanent barrier agst. every pernicious innovation, whether attempted on the part of the Crown or of the Commons. No temporary Senate will have the firmness eno' to answer the purpose. . . . Gentlemen differ in their opinions concerning the necessary checks, from the different estimates they form of the human passions. They suppose seven years a sufficient period to give the senate an adequate firmness, from not duly considering the amazing violence & turbulence of the democratic spirit. When a great object of Govt. is pursued, which seizes the popular passions, they spread like wild fire, and become irresistable. He appealed to the gentlemen from the N. England States whether experience had not there verified the remark. As to the Executive, it seemed to be admitted that no good one could be established on Republican principles. Was not this giving up the merits of the question: for can there be a good Govt. without a good Executive.

The English model was the only good one on this subject. The Hereditary interest of the King was so interwoven with that of the Nation, and his personal emoluments so great, that he was placed above the danger of being corrupted from abroad—and at the same time was both sufficiently independent and sufficiently controuled, to answer the purpose of the institution at home. one of the weak sides of Republics was their being liable to foreign influence & corruption. Men of little character, acquiring great power become easily the tools of intermedling Neibours. . . . What is the inference from all these observations? That we ought to go as far in order to attain stability and permanency, as republican principles will admit. Let one branch of the Legislature hold their places for life or at least during good behaviour. Let the Executive also be for life. He appealed to the feelings of the members present whether a term of seven years, would induce the sacrifices of private affairs which an acceptance of public trust would require, so as to ensure the services of the best Citizens. On this plan we should have in the Senate a permanent will, a weighty interest, which would answer essential purposes. But is this a Republican Govt., it will be asked? Yes if all the Magistrates are appointed, and vacancies are filled, by the people, or a process of election originating with the people. He was sensible that an Executive constituted as he proposed would have in fact but little of the power and independence that might be necessary. On the other plan of appointing him for 7 years, he thought the Executive ought to have but little power. He would be ambitious, with the means of making creatures; and as the object of his ambition wd. be to *prolong* his power, it is probable that in case of a war, he would avail himself of the emergence, to evade or refuse a degradation from his place. An Executive for life has not this motive for forgetting his fidelity, and will therefore be a safer depository of power. . . . Having made these observations he would read to the Committee a sketch of a plan which he shd. prefer to either of those under consideration. He was aware that it went beyond the ideas of most members. But will such a plan be adopted out of doors? In return he would ask will the people adopt the other plan? At present they will adopt neither. But he sees the Union dissolving or already dissolved— he sees evils operating in the States which must soon cure the people of their fondness for democracies—he sees that a great progress has been already made & is still going on in the public mind. He thinks therefore that the people will in time be unshackled from their prejudices; and whenever that happens, they will themselves not be satisfied at stopping where the plan of Mr. R. wd. place them, but be ready to go as far at least as he proposes. He did not mean to offer the paper he had sketched as a proposition to the Committee. It was meant only to give a more correct view of his ideas, and to suggest the amendments which he should probably propose to the plan of Mr. R. in the proper stages of its future discussion.

ROBERT YATES' VERSION [8]

Mr. Hamilton. . . . I have well considered the subject, and am convinced that no amendment of the confederation can answer the purpose of a good government, so long as state sovereignties do, in any shape, exist; and I have great doubts whether a national government on the Virginia plan can be made effectual. What is federal? An association of several independent states into one. . . .

. . . What, for example, will be the inducementes for gentlemen of fortune and abilities to leave their houses and business to attend annually and long [in the national legislature]? It cannot be the wages; for these, I presume, must be small. Will not the power, therefore, be thrown into the hands of the demagogue or middling politician, who, for the sake of a small stipend and the hopes of advancement, will offer himself as a candidate, and the real men of weight and influence, by remaining at home, add strength to the state governments? I am at a loss to know what must be done; I despair that a republican form of government can remove the difficulties. Whatever may be my opinion, I would hold it however unwise to change that form of government. I believe the British government forms the best model the world ever produced, and such has been its progress in the minds of the many, that this truth gradually gains ground. This government has for its object *public strength* and *individual security*. It is said with us to be unattainable. If it was once formed it would maintain itself. All communities divide themselves into the few and the many. The first are the rich and well born, the other the mass of the people. The voice of the people has been said to be the voice of God; and however generally this maxim has been quoted and believed, it is not true in fact. The people are turbulent and changing; they seldom judge or determine right. Give therefore to the first class a distinct, permanent share in the government. They will check the unsteadiness of the second, and as they cannot receive any advantage by a change, they therefore will ever maintain good government. Can a democratic assembly, who annually revolve in the mass of the people, be supposed steadily to pursue the public good? Nothing but a permanent body can check the imprudence of democracy. Their turbulent and uncontrouling disposition requires checks. The senate of New-York, although chosen for four years, we have found to be inefficient. Will, on the Virginia plan, a continuance of seven years do it? It is admitted, that you cannot have a good executive upon a democratic plan. See the excellency of the British executive. He is placed above temptation. He can have no distinct interests from the public welfare. Nothing short of such an executive can be efficient. The weak side of a republican government is the danger of

[8] From Robert Yates' version of Hamilton's "Speech on a Plan of Government," June 18, 1787. From *The Papers of Alexander Hamilton,* vol. 4.

foreign influence. This is unavoidable, unless it is so constructed as to bring forward its first characters in its support. I am therefore for a general government, yet would wish to go to the full length of republican principles.

Let one body of the legislature be constituted during good behaviour or life.

Let one executive be appointed who dares execute his powers.

It may be asked is this a republican system? It is strictly so, as long as they remain elective.

And let me observe, that an executive is less dangerous to the liberties of the people when in office during life, than for seven years.

It may be said, this constitutes an elective monarchy? Pray, what is a monarchy? May not the governors of the respective states be considered in that light? But by making the executive subject to impeachment, the term monarchy cannot apply. . . . Let electors be appointed in each of the states to elect the executive—(*Here Mr. H. produced his plan, a copy whereof is hereunto annexed,*)[9] to consist of two branches—and I would give them the unlimited power of passing *all laws* without exception. The assemby to be elected for three years by the people in districts— the senate to be elected by the electors to be chosen for that purpose by the people, and to remain in office during life. The executive to have the power of negativing all laws—to make war or peace, with the advice of the senate—to make treaties with their advice, but to have the sole direction of all military operations, and to send ambassadors and appoint all military officers, and to pardon all offenders, treason excepted, unless by advice of the senate. On his death or removal, the president of the senate to officiate, with the same powers, until another is elected. Supreme judicial officers to be appointed by the executive and the senate. The legislature to appoint courts in each state, so as to make the state governments unnecessary to it.

All state laws to be absolutely void which contravene the general laws. An officer to be appointed in each state to have a negative on all state laws. All the militia and the appointment of officers to be under the national government.

I confess that this plan and that from Virginia are very remote from the idea of the people. Perhaps the Jersey plan is nearest their expectation. But the people are gradually ripening in their opinions of government—they begin to be tired of an excess of democracy—and what even is the Virginia plan, but *pork still, with a little change of the sauce.*

[9] See "Constitutional Convention. Plan of Government," June 18, 1787.

3

Arguments for Ratification
of the Constitution

Hamilton's contributions to the eighty-five Federalist Papers were part of the same seamless web of his thought on the nature of effective and viable government. These papers, written in great haste and secrecy, were jointly authored by Jay, Madison and Hamilton, with the last being the key figure, composing nearly two thirds (fifty-one numbers) of them. Indeed, it was his energy and organizational skill that made them possible. They were written over the signature of "Publius," a happy choice of Hamilton's, referring as it did to the Roman hero, Publius Valerius, who established just and stable republican government.

Published in the Independent Journal: or the General Advertiser *of New York, these papers were the earliest and remained the most effective defense of and commentaries upon the new Constitution (the best, according to Jefferson, "on the principles of government which ever was written"). They did a brilliant public relations job, successfully parrying the anti-nationalist Clintonians and enlisting support for the new instrument of government. They would help persuade a majority of New York's delegates, then locked in the critical ratification struggle at Poughkeepsie.*

The Federalist Papers skillfully combined a quartet of issues and arguments: they explained the virtues of federal government, condemned the Articles, analyzed and defended the new Constitution, and provided a luminous and penetrating exposition on the pleasures and dangers of democratic government. They sought to rescue America's experiment in political liberty—to be done, the authors believed, only by creating strong and energetic national government and by giving it great power and prestige; they sought, in other words, to create "a more perfect union." Taken together, they were a brilliant treatise in political science.

Nor is there any reason why these papers should not be taken together, as a unified commentary on the need to enlarge the scope of national power. After all, they read as if composed by one hand. They are all characterized by a moderate tone, one of almost Olympian calm. Those of Hamilton, for instance, are restrained and unemotional—in sharp contrast to his earlier and heated work as well as to the rough-and-tumble political scene. The appeal is to reason throughout. Like those of his co-authors, Hamilton's contributions are simple in eloquence, faultlessly clear in language, elementary but not shrill or slick; they are Hamilton at his best, with nothing of the sly or dishonest about them. Finally, all their essays were written in haste, but their surfaces do not betray it and they were surely not the result of hasty thought. Hamilton, for example, was assigned the chore of exposing weaknesses in the Articles, a subject which he had thought about for nearly a decade.

For reasons which should be obvious, Hamilton never intimated his own deep misgivings about the new document and sought, in the first number, to soothe the fears of "the cultivators of the land"; in another, he warned that anarchy was the only alternative to ratification and reassured those fearful of Leviathan; in a third, he denounced the arguments of "the credulous votaries of state power"; in still one more essay he explored the importance and functions of the federal judiciary, stressing the need for a final arbiter between the varied classes and interests as well as between states and national governments; and any number were stained by a pessimistic awareness of the frailties of men. Even the best of men, Hamilton acknowledged, possessed "natural depravity"—which expressed itself in hatred, envy, dishonesty, treachery, hypocrisy, covetousness and bellicosity. Lamenting the "folly and wickedness of mankind," he enjoined his readers to approve institutional devices which would protect society by curbing these selfish and irrational impulses in human beings.

Hamilton, then, never indulged in the Jeffersonian dream of man's perfectibility. On the other hand, he was no Hobbesian. He maintained that men also possessed estimable qualities—of bravery, generosity, humanity, love of liberty. Admittedly, he declared that vice and self-interest dominated. But, much like Madison, Jefferson and John Adams among others, he believed the passions and interests of men could be restrained and channeled in the interest of the "public good."

THE FEDERALIST NO. 1 [1]

[New York, October 27, 1787]

To the People of the State of New York.

Among the most formidable of the obstacles which the new Constitution will have to encounter, may readily be distinguished the obvious

[1] From *The Papers of Alexander Hamilton*, vol. 4.

interest of a certain class of men in every State to resist all changes which may hazard a diminution of the power, emolument and consequence of the offices they hold under the State-establishments—and the perverted ambition of another class of men, who will either hope to aggrandise themselves by the confusions of their country, or will flatter themselves with fairer prospects of elevation from the subdivision of the empire into several partial confederacies, than from its union under one government.

It is not, however, my design to dwell upon observations of this nature. I am well aware that it would be disingenuous to resolve indiscriminately the opposition of any set of men (merely because their situations might subject them to suspicion) into interested or ambitious views: Candour will oblige us to admit, that even such men may be actuated by upright intentions; and it cannot be doubted, that much of the opposition which has made its appearance, or may hereafter make its appearance, will spring from sources, blameless at least, if not respectable, the honest errors of minds led astray by preconceived jealousies and fears. So numerous indeed and so powerful are the causes, which serve to give a false bias to the judgment, that we upon many occasions, see wise and good men on the wrong as well as on the right side of questions, of the first magnitude to society. . . . Ambition, avarice, personal animosity, party opposition, and many other motives, not more laudable than these, are apt to operate as well upon those who support as upon those who oppose the right side of a question. Were there not even these inducements to moderation, nothing could be more illjudged than that intolerant spirit, which has, at all times, characterised political parties. For, in politics as in religion, it is equally absurd to aim at making proselytes by fire and sword. Heresies in either can rarely be cured by persecution. . . .

An enlightened zeal for the energy and efficiency of government will be stigmatised, as the off-spring of a temper fond of despotic power and hostile to the principles of liberty. An overscrupulous jealousy of danger to the rights of the people, which is more commonly the fault of the head than of the heart, will be represented as mere pretence and artifice; the bait for popularity at the expence of public good. It will be forgotten, on the one hand, that jealousy is the usual concomitant of violent love, and that the noble enthusiasm of liberty is too apt to be infected with a spirit of narrow and illiberal distrust. On the other hand, it will be equally forgotten, that the vigour of government is essential to the security of liberty; that, in the contemplation of a sound and well informed judgment, their interest can never be separated; and that a dangerous ambition more often lurks behind the specious mask of zeal for the rights of the people, than under the forbidding appearance of zeal for the firmness and efficiency of government. History will teach us, that the former has been found a much more certain road to the introduction of despotism, than the latter, and that of those men who have overturned the liberties of republics the greatest number have begun their carreer, by paying an obsequious court to the people, commencing Demagogues and ending Tyrants.

In the course of the preceeding observations I have had an eye, my Fellow Citizens, to putting you upon your guard against all attempts, from whatever quarter, to influence your decision in a matter of the utmost moment to your welfare by any impressions other than those which may result from the evidence of truth. You will, no doubt, at the same time, have collected from the general scope of them that they proceed from a source not unfriendly to the new Constitution. Yes, my Countrymen, I own to you, that, after having given it an attentive consideration, I am clearly of opinion, it is your interest to adopt it. I am convinced, that this is the safest course for your liberty, your dignity, and your happiness. I effect not reserves, which I do not feel. I will not amuse you with an appearance of deliberation, when I have decided. I frankly acknowledge to you my convictions, and I will freely lay before you the reasons on which they are founded. The consciousness of good intentions disdains ambiguity. I shall not however multiply professions on this head. My motives must remain in the depository of my own breast: My arguments will be open to all, and may be judged of by all. They shall at least be offered in a spirit, which will not disgrace the cause of truth.

I propose in a series of papers to discuss the following interesting particulars—*The utility of the UNION to your political prosperity—The insufficiency of the present Confederation to preserve that Union—The necessity of a government at least equally energetic with the one proposed to the attainment of this object—The conformity of the proposed constitution to the true principles of republican government—Its analogy to your own state constitution*—and lastly, *The additional security, which its adoption will afford the preservation of that species of government, to liberty and to property.*

In the progress of this discussion I shall endeavour to give a satisfactory answer to all the objections which shall have made their appearance that may seem to have any claim to your attention.

It may perhaps be thought superfluous to offer arguments to prove the utility of the UNION, a point, no doubt, deeply engraved on the hearts of the great body of the people in every state, and one, which it may be imagined has no adversaries. But the fact is, that we already hear it whispered in the private circles of those who oppose the new constitution, that the Thirteen States are of too great extent for any general system, and that we must of necessity resort to separate confederacies of distinct portions of the whole. This doctrine will, in all probability, be gradually propagated, till it has votaries enough to countenance an open avowal of it. For nothing can be more evident, to those who are able to take an enlarged view of the subject than the alternative of an adoption of the new Constitution, or a dismemberment of the Union. It will therefore be of use to begin by examining the advantages of that Union, the certain evils and the probable dangers, to which every State will be exposed from its dissolution. This shall accordingly constitute the subject of my next address.

PUBLIUS.

THE FEDERALIST NO. 9 [2]

The efficacy of various principles is now well understood, which were either not known at all, or imperfectly known to the ancients. The regular distribution of power into distinct departments—the introduction of legislative ballances and checks—the institution of courts composed of judges, holding their offices during good behaviour—the representation of the people in the legislature by deputies of their own election—these are either wholly new discoveries or have made their principal progress towards perfection in modern times. They are means, and powerful means, by which the excellencies of republican government may be retained and its imperfections lessened or avoided. . . .

The utility of a confederacy, as well to suppress faction and to guard the internal tranquillity of States, as to increase their external force and security, is in reality not a new idea. It has been practiced upon in different countries and ages, and has received the sanction of the most applauded writers, on the subjects of politics. The opponents of the PLAN proposed have with great assiduity cited and circulated the observations of Montesquieu on the necessity of a contracted territory for a republican government. But they seem not to have been apprised of the sentiments of that great man expressed in another part of his work, nor to have adverted to the consequences of the principle to which they subscribe, with such ready acquiescence. . . .

The proposed Constitution, so far from implying an abolition of the State Governments, makes them constituent parts of the national sovereignty by allowing them a direct representation in the Senate, and leaves in their possession certain exclusive and very important portions of sovereign power. This fully corresponds, in every rational import of the terms, with the idea of a Fœderal Government.

THE FEDERALIST NO. 11 [3]

Under a vigorous national government, the natural strength and resources of the country, directed to a common interest, would baffle all the combinations of European jealousy to restrain our growth. This situation would even take away the motive to such combinations, by inducing

[2] From *The Papers of Alexander Hamilton*, vol. 4.
[3] From *The Papers of Alexander Hamilton*, vol. 4.

an impracticability of success. An active commerce, an extensive navigation, and a flourishing marine would then be the inevitable offspring of moral and physical necessity. We might defy the little arts of little politicians to controul, or vary, the irresistible and unchangeable course of nature.

But in a state of disunion these combinations might exist, and might operate with success. It would be in the power of the maritime nations, availing themselves of our universal impotence, to prescribe the conditions of our political existence; and as they have a common interest in being our carriers, and still more in preventing our being theirs, they would in all probability combine to embarrass our navigation in such a manner, as would in effect destroy it, and confine us to a PASSIVE COMMERCE. We should thus be compelled to content ourselves with the first price of our commodities, and to see the profits of our trade snatched from us to enrich our enemies and persecutors. That unequalled spirit of enterprise, which signalises the genius of the American Merchants and Navigators, and which is in itself an inexhaustible mine of national wealth, would be stifled and lost; and poverty and disgrace would overspread a country, which with wisdom might make herself the admiration and envy of the world.

There are rights of great moment to the trade of America, which are rights of the Union. I allude to the fisheries, to the navigation of the Western lakes and to that of the Mississippi. The dissolution of the confederacy would give room for delicate questions, concerning the future existence of these rights; which the interest of more powerful partners would hardly fail to solve to our disadvantage. The disposition of Spain with regard to the Mississippi needs no comment. France and Britain are concerned with us in the fisheries; and view them as of the utmost moment to their navigation. They, of course, would hardly remain long indifferent to that decided mastery of which experience has shewn us to be possessed in this valuable branch of traffic; and by which we are able to undersell those nations in their own markets. What more natural, than that they should be disposed to exclude, from the lists, such dangerous competitors?

This branch of trade ought not to be considered as a partial benefit. All the navigating States may in different degrees advantageously participate in it and under circumstances of a greater extension of mercantile capital would not be unlikely to do it. As a nursery of seamen it now is, or when time shall have more nearly assimilated the principles of navigation in the several States, will become an universal resource. To the establishment of a navy it must be indispensible. . . .

An unrestrained intercourse between the States themselves will advance the trade of each, by an interchange of their respective productions, not only for the supply of reciprocal wants at home, but for exportation to foreign markets. The veins of commerce in every part will be replenished, and will acquire additional motion and vigour from a free circulation of the commondities of every part. Commercial enterprise will have much greater scope, from the diversity in the productions of different States. When the staple of one fails, from a bad harvest or unproductive crop, it can call to its aid the staple of another. The variety not less than the value of products for exportation, contributes to the activity of foreign commerce. It can be conducted upon much better terms, with a large number of materials of a given value, than with a small number of materials of the same value; arising from the competitions of trade and from the fluctuations of markets. Particular articles may be in great demand, at certain periods, and unsaleable at others; but if there be a variety of articles it can scarcely happen that they should all be at one time in the latter predicament; and on this account the operations of the merchant would be less liable to any considerable obstruction, or stagnation. The speculative trader will at once perceive the force of these observations; and will acknowledge that the aggregate ballance of the commerce of the United States would bid fair to be much more favorable, than that of the thirteen States, without union, or with partial unions.

It may perhaps be replied to this, that whether the States are united, or disunited, there would still be an intimate intercourse between them which would answer the same ends: But this intercourse would be fettered, interrupted and narrowed by a multiplicity of causes; which in the course of these Papers have been amply detailed. An unity of commercial, as well as political interests, can only result from an unity of government.

There are other points of view, in which this subject might be placed, of a striking and animating kind. But they would lead us too far into the regions of futurity, and would involve topics not proper for a Newspaper discussion. I shall briefly observe, that our situation invites, and our interest prompt us, to aim at an ascendant in the system of American affairs. The world may politically, as well as geographically, be divided into four parts, each having a distinct set of interests. Unhappily for the other three, Europe by her arms and by her negociations, by force and by fraud, has, in different degrees, extended her dominion over them all. Africa, Asia, and America have successively felt her domination. The superiority, she has long maintained, has tempted her to plume herself as the Mistress of the World, and to consider the rest of mankind as created for her benefit. Men admired as profound philosophers have, in direct terms, attributed to her inhabitants a physical superiority; and have gravely asserted that all animals, and with them the human species, degenerate in America—that even dogs cease to bark after having breathed a while in our atmosphere. Facts have too long supported these arrogant pretensions of the European: It belongs to us to vindicate the honor of the human race, and to teach that assuming brother moderation. Union will enable us to do it. Disunion will add another victim to his triumphs. Let Americans disdain to be the instruments of European greatness! Let the thirteen States, bound together in a strict and indissoluble union, concur in erecting one great American system, superior to the controul of all trans-atlantic force or influence, and able to dictate the terms of the connection between the old and the new world!

PUBLIUS.

THE FEDERALIST NO. 12 [4]

[New York, November 27, 1787]

To the People of the State of New-York.

The prosperity of commerce is now perceived and acknowledged, by all enlightened statesmen, to be the most useful as well as the most productive source of national wealth; and has accordingly become a primary object of their political cares. By multiplying the means of gratification, by promoting the introduction and circulation of the precious metals, those darling objects of human avarice and enterprise, it serves to vivify and invigorate the channels of industry, and to make them flow with greater activity and copiousness. The assiduous merchant, the laborious husbandman, the active mechanic, and the industrious manufacturer, all orders of men look forward with eager expectation and growing alacrity to this pleasing reward of their toils. The often-agitated question, between agriculture and commerce, has from indubitable experience received a decision, which has silenced the rivalships, that once subsisted between them, and has proved to the satisfaction of their friends, that their interests are intimately blended and interwoven. It has been found, in various countries, that in proportion as commerce has flourished, land has risen in value. And how could it have happened otherwise? Could that which procures a free vent for the products of the earth—which furnishes new incitements to the cultivators of land—which is the most powerful instrument in encreasing the quantity of money in a state—could that, in fine, which is the faithful handmaid of labor and industry in every shape, fail to augment the value of that article, which is the prolific parent of far the greatest part of the objects upon which they are exerted? It is astonishing, that so simple a truth should ever have had an adversary; and it is one among a multitude of proofs, how apt a spirit of ill-informed jealousy, or of too great abstraction and refinement is to lead men astray from the plainest paths of reason and conviction.

The ability of a country to pay taxes must always be proportioned, in a great degree, to the quantity of money in circulation, and to the celerity with which it circulates. Commerce, contributing to both these objects, must of necessity render the payment of taxes easier, and facilitate the requisite supplies to the treasury. . . .

[4] From *The Papers of Alexander Hamilton*, vol. 4.

THE FEDERALIST NO. 15 [5]

[New York, December 1, 1787]

In pursuance of the plan, which I have laid down for the discussion of the subject, the point next in order to be examined is the "insufficiency of the present confederation to the preservation of the Union." . . .

We may indeed with propriety be said to have reached almost the last stage of national humiliation. There is scarcely any thing that can wound the pride, or degrade the character of an independent nation, which we do not experience. Are there engagements to the performance of which we are held by every tie respectable among men? These are the subjects of constant and unblushing violation. Do we owe debts to foreigners and to our own citizens contracted in a time of imminent peril, for the preservation of our political existence? These remain without any proper or satisfactory provision for their discharge. Have we valuable territories and important posts in the possession of a foreign power, which by express stipulations ought long since to have been surrendered? These are still retained, to the prejudice of our interests not less than of our rights. Are we in a condition to resent, or to repel the aggression? We have neither troops nor treasury nor government. Are we even in a condition to remonstrate with dignity? The just imputations on our own faith, in respect to the same treaty, ought first to be removed. Are we entitled by nature and compact to a free participation in the navigation of the Mississippi? Spain excludes us from it. Is public credit an indispensable resource in time of public danger? We seem to have abandoned its cause as desperate and irretrivable. Is commerce of importance to national wealth? Ours is at the lowest point of declension. Is respectability in the eyes of foreign powers a safe guard against foreign encroachments? The imbecility of our Government even forbids them to treat with us: Our ambassadors abroad are the mere pageants of mimic sovereignty. Is a violent and unnatural decrease in the value of land a symptom of national distress? The price of improved land in most parts of the country is much lower than can be accounted for by the quantity of waste land at market, and can only be fully explained by that want of private and public confidence, which are so alarmingly prevalent among all ranks and which have a direct tendency to depreciate property of every kind. Is private credit the friend and patron of industry? That most useful kind which relates to borrowing and lending is reduced within the narrowest limits, and this still more from an opinion of insecurity than from the scarcity of money. To shorten an enumeration of particulars which can afford neither pleasure nor instruction it may in general be demanded, what indication is there of national disorder, poverty and insignificance that could befall a community so peculiarly blessed with natural advantages as we are, which does not form a part of the dark catalogue of our public misfortunes?

This is the melancholy situation, to which we have been brought by those very maxims and councils, which would now deter us from adopting the proposed constitution; and which not content with having conducted us to the brink of a precipice, seem resolved to plunge us into the abyss, that awaits us below. Here, my Countrymen, impelled by every motive that ought to influence an enlightened people, let us make a firm stand for our safety, our tranquillity, our dignity, our reputation. Let us at last break the fatal charm which has too long seduced us from the paths of felicity and prosperity.

It is true, as has been before observed, that facts too stubborn to be resisted have produced a species of general assent to the abstract proposition that there exist material defects in our national system; but the usefulness of the concession, on the part of the old adversaries of fœderal measures, is destroyed by a strenuous opposition to a remedy, upon the only principles, that can give it a chance of success. While they admit that the Government of the United States is destitute of energy; they contend against conferring upon it those powers which are requisite to supply that energy: They seem still to aim at things repugnant and irreconcilable—at an augmentation of Fœderal authority without a diminution of State authority—at sovereignty in the Union and complete independence in the members. They still in fine seem to cherish with blind devotion the political monster of an *imperium in imperio*. This renders a full display of the principal defects of the confederation necessary, in order to shew, that the evils we experience do not proceed from minute or partial imperfections, but from fundamental errors in the structure of the building which cannot be amended otherwise than by an alteration in the first principles and main pillars of the fabric. . . .

If the particular States in this country are disposed to stand in a similar relation to each other, and to drop the project of a general DISCRETIONARY SUPERINTENDENCE, the scheme would indeed be pernicious, and would entail upon us all the mischiefs that have been enumerated under the first head; but it would have the merit of being at least consistent and practicable. Abandoning all views towards a confederate Government, this would bring us to a simple alliance offensive and defensive; and would place us in a situation to be alternately friends and enemies of each other as our mutual jealousies and rivalships nourished by the intrigues of foreign nations should prescribe to us.

But if we are unwilling to be placed in this perilous situation; if we will still adhere to the design of a national government, or which is the same thing of a superintending power under the direction of a common Council, we must resolve to incorporate into our plan those ingredients which may be considered as forming the characteristic difference between a league and a government; we must extend the authority of the union to the persons of the citizens,—the only proper objects of government. . . .

In our case, the concurrence of thirteen distinct sovereign wills is requisite under the confederation to the complete execution of every important measure, that proceeds from the Union. It has happened as was to have been foreseen. The measures of the Union have not been executed; and the delinquencies of the States have step by step matured themselves to an extreme; which has at length arrested all the wheels of the national government, and brought them to an awful stand. Congress at this time scarcely possess the means of keeping up the forms of administration; 'till the States can have time to agree upon a more substantial substitute for the present shadow of a fœderal government. Things did not come to this desperate extremity at once. The causes which have been specified produced at first only unequal and disproportionate degrees of compliance with the requisitions of the Union. The greater deficiencies of some States furnished the pretext of example and the temptation of interest to the complying, or to the least delinquent States. Why should we do more in proportion than those who are embarked with us in the same political voyage? Why should we consent to bear more than our proper share of the common burthen? These were suggestions which human selfishness could not withstand, and which even speculative men, who looked forward to remote consequences, could not, without hesitation, combat. Each State yielding to the persuasive voice of immediate interest and convenience has successively withdrawn its support, 'till the frail and tottering edifice seems ready to fall upon our heads and to crush us beneath its ruins.

PUBLIUS.

THE FEDERALIST NO. 16 [6]

[New York, December 4, 1787]

To the People of the State of New-York.

If a large and influential State should happen to be the aggressing member, it would commonly have weight enough with its neighbours, to win over some of them as associates to its cause. Specious arguments of danger to the common liberty could easily be contrived; plausible excuses for the deficiencies of the party, could, without difficulty be invented, to alarm the apprehensions, inflame the passions, and conciliate the good will even of those States which were not chargeable with any violation, or omission of duty. This would be the more likely to take place, as the delinquencies of the larger members might be expected sometimes to proceed from an ambitious premeditation in their rulers, with a view to getting rid of all external controul upon their designs of personal

[6] From *The Papers of Alexander Hamilton*, vol. 4.

aggrandizement; the better to effect which, it is presumable they would tamper beforehand with leading individuals in the adjacent States. If associates could not be found at home, recourse would be had to the aid of foreign powers, who would seldom be disinclined to encouraging the dissentions of a confederacy, from the firm Union of which they had so much to fear. When the sword is once drawn, the passions of men observe no bounds of moderation. The suggestions of wounded pride, the instigations of irritated resentment, would be apt to carry the States, against which the arms of the Union were exerted to any extremes necessary to revenge the affront, or to avoid the disgrace of submission. The first war of this kind would probably terminate in a dissolution of the Union.

This may be considered as the violent death of the confederacy. Its more natural death is what we now seem to be on the point of experiencing, if the fœderal system be not speedily renovated in a more substantial form. . . .

Whoever considers the populousness and strength of several of these States singly at the present juncture, and looks forward to what they will become, even at the distance of half a century, will at once dismiss as idle and visionary any scheme, which aims at regulating their movements by laws, to operate upon them in their collective capacities, and to be executed by a coertion applicable to them in the same capacities. A project of this kind is little less romantic than that monster-taming spirit, which is attributed to the fabulous heroes and demi-gods of antiquity.

Even in those confederacies, which have been composed of members smaller than many of our countries, the principle of legislation for sovereign States, supported by military coertion, has never been found effectual. It has rarely been attempted to be employed, but against the weaker members. And in most instances attempts to coerce the refractory and disobedient, have been the signals of bloody wars; in which one half of the confederacy has displayed its banners against the other half.

The result of these observations to an intelligent mind must be clearly this, that if it be possible at any rate to construct a Fœderal Government capable of regulating the common concerns and preserving the general tranquility, it must be founded, as to the objects committed to its care, upon the reverse of the principle contended for by the opponents of the proposed constitution. It must carry its agency to the persons of the citizens. It must stand in need of no intermediate legislations; but must itself be empowered to employ the arm of the ordinary magistrate to execute its own resolutions. The majesty of the national authority must be manifested through the medium of the Courts of Justice. The government of the Union, like that of each State, must be able to address itself immediately to the hopes and fears of individuals; and to attract to its support, those passions, which have the strongest influence upon the human heart. It must in short, possess all the means and have a right to resort to all the methods of executing the powers, with which it is entrusted, that are possessed and exercised by the governments of the particular States.

THE FEDERALIST NO. 21 [7]

[New York, December 12, 1787]

To the People of the State of New-York.

I shall now proceed in the enumeration of the most important of those defects, which have hitherto disappointed our hopes from the system established among ourselves. To form a safe and satisfactory judgment of the proper remedy, it is absolutely necessary that we should be well acquainted with the extent and malignity of the disease.

The next most palpable defect of the subsisting confederation is the total want of a SANCTION to its laws. The United States as now composed, have no power to exact obedience, or punish disobedience to their resolutions, either by pecuniary mulcts by a suspension or divestiture of privileges, or in any other constitutional mode. There is no express delegation of authority to them to use force against delinquent members; and if such a right should be ascribed to the fœderal head, as resulting from the nature of the social compact between the States, it must be by inference and construction, in the face of that part of the second article, by which it is declared, "each State shall retain every power, jurisdiction and right, not *expressly* delegated to the United States in Congress assembled." . . .

Without a guarantee, the assistance to be derived from the Union in repelling those domestic dangers, which may sometimes threaten the existence of the State constitutions, must be renounced. Usurpation may rear its crest in each State, and trample upon the liberties of the people; while the national government could legally do nothing more than behold its encroachments with indignation and regret. A successful faction may erect a tyranny on the ruins of order and law, while no succour could constitutionally be afforded by the Union to the friends and supporters of the government. The tempestuous situation, from which Massachusetts has scarcely emerged, evinces that dangers of this kind are not merely speculative.[8] Who can determine what might have been the issue of her late convulsions, if the mal-contents had been headed by a Caesar or by a Cromwell? Who can predict what effect a despostism established in Massachusetts, would have upon the liberties of New-Hampshire or Rhode-Island; of Connecticut or New-York?

The inordinate pride of State importance has suggested to some minds an objection to the principle of a guarantee in the fœderal Government; as involving an officious interference in the domestic concerns of the

---

[7] From *The Papers of Alexander Hamilton,* vol. 4.
[8] H is referring to Shay's Rebellion.

members. A scruple of this kind would deprive us of one of the principal advantages to be expected from Union; and can only flow from a misapprehension of the nature of the provision itself. It would be no impediment to reforms of the State Constitutions by a majority of the people in a legal and peaceable mode. This right would remain undiminished. The guarantee could only operate against changes to be effected by violence. Towards the prevention of calamities of this kind too many checks cannot be provided. The peace of society, and the stability of government, depend absolutely on the efficacy of the precautions adopted on this head. Where the whole power of the government is in the hands of the people, there is the less pretence for the use of violent remedies, in partial or occasional distempers of the State. The natural cure for an ill administration, in a popular or representative constitution, is a change of men. A guarantee by the national authority would be as much levelled against the usurpations of rulers, as against the ferments and outrages of faction and sedition in the community.

THE FEDERALIST NO. 22 [9]

[New York, December 14, 1787]
To the People of the State of New-York.
IN addition to the defects already enumerated in the existing Fœderal system, there are others of not less importance, which concur in rendering it altogether unfit for the administration of the affairs of the Union.

The want of a power to regulate commerce is by all parties allowed to be of the number. . . . It is indeed evident, on the most superficial views, that there is no object, either as it respects the interests of trade or finance that more strongly demands a Fœderal superintendence. The want of it has already operated as a bar to the formation of beneficial treaties with foreign powers; and has given occasions of dissatisfaction between the States. . . .

The interfering and unneighbourly regulations of some States, contrary to the true spirit of the Union, have in different instances given just cause of umbrage and complaint to others; and it is to be feared that examples of this nature, if not restrained by a national controul, would be multiplied and extended till they became not less serious sources of animosity and discord, than injurious impediments to the intercourse between the different parts of the confederacy. . . . [Y]et we may reasonably expect, from the gradual conflicts of State regulations, that the citizens of each, would at length come to be considered and treated by the others in no better light than that of foreigners and aliens.

The power of raising armies, by the most obvious construction of the articles of the confederation, is merely a power of making requisitions upon the States for quotas of men. This practice, in the course of the late war, was found replete with obstructions to a vigorous and to an œconomical system of defence. It gave birth to a competition between the States, which created a kind of auction for men. In order to furnish the quotas required of them, they outbid each other, till bounties grew to an enormous and insupportable size. . . .

This method of raising troops is not more unfriendly to œconomy and vigor, than it is to an equal distribution of the burthen. The States near the seat of war, influenced by motives of self preservation, made efforts to furnish their quotas, which even exceeded their abilities, while those at a distance from danger were for the most part as remiss as the others were diligent in their exertions. The immediate pressure of this inequality was not in this case, as in that of the contributions of money, alleviated by the hope of a final liquidation. . . .

The right of equal suffrage among the States is another exceptionable part of the confederation. Every idea of proportion, and every rule of fair representation conspire to condemn a principle, which gives to Rhode-Island an equal weight in the scale of power with Massachusetts, or Connecticut, or New-York; and to Delaware, an equal voice in the national deliberations with Pennsylvania or Virginia, or North-Carolina. Its operation contradicts that fundamental maxim of republican government, which requires that the sense of the majority should prevail. . . .

But this is not all; what at first sight may seem a remedy, is in reality a poison. To give a minority a negative upon the majority (which is always the case where more than a majority is requisite to a decision) is in its tendency to subject the sense of the greater number to that of the lesser number. Congress from the non-attendance of a few States have been frequently in the situation of a Polish Diet, where a single veto has been sufficient to put a stop to all their movements. A sixtieth part of the Union, which is about the proportion of Delaware and Rhode-Island, has several times been able to oppose an intire bar to its operations. This is one of those refinements which in practice has an effect, the reverse of what is expected from it in theory. The necessity of unanimity in public bodies, or of something approaching towards it, has been founded upon a supposition that it would contribute to security. But its real operation is to embarrass the administration, to destroy the energy of government, and to substitute the pleasure, caprice or artifices of an insignificant, turbulent or corrupt junto, to the regular deliberations and decisions of a respectable majority. . . .

A circumstance, which crowns the defects of the confederation, remains yet to be mentioned—the want of a judiciary power. Laws are a dead letter without courts to expound and define their true meaning and operation. The treaties of the United States to have any force at all, must be considered as part of the law of the land. Their true import as far as respects individuals, must, like all other laws, be ascertained by judicial determinations. To produce uniformity in these determinations, they ought to be submitted in the last resort, to one SUPREME TRIBU-NAL. . . .

This is the more necessary where the frame of the government is so compounded, that the laws of the whole are in danger of being contravened by the laws of the parts. In this case if the particular tribunals are invested with a right of ultimate jurisdiction, besides the contradictions to be expected from difference of opinion, there will be much to fear from the bias of local views and prejudices, and from the interference of local regulations. As often as such an interference was to happen, there would be reason to apprehend, that the provisions of the particular laws might be preferred to those of the general laws; for nothing is more natural to men in office, than to look with peculiar deference towards that authority to which they owe their official existence.

The treaties of the United States, under the present constitution, are liable to the infractions of thirteen different Legislatures, and as many different courts of final jurisdiction, acting under the authority of those Legislatures. The faith, the reputation, the peace of the whole union, are thus continually at the mercy of the prejudices, the passions, and the interests of every member of which it is composed. Is it possible that foreign nations can either respect or confide in such a government? Is it possible that the People of America will longer consent to trust their honor, their happiness, their safety, on so precarious a foundation? . . .

It has not a little contributed to the infirmities of the existing fœderal system, that it never had a ratification by the PEOPLE. Resting on no better foundation than the consent of the several Legislatures; it has been exposed to frequent and intricate questions concerning the validity of its powers; and has in some instances given birth to the enormous doctrine of a right of legislative repeal. Owing its ratification to the law of a State, it has been contended, that the same authority might repeal the law by which it was ratified. However gross a heresy it may be, to maintain that *a party* to *a compact* has a right to revoke that *compact*, the doctrine itself has had respectable advocates. The possibility of a question of this nature, proves the necessity of laying the foundations of our national government deeper than in the mere sanction of delegated authority. The fabric of American Empire ought to rest on the solid basis of THE CONSENT OF THE PEOPLE. The streams of national power ought to flow immediately from that pure original fountain of all legitimate authority.

PUBLIUS.

4

On Banks and Finances

Perhaps the most intractable problem facing the Conti-
nental Congress was that of maintaining financial stability and, in-
timately related, carrying the Revolution forward. Inflation was
rampant in 1780, paper money having deteriorated to about one
fortieth its face value. Congress was unable adequately to feed or
pay the army. It lacked any accumulated funds and had to conduct
military operations on credit. By 1780, however, government credit
was nonexistent, American as well as foreign creditors having no
faith in the nation's future. Hamilton's letters to John Duane and
Robert Morris, the Superintendent of Finance, offered comprehensive
measures toward the end of rescuing and reinvigorating the econ-
omy. Though private correspondence, they were in effect his first
state papers, documents looking forward to the Annapolis Conven-
tion, to his major speech at the Constitutional Convention, and to
his first Reports as Secretary of the Treasury. With a sweep and
audacity which he above all others possessed, Hamilton sketched
the organic relation between economic rehabilitation and consoli-
dated government; it would be a steady theme.

Hamilton was offered a matchless opportunity to implement his
views about political economy in September 1789, some six months
after the new government was inaugurated, when appointed Secre-
tary of the Treasury. The national scene was such as to challenge
even his extraordinary powers. The fiscal ineptitude of the govern-
ment, which had been primarily responsible for events leading up to
the Constitution, continued. Only the fact of prosperity marked
this post-1787 period off from events prior to it. The debts remained
—a large foreign debt, a complicated domestic one which consisted
of a bewildering array of certificates and bills of credit, and a hope-
lessly tangled state debt. (The foreign debt, mostly owed to France
and Holland was about $12,000,000. The domestic debt, states and
national, totalled about $65,000,000, according to Hamilton, a sub-
stantial amount for four million farmers.) Hamilton determined to
honor the Constitutional provision that "all debts contracted and
engagements entered into before the adoption of the Constitution
shall be as valid against the United States under this Constitution as
under the Confederation." Fulfillment of this pledge fell to Hamil-

ton and his recommendations would create fierce factional rivalry in the first decade of our national history.

On September 21, 1789, the House of Representatives, aware that "an adequate provision for the support of the public credit" was "a matter of high importance to the national honor and prosperity," directed Hamilton to "prepare a plan for that purpose." The secretary did as directed and his first careful blueprint, a bold and imaginative proposal, was the "Report Relative to a Provision for the Support of Public Credit." It initially commanded strong support. Not even the agrarian spokesmen, such as Madison or Jefferson, entertained any thought of repudiating the honest debts of their virtually friendless government. Hamilton's appeal to the national honor was most persuasive; and he pressed his case with charm, eloquence, and cogency.

If no opposition was voiced to payment of the foreign debt and funding the domestic debt, interest and principal was another matter. The old debt holders, often artisans and small farmers, had frequently sold their certificates of indebtedness at the going rate of one seventh of the original face value. Now these former owners of the scrip charged that Hamilton's plan to fund the national debt at par would in effect benefit only the present holders, mostly speculators who had purchased these evidences of debt for a song; that is, it would "swindle" the original holders and compound the felony by taxing them, those least able to pay, to refund speculators at one hundred cents on the dollar.

At first there was only a low murmur of opposition, partly because it was disorganized and because Hamilton had done his work well. This Report was, above all, a laborious inquiry into the state of the economy. It opened by establishing the principle—moral and economic as well as legal—that a nation's debts should be honored; and only then did it turn to the means by which revenue would be collected. Funding, it emphasized throughout, would be productive of loans and commercial growth.

But Madison proposed that this Report be amended so as to discriminate "between original holders of the public securities and present possessors by purchase." Justice and good faith demanded, he stated, some sort of compromise; and he proposed that "the present holders . . . have the highest price which has prevailed on the market" with the "residue," that is, the difference between market and face value being paid to the "original sufferers." Hamilton objected; this proposal would be "unjust and impolitic" as well as a breach of contract. Thus a debate was touched off which, as John Marshall said, "seemed to unchain all those fierce passions which a high respect for the government" had heretofore restrained. The measure passed; but those most aggrieved—the former soldier, the *yoeman farmer, the urban artisan*—had begun to sense their organized political power.

Conflict over the debt deepened when another portion of Hamilton's Report came under public scrutiny; the requirement that the debts of the several states be assumed by the national government. This proposal, Hamilton claimed, would give state creditors "the same interests as federal creditors" and also induce them to "support . . . the fiscal arrangements of the government." But Southern agrarians demurred. Such a measure, ran the gravamen of their charge, would weaken the states and enfeeble local sovereignty. Equally intolerable, many states had already discharged much of their debt and would now have an additional tax burden levied, which would be applied to the debts of those states, mostly northern, still in arrears. Again, after a sectional bargain, the measure passed but also at a high price: deep and enduring economic as well as sectional division.

Contrary to Hamilton's expectations, therefore, the national debt did not serve as a unifying device. Rather it brought an end to the spirit of good will that had reigned in the first session of Congress and sparked open warfare between Federalists and anti-Federalists, each accusing the other of undermining the Constitution and the national welfare. Nor did Hamilton's report on a National Bank restore unity or tranquility. To the contrary, it further exacerbated divisions in his troubled land. His own party, already sundered over funding and assumption, was further splintered, with Southern Federalists deserting the ranks.

Hamilton had written about a national bank as early as 1779, when he was only twenty-two—in a letter to John Sullivan. And thereafter, in correspondence, addresses, debates, he pressed home the message that such a bank was essential if financial stability were to be achieved. He proposed it in letters to Schuyler, Duane and Morris —at a time when there was no national bank or indeed any means to neutralize the seemingly chronic inflation and indebtedness. The usefulness of such a bank was confirmed in the intervening years and by three intervening banks up to 1791. Like the Bank of England upon which it was modelled, the new Bank would conduct commercial operations as well as administer public finances, provide the Treasury with loans, and help the government to collect taxes.

Opposition to Hamilton's plan was predictable, considering the storm which broke over the first Report and the agrarian attack on the Bank of North America in the Pennsylvania assembly some five years earlier. But even he may not have anticipated the intensity of this bombshell, which proved even more explosive than assumed. The Bank opposition, mostly agrarian, had marshalled its forces, its suspicions about central government and business interests now

fully confirmed. Hamilton's rebuttal was as audacious as his 1779
letter to Sullivan and as comprehensive as the 1790 Report itself,
being nothing less than a bold and sweeping assertion of federal
sovereignty.

TO DUANE, SEPTEMBER 3, 1780 [1]

How far it may be practicable to erect a bank on the joint credit
of the public and of individuals can only be certainly determined by the
experiment: but it is of so much importance that the experiment ought
to be fully tried. . . .

And why can we not have an American bank? Are our monied men less
enlightened to their own interest or less enterprising in the persuit? I believe the fault is in our government which does not exert itself to engage
them in such a scheme. It is true, the individuals in America are not very
rich, but this would not prevent their instituting a bank; it would only
prevent its being done with such ample funds as in other countries. Have
they not sufficient confidence in the government and in the issue of the
cause? Let the Government endeavour to inspire that confidence, by
adopting the measures I have recommended or others equivalent to them.
Let it exert itself to procure a solid confederation, to establish a good plan
of executive administration, to form a permanent military force, to obtain
at all events a foreign loan. If these things were in a train of vigorous
execution, it would give a new spring to our affairs; government would
recover its respectability and individuals would renounce their diffi-
dence. . . .

The first step to establishing the bank will be to engage a number of
monied men of influence to relish the project and make it a business. The
subscribers to that lately established are the fittest persons that can be
found; and their plan may be interwoven.

The outlines of my plan would be to open subscriptions in all the states
for the stock, which we will suppose to be one million of pounds. Real
property of every kind, as well as specie should be deemed good stock, but
at least a fourth part of the subscription should be in specie or plate.
There should be one great company in three divisions in Virginia, Philadelphia, and at Boston or two at Philadelphia and Boston. The bank
should have a right to issue bank notes bearing two per Cent interest for
the whole of their stock; but not to exceed it. These notes may be payable
every three months or oftener, and the faith of government must be pledged
for the support of the bank. It must therefore have a right from time to
time to inspect its operations, and must appoint inspectors for the purpose. . . .

[1] From *The Papers of Alexander Hamilton,* vol. 1.

. . . If government could engage the states to raise a sum of money in specie to be deposited in bank in the same manner, it would be of the greatest consequence. If government could prevail on the enthusiasm of the people to make a contribution in plate for the same purpose it would be a master stroke. Things of this kind sometimes succeed in popular contests; and if undertaken with address; I should not despair of its success; but I should not be sanguine.

The bank may be instituted for a term of years by way of trial and the particular privilege of coining money be for a term still shorter. A temporary transfer of it to a particular company can have no inconvenience as the government are in no condition to improve this resource nor could it in our circumstances be an object to them, though with the industry of a knot of individuals it might be.

A bank of this kind even in its commencement would answer the most valuable purposes to government and to the proprietors; in its progress the advantages will exceed calculation. It will promote commerce by furnishing a more extensive medium which we greatly want in our circumstances. I mean a more extensive valuable medium. We have an enormous nominal one at this time; but it is only a name.

TO ROBERT MORRIS, APRIL 30, 1781 [2]

. . . I mean the institution of a National Bank. This I regard, in some shape or other as an expedient essential to our safety and success, unless by a happy turn of European affairs the war should speedily terminate in a manner upon which it would be unwise to reckon. There is no other that can give to government that extensive and systematic credit, which the defect of our revenues makes indispensably necessary to its operations. The longer it is delayed, the more difficult it becomes; our affairs grow every day more relaxed and more involved; public credit hastens to a more irretrievable catastrophe; the means for executing the plan are exhausted in partial and temporary efforts. The loan now making in Massachusettes would have gone a great way in establishing the funds on which the bank must stand. . . .

We have little specie; the paper we have is of small value and rapidly descending to less; we are immersed in a war for our existence as a nation, for our liberty and happiness as a people; we have no revenues nor no credit. A bank if practicable is the only thing that can give us either the one or the other. . . .

In the present system of things the health of a state particularly a commercial one depends on a due quantity and regular circulation of Cash, as much as the health of an animal body depends upon the due quantity and regular circulation of the blood. There are indisputable indications that we have not a sufficient medium and what we have is in continual fluctuation. The only cure to our public disorders is to fix the value of the currency we now have and increase it to a proper standard in a species that will have the requisite stability.

The error of those who would explode paper money altogether originates in not making proper distinctions. Our paper was in its nature liable to depreciations, because it had no funds for its support and was not upheld by private credit. . . . 'Tis in a National Bank alone that we can find the ingredients to constitute a wholesome, solid and beneficial paper credit. . . .

I see nothing to prevent the practicability of a plan of this kind but a distrust of the final success of the War, which may make men afraid to risk any considerable part of their fortunes in the public funds, but without being an enthusiast, I will venture to assert, that with such a resource as is here proposed, the loss of our Independence is impossible. All we have to fear is that the want of money may disband the army, or so perplex and enfeeble our operations as to create in the people a general disgust and alarm, which may make them clamour for peace on any terms. But if a judicious administration of our finances, assisted by a bank takes place, and the ancient security of property is restored, no convulsion is to be apprehended; our opposition will soon assume an aspect of system and vigor that will relieve and encourage the people and put an end to the hopes of the enemy. . . .

A national debt if it is not excessive will be to us a national blessing; it will be powerful cement of our union. It will also create a necessity for keeping up taxation to a degree which without being oppressive, will be a spur to industry; remote as we are from Europe and shall be from danger.

REPORT RELATIVE TO PUBLIC CREDIT, JANUARY 9, 1790 [3]

. . . the momentous nature of the truth contained in the resolution under which his investigations have been conducted, "That an *adequate* provision for the support of the Public Credit, is a matter of high importance to the honor and prosperity of the United States." . . .

In the opinion of the Secretary, the wisdom of the House, in giving their explicit sanction to the proposition which has been stated, cannot be applauded by all, who will seriously consider, and trace through their obvious consequences, these plain and undeniable truths

That exigencies are to be expected to occur, in the affairs of nations, in which there will be a necessity for borrowing.

That loans in times of public danger, especially from foreign war, are found an indispensable resource, even to the wealthiest of them.

And that in a country, which, like this, is possessed of little active

[3] From *The Reports of Alexander Hamilton.*

wealth, or in other words, little monied capital, the necessity for that resource, must, in such emergencies, be proportionably urgent.

And as on the one hand, the necessity for borrowing in particular emergencies cannot be doubted, so on the other, it is equally evident, that to be able to borrow upon *good terms*, it is essential that the credit of a nation should be well established.

For when the credit of a country is in any degree questionable, it never fails to give an extravagant premium, in one shape or another, upon all the loans it has occasion to make. Nor does the evil end here; the same disadvantage must be sustained upon whatever is to be bought on terms of future payment.

From this constant necessity of *borrowing* and *buying dear*, it is easy to conceive how immensely the expences of a nation, in a course of time, will be augmented by an unsound state of the public credit. . . .

If the maintenance of public credit, then, be truly so important, the next enquiry which suggests itself is, by what means it is to be effected? The ready answer to which question is, by good faith, by a punctual performance of contracts. States, like individuals, who observe their engagements, are respected and trusted: while the reverse is the fate of those, who pursue an opposite conduct.

Every breach of the public engagements, whether from choice or necessity, is in different degrees hurtful to public credit. When such a necessity does truly exist, the evils of it are only to be palliated by a scrupulous attention, on the part of the government, to carry the violation no farther than the necessity absolutely requires, and to manifest, if the nature of the case admits of it, a sincere disposition to make reparation, whenever circumstances shall permit. . . .

This reflection derives additional strength from the nature of the debt of the United States. It was the price of liberty. The faith of America has been repeatedly pledged for it, and with solemnities, that give peculiar force to the obligation. There is indeed reason to regret that it has not hitherto been kept; that the necessities of the war, conspiring with inexperience in the subjects of finance, produced direct infractions; and that the subsequent period has been a continued scene of negative violation, or non-compliance. But a diminution of this regret arises from the reflection, that the last seven years have exhibited an earnest and uniform effort, on the part of the government of the union, to retrieve the national credit, by doing justice to the creditors of the nation; and that the embarrassments of a defective constitution, which defeated this laudable effort, have ceased.

From this evidence of a favorable disposition, given by the former government, the institution of a new one, cloathed with powers competent to calling forth the resources of the community, has excited correspondent expectations. A general belief, accordingly, prevails, that the credit of the United States will quickly be established on the firm foundation of an effectual provision for the existing debt. The influence, which this has had at home, is witnessed by the rapid increase, that has taken place in the market value of the public securities. . . .

The most enlightened friends of good government are those, whose expectations are the highest.

To justify and preserve their confidence; to promote the encreasing respectability of the American name; to answer the calls of justice; to restore landed property to its due value; to furnish new resources both to agriculture and commerce; to cement more closely the union of the states; to add to their security against foreign attack; to establish public order on the basis of an upright and liberal policy. These are the great and invaluable ends to be secured, by a proper and adequate provision, at the present period, for the support of public credit. . . .

The advantage to the public creditors from the increased value of that part of their property which constitutes the public debt, needs no explanation.

But there is a consequence of this, less obvious, though not less true, in which every other citizen is interested. It is a well known fact, that in countries in which the national debt is properly funded, and an object of established confidence, it answers most of the purposes of money. Transfers of stock or public debt are there equivalent to payments in specie; or in other words, stock, in the principal transactions of business, passes current as specie. The same thing would, in all probability happen here, under the like circumstances.

The benefits of this are various and obvious.

First. Trade is extended by it. . . .

Secondly. Agriculture and manufactures are also promoted by it. . . .

Thirdly. The interest of money will be lowered by it. . . .

And from the combination of these effects, addition aids will be furnished to labour, to industry, and to arts of every kind. . . .

The effect, which the funding of the public debt, on right principles, would have upon landed property, is one of the circumstances attending such an arrangement, which has been least adverted to, though it deserves the most particular attention. The present depreciated state of that species of property is a serious calamity. The value of cultivated lands, in most of the states, has fallen since the revolution from 25 to 50 per cent. In those farthest south, the decrease is still more considerable. Indeed, if the representations, continually received from that quarter, may be credited, lands there will command no price, which may not be deemed an almost total sacrifice.

This decrease, in the value of lands, ought, in a great measure, to be attributed to the scarcity of money. Consequently whatever produces an augmentation of the monied capital of the country, must have a proportional effect in raising that value. . . .

Having now taken a concise view of the inducements to a proper provision for the public debt, the next enquiry which presents itself is, what ought to be the nature of such a provision? This requires some preliminary discussions.

It is agreed on all hands, that that part of the debt which has been contracted abroad, and is denominated the foreign debt, ought to be provided for, according to the precise terms of the contracts relating to it. The discussions, which can arise, therefore, will have reference essentially to the domestic part of it, or to that which has been contracted at home. It is to be regretted, that there is not the same unanimity of sentiment on this part, as on the other.

The Secretary has too much deference for the opinions of every part of the community, not to have observed one, which has, more than once, made its appearance in the public prints, and which is occasionally to be met with in conversation. It involves this question, whether a discrimination ought not be made between original holders of the public securities, and present possessors, by purchase. Those who advocate a discrimination are for making a full provision for the securities of the former, at their nominal value; but contend, that the latter ought to receive no more than the cost to them, and the interest: And the idea is sometimes suggested of making good the difference to the primitive possessor.

In favor of this scheme, it is alleged, that it would be unreasonable to pay twenty shillings in the pound, to one who had not given more for it than three or four. And it is added, that it would be hard to aggravate the misfortune of the first owner, who, probably through necessity, parted with his property at so great a loss, by obliging him to contribute to the profit of the person, who had speculated on his distresses.

The Secretary, after the most mature reflection on the force of this argument, is induced to reject the doctrine it contains, as equally unjust and impolitic, as highly injurious, even to the original holders of public securities; as ruinous to public credit.

It is inconsistent with justice, because in the first place, it is a breach of contract; in violation of the rights of a fair purchaser.

The nature of the contract in its origin, is, that the public will pay the sum expressed in the security, to the first holder, or his *assignee*. The *intent*, in making the security assignable, is, that the proprietor may be able to make use of his property, by selling it for as much as it *may be worth in the market*, and that the buyer may be *safe* in the purchase.

Every buyer therefore stands exactly in the place of the seller, has the same rights with him to the identical sum expressed in the security, and having acquired that right, by fair purchase, and in conformity to the original *agreement* and *intention* of the government, his claim cannot be disputed, without manifest injustice.

That he is to be considered as a fair purchaser, results from this: Whatever necessity the seller may have been under, was occasioned by the government, in not making a proper provision for its debts. The buyer had no agency in it, and therefore ought not to suffer. He is not even charge-able with having taken an undue advantage. He paid what the commodity was worth in the market, and took the risks of reimbursement upon him-self. He of course gave a fair equivalent, and ought to reap the benefit of his hazard; a hazard which was far from inconsiderable, and which, perhaps, turned on little less than a revolution in government.

That the case of those, who parted with their securities from necessity, is a hard one, cannot be denied. But whatever complaint of injury, or claim of redress, they may have, respects the government solely. . . .

But though many of the original holders sold from necessity, it does not follow, that this was the case with all of them. It may well be sup-posed, that some of them did it either through want of confidence in an eventual provision, or from the allurements of some profitable specula-tion. How shall these different classes be discriminated from each other? . . .

Questions of this sort, on a close inspection, multiply themselves with-out end, and demonstrate the injustice of a discrimination, even on the most subtile calculations of equity, abstracted from the obligation of con-tract.

The difficulties too of regulating the details of a plan for that purpose, which would have even the semblance of equity, would be found im-mense. . . .

It will be perceived at first sight, that the transferable quality of stock is essential to its operation as money, and that this depends on the idea of complete security to the transferree, and a firm persuasion, that no dis-tinction can in any circumstances be made between him and the original proprietor. . . .

It is equally unnecessary to add any thing to what has been already said to demonstrate the fatal influence, which the principle of discrimination would have on the public credit.

But there is still a point in view in which it will appear perhaps even more exceptionable, than in either of the former. It would be repugnant to an express provision of the Constitution of the United States. This pro-vision is, that "all debts contracted and engagements entered into before the adoption of that Constitution shall be as valid against the United States under it, as under the confederation," which amounts to a consti-tutional ratification of the contracts respecting the debt, in the state in which they existed under the confederation. And resorting to that stand-ard, there can be no doubt, that the rights of assignees and original hold-ers, must be considered as equal.

In exploding thus fully the principle of discrimination, the Secretary is happy in reflecting, that he is only the advocate of what has been already sanctioned by the formal and express authority of the government of the Union. . . .

The Secretary concluding, that a discrimination, between the different classes of creditors of the United States, cannot with propriety be *made*, proceeds to examine whether a difference ought to be permitted to *remain* between them, and another description of public creditors—Those of the states individually.

The Secretary, after mature reflection on this point, entertains a full conviction, that an assumption of the debts of the particular states by the union, and a like provision for them, as for those of the union, will be a measure of sound policy and substantial justice.

It would, in the opinion of the Secretary, contribute, in an eminent degree, to an orderly, stable and satisfactory arrangement of the national finances.

Admitting, as ought to be the case, that a provision must be made in some way or other, for the entire debt; it will follow, that no greater revenues will be required, whether that provision be made wholly by the United States, or partly by them, and partly by the states separately. . . .

This sum [current expenses] may, in the opinion of the Secretary, be obtained from the present duties on imports and tonnage, with the additions, which without any possible disadvantages either to trade, or agriculture, may be made on wines, spirits, including those distilled within the United States, teas and coffee.[4]

The Secretary conceives, that it will be sound policy, to carry the duties upon articles of this kind, as high as will be consistent with the practicability of a safe collection. This will lessen the necessity, both of having recourse to direct taxation, and of accumulating duties where they would be more inconvenient to trade, and upon objects, which are more to be regarded as necessaries of life.

That the articles which have been enumerated, will, better than most others, bear high duties, can hardly be a question. They are all of them, in reality—luxuries—the greatest part of them foreign luxuries; some of them, in the excess in which they are used, pernicious luxuries. And there is, perhaps, none of them, which is not consumed in so great abundance, as may, justly, denominate it, a source of national extravagance and impoverishment. The consumption of ardent spirits particularly, no doubt very much on account of their cheapness, is carried to an extreme, which is truly to be regretted, as well in regard to the health and the morals, as to the œconomy of the community.

Should the increase of duties tend to a decrease of the consumption of those articles, the effect would be, in every respect desirable. The saving which it would occasion, would leave individuals more at their ease, and promote a more favourable balance of trade. As far as this decrease might be applicable to distilled spirits, it would encourage the substitution of

---

[4] The estimated income from these sources was included in "Schedule K" which Hamilton attached to his report. He estimated the product of duties on imports and tonnage at $1,140,000 and the product of proposed duties at $1,703,400.

cyder and malt liquors, benefit agriculture, and open a new and productive source of revenue.

It is not however, probable, that this decrease would be in a degree, which would frustrate the expected benefit to the revenue from raising the duties. Experience has shewn, that luxuries of every kind, lay the strongest hold on the attachments of mankind, which, especially when confirmed by habit, are not easily alienated from them. . . .

And when it is considered, that the object of the proposed system is the firm establishment of public credit; that on this depends the character, security and prosperity of the nation; that advantages in every light important, may be expected to result from it; that the immediate operation of it will be upon an enlightened class of citizens, zealously devoted to good government, and to a liberal and enlarged policy, and that it is peculiarly the interest of the virtuous part of them to co-operate in whatever will restrain the spirit of illicit traffic; there will be perceived to exist, the justest ground of confidence, that the plan, if eligible in itself, will experience the chearful and prompt acquiescence of the community. . . .

The Secretary would propose, that the duties on distilled spirits, should be applied in the first instance, to the payment of the interest of the foreign debt.

That reserving out of the residue of those duties an annual sum of six hundred thousand dollars, for the current service of the United States; the surplus, together with the product of the other duties, be applied to the payment of the interest on the new loan, by an appropriation, co-extensive with the duration of the debt.

And that if any part of the debt should remain unsubscribed, the excess of the revenue be divided among the creditors of the unsubscribed part, by a temporary disposition; with a limitation, however, to four per cent.

It will hardly have been unnoticed, that the Secretary had been thus far silent on the subject of the post-office. The reason is, that he has had in view the application of the revenue arising from that source, to the purposes of a sinking fund. . . .

Persuaded as the Secretary is, that the proper funding of the present debt, will render it a national blessing: Yet he is so far from acceding to the position, in the latitude in which it is sometimes laid down, that "public debts are public benefits," a position inviting to prodigality, and liable to dangerous abuse,—that he ardently wishes to see it incorporated, as a fundamental maxim, in the system of public credit of the United States, that the creation of debt should always be accompanied with the means of extinguishment. This he regards as the true secret for rendering public credit immortal. . . .

The Secretary now proceeds, in the last place, to offer to the consideration of the House, his ideas, of the steps, which ought at the present session, to be taken, towards the assumption of the state debts.

These are briefly, that concurrent resolutions of the two Houses, with the approbation of the President, be entered into, declaring in substance,

That the United States do assume, and will at the first session in the year 1791, provide, on the same terms with the present debt of the United States, for all such part of the debts of the respective states, or any of them, as shall, prior to the first day of January in the said year 1791, be subscribed towards a loan to the United States, upon the principles of either of the plans, which shall have been adopted by them, for obtaining a re-loan of their present debt. . . .

Deeply impressed, as the Secretary is, with a full and deliberate conviction, that the establishment of public credit, upon the basis of a satisfactory provision, for the public debt, is, under the present circumstances of this country, the true desideratum towards relief from individual and national embarrassments; that without it, these embarrassments will be likely to press still more severely upon the community—He cannot but indulge an anxious wish, that an effectual plan for that purpose may, during the present session, be the result of the united wisdom of the legislature.

He is fully convinced, that it is of the greatest importance, that no further delay should attend the making of the requisite provision; not only, because it will give a better impression of the good faith of the country, and will bring earlier relief to the creditors; both which circumstances are of great moment to public credit: but, because the advantages to the community, from raising stock, as speedily as possible, to its natural value, will be incomparably greater, than any that can result from its continuance below that standard. No profit, which could be derived from purchases in the market, on account of the government, to any practicable extent, would be an equivalent for the loss, which would be sustained by the purchases of foreigners, at a low value. Not to repeat, that governmental purchases, to be honorable, ought to be preceded by a provision. Delay, by disseminating doubt, would sink the price of stock; and as the temptation to foreign speculations, from the lowness of the price, would be too great to be neglected, millions would probably be lost to the United States.

THE SECOND REPORT ON THE FURTHER PROVISION NECESSARY FOR ESTABLISHING PUBLIC CREDIT (REPORT ON A NATIONAL BANK), DECEMBER 13th, 1790 [5]

To the Speaker of the House of Representatives

In obedience to the order of the House of Representatives of the ninth day of August last, requiring the Secretary of the Treasury to prepare and report on this day such further provision as may, in his opinion, be necessary for establishing the public Credit. . . .

[5] From *The Reports of Alexander Hamilton.*

That from a conviction (as suggested in his report No. 1 herewith presented) That a National Bank is an Institution of primary importance to the properous administration of the Finances, and would be of the greatest utility in the operations connected with the support of the Public Credit. . . .

The following are among the principal advantages of a Bank.

First. The augmentation of the active or productive capital of a country. Gold and Silver, when they are employed merely as the instruments of exchange and alienation, have been not improperly denominated dead Stock; but when deposited in Banks, to become the basis of a paper circulation, which takes their character and place, as the signs or representatives of value, they then acquire life, or, in other words, an active and productive quality. . . .

Secondly. Greater facility to the Government in obtaining pecuniary aids, especially in sudden emergencies. . . .

Thirdly. The facilitating of the payment of taxes. . . .

It would be to intrude too much on the patience of the house, to prolong the details of the advantages of Banks; especially as all those, which might still be particularized are readily to be inferred as consequences from those, which have been enumerated. Their disadvantages, real or supposed, are now to be reviewed. The most serious of the charges which have been brought against them are—

That they serve to increase usury:

That they tend to prevent other kinds of lending:

That they furnish temptations to overtrading:

That they afford aid to ignorant adventurers who disturb the natural and beneficial course of trade:

That they give to bankrupt and fraudulent traders a fictitious credit, which enables them to maintain false appearances and to extend their impositions: And lastly

That they have a tendency to banish gold and silver from the country.

There is great reason to believe, that on a close and candid survey, it will be discovered, that these charges are either destitute of foundation; or that, as far as the evils, they suggest, have been found to exist, they have proceeded from other, or partial, or temporary causes, are not inherent in the nature and permanent tendency of such institutions; or are more than counterbalanced by opposite advantages. . . .

But the last and heaviest charge is still to be examined. This is, that Banks tend to banish the gold and silver of the Country.

The force of this objection rests upon their being an engine of paper credit, which by furnishing a substitute for the metals, is supposed to promote their exportation. It is an objection, which if it has any foundation, lies not against Banks, peculiarly, but against every species of paper credit. . . .

A nation, that has no mines of its own, must derive the precious metals from others; generally speaking, in exchange for the products of its labor and industry. The quantity, it will possess, will therefore, in the ordinary course of things, be regulated by the favourable, or unfavourable balance of its trade; that is, by the proportion between its abilities to supply foreigners, and its wants of them; between the amount of its exportations and that of its importations. Hence the state of its agriculture and manufactures, the quantity and *quality* of its labor and industry must, in the main, influence and determine the increase or decrease of its gold and silver.

If this be true, the inference seems to be, that well constituted Banks favour the increase of the precious metals. It has been shewn, that they augment in different ways, the active capital of the country. This, it is, which generates employment; which animates and expands labor and industry. Every addition, which is made to it, by contributing to put in motion a greater quantity of both, tends to create a greater quantity of the products of both: And, by furnishing more materials for exportation, conduces to a favourable balance of trade and consequently to the introduction and increase of gold and silver. . . .

The emitting of paper money by the authority of Government is wisely prohibited to the individual States, by the National Constitution. And the spirit of that prohibition ought not to be disregarded, by the Government of the United States. Though paper emissions, under a general authority, might have some advantages, not applicable, and be free from some disadvantages, which are applicable, to the like emissions by the States separately; yet they are of a nature so liable to abuse, and it may even be affirmed so certain of being abused, that the wisdom of the Government will be shewn in never trusting itself with the use of so seducing and dangerous an expedient. In times of tranquillity, it might have no ill consequence, it might even perhaps be managed in a way to be productive of good; but in great and trying emergencies, there is almost a moral certainty of its becoming mischievous. The stamping of paper is an operation so much easier than the laying of taxes, that a government, in the practice of paper emissions, would rarely fail in any such emergency to indulge itself too far, in the employment of that resource, to avoid as much as possible one less auspicious to present popularity. . . .

The payment of the interest of the public debt, at thirteen different places, is a weighty reason, peculiar to our immediate situation, for desiring a Bank circulation. Without a paper, in general currency, equivalent to gold and silver, a considerable proportion of the specie of the country must always be suspended from circulation and left to accumulate, preparatorily to each day of payment; and as often as one approaches, there must in several cases be an actual transportation of the metals at both expence and risk, from their natural and proper reservoirs to distant places. This necessity will be felt very injuriously to the trade of some of the States; and will embarrass not a little the operations of the Treasury in those States. It will also obstruct those negociations, between different parts of the Union. . . .

Considerations of public advantage suggest a further wish, which is, that the Bank could be established upon principles, that would cause the profits of it to redound to the immediate benefit of the State. This is contemplated by many, who speak of a National Bank, but the idea seems liable to insuperable objections. To attach full confidence to an institution of this nature, it appears to be an essential ingredient in its structure, that it shall be under a *private* not a *public* Direction, under the guidance of *individual interest,* not of *public policy;* which would be supposed to be, and in certain emergencies, under a feeble or too sanguine administration would, really, be, liable to being too much influenced by *public necessity.* The suspicion of this would most probably be a canker, that would continually corrode the vitals of the credit of the Bank, and would be most likely to prove fatal in those situations, in which the public good would require, that they should be most sound and vigorous. It would indeed be little less, than a miracle, should the credit of the Bank be at the disposal of the Government, if in a long series of time, there was not experienced a calamitous abuse of it. It is true, that it would be the real interest of the Government not to abuse it; its genuine policy to husband and cherish it with the most guarded circumspection as an inestimable treasure. But what Government ever uniformly consulted its true interest, in opposition to the temptations of momentary exigencies? What nation was ever blessed with a constant succession of upright and wise Administrators?

The keen, steady, and, as it were, magnetic sense, of their own interest, as proprietors, in the Directors of a Bank, pointing invariably to its true pole, the prosperity of the institution, is the only security, that can always be relied upon, for a careful and prudent administration. It is therefore the only basis on which an enlightened, unqualified and permanent confidence can be expected to be erected and maintained. . . .

It will not follow, from what has been said, that the State may not be the holder of a part of the Stock of a Bank, and consequently a sharer in the profits of it. It will only follow, that it ought not to desire any participation in the Direction of it, and therefore ought not to own the whole or a principal part of the Stock; for if the mass of the property should belong to the public, and if the direction of it should be in private hands, this would be to commit the interests of the State to persons, not interested, or not enough interested in their proper management. . . .

The following plan for the constitution of a National Bank is respectfully submitted to the consideration of the House.

I. The capital Stock of the Bank shall not exceed ten Millions of Dollars, divided into Twenty five thousand shares, each share being four hundred Dollars; to raise which sum, subscriptions shall be opened on the first monday of april next, and shall continue open, until the whole shall be subscribed. Bodies politic as well as individuals may subscribe.

II. The amount of each share shall be payable, one fourth in gold and silver coin, and three fourths in that part of the public debt, which according to the loan proposed by the Act making provision for the debt of the United States, shall bear an accruing interest at the time of payment of six per centum per annum.

5

On Manufacturing

There is still one more Hamilton, the prophet of American industry, the visionary who lived in a future which we have only recently secured. This Hamilton, in June 1791, sent a circular letter to all his supervisors of revenues, asking them to gather information on the condition of manufacturing in their respective states. Forwarded to the Treasury Department was an enormous body of material which Hamilton incorporated into his last and perhaps greatest report, that on manufacturing. A breathtaking and even prophetic set of recommendations for encouraging industrial and commercial growth, this report was the capstone to his thinking. It had germinated in countless earlier letters and essays as well as in The Federalist, where Hamilton imaginatively projected America's future economy. It was also a declaration of economic independence from the Old World—to be implemented by means of a well-balanced national economy and to be attained by means of a government-protected and encouraged industry. Nor did this "well-balanced" economy exclude agriculture, or tack it on for politic reasons. For Hamilton believed it primary to the national scene; he simply denied its exclusiveness.

Hamilton is, in this Report, hardly antifarmer or probusiness, though tending instinctively in these directions. Rather he gives priority to whatever policy best promoted economic growth. It seemed urgent for the government to support "infant industries" by, inter alia, tariffs and bounties. Even the farmers would be assisted by such a program, he insisted, and his reasoning was not placatory in intent: home manufactures and industrial diversification could only be a boon to agrarians. Such developments would increase the demand for farm products and increase farm purchasing power, since American-manufactured goods (not having to bear the cost of ocean-going transport) could be sold more cheaply than European. There is no denying, however, that Hamilton opted for the new rather than for the tradition-bound, for a rising capitalist economy, one which by its very nature would inevitably undermine the old agrarian order.

Hamilton's advocacy of American manufacturing, coupled with beneficent governmental guidance, may seem labored and obvious to today's student; but if such is the case it is because Richard Morris *is correct in finding that Hamilton "anticipated America." It is also because they have torn Hamilton's words out of their inextricable historic context and are guilty of what John Roche has called "retrospective symmetry." For the average man of Hamilton's day lived, by and large, in a rural society, and agriculture seemed infinitely preferable to manufacturing or to urban living. Jefferson and Madison, for example, thought so, and they saw only the potential malevolence of this Report. Hamilton, to them, was engaged in one more effort to strengthen the government and to create a moneyed aristocracy, sufficient reason for them to rally the opposition. But their time in the political sun was still a decade away and Hamilton, with his appeal to the business community and his determination upon national self-sufficiency carried the day, the "better sort" again hailing him as America's benefactor.*

REPORT ON MANUFACTURES, DECEMBER 5, 1791 [1]

The Secretary of the Treasury, in obedience to the order of ye House of Representatives, of the 15th day of January, 1790, has applied his attention, at as early a period as his other duties would permit, to the subject of Manufactures; and particularly to the means of promoting such as will tend to render the United States, independent on foreign nations for military and other essential supplies. . . .

It ought readily to be conceded that the cultivation of the earth—as the primary and most certain source of national supply—as the immediate and chief source of subsistence to man—as the principal source of those materials which constitute the nutriment of other kinds of labor—as including a state most favourable to the freedom and independence of the human mind—one, perhaps, most conducive to the multiplication of the human species—has *intrinsically a strong claim to pre-eminence over every other kind of industry.* . . .

. . . Tillage ought to be no obstacle to listening to any substantial inducements to the encouragement of manufactures, which may be otherwise perceived to exist, through an apprehension; that they may have a tendency to divert labour from a more to a less profitable employment. . . .

To affirm, that the labour of the Manufacturer is unproductive, because he consumes as much of the produce of land, as he adds value to the raw materials which he manufactures, is not better founded, than it would be to affirm, that the labour of the farmer, which furnishes materials to the manufacturer is unproductive, *because he consumes an equal value of manufactured articles.* Each furnishes a certain portion of the produce

---

[1] From *The Reports of Alexander Hamilton.*

of his labor to the other, and each destroys a correspondent portion of the produce of the labour of the other. In the mean time the maintenance of two Citizens, instead of one, is going on; the State has two members instead of one; and they together consume twice the value of what is produced from the land. . . .

The labour of the Artificer replaces to the farmer that portion of his labour, with which he provides the materials of exchange with the Artificer, and which he would otherwise have been compelled to apply to manufactures: and while the Artificer thus enables the farmer to enlarge his stock of Agricultural industry, a portion of which he purchases for his own use, *he also supplies himself with the manufactured articles of which he stands in need.* He does still more—Besides this equivalent which he gives for the portion of Agricultural labour consumed by him, and this supply of manufactured commodities for his own consumption—he furnishes still a surplus, which compensates for the use of the Capital advanced either by himself or some other person, for carrying on the business. This is the ordinary profit of the Stock employed in the manufactory, and is, in every sense, as effective an addition to the income of the Society, as the rent of the land.

The produce of the labour of the Artificer consequently, may be regarded as composed of three parts: one by which the provisions for his subsistence and the materials for his work are purchased of the farmer, one by which he supplies himself with manufactured necessities, and a third which constitutes the profit on the Stock employed. The two last portions seem to have been overlooked in the system, which represents manufacturing industry as barren and unproductive. . . .

It is now proper to proceed a step further, and to enumerate the principal circumstances, from which it may be inferred—that manufacturing establishments not only occasion a positive augmentation of the Produce and Revenue of the Society, but that they contribute essentially to rendering them greater than they could possibly be, without such establishments. These circumstances are—

1. The division of labour.
2. An extension of the use of Machinery.
3. Additional employment to classes of the community not ordinarily engaged in the business.
4. The promoting of emigration from foreign Countries.
5. The furnishing greater scope for the diversity of talents and dispositions which discriminate men from each other.
6. The affording a more ample and various field for enterprize.
7. The creating in some instances a new, and securing in all, a more certain and steady demand for the surplus produce of the soil. . . .

I. As to the Division of Labour

It has justly been observed, that there is a scarcely any thing of greater moment in the œconomy of a nation than the proper division of labour. The separation of occupations causes each to be carried to a much greater perfection, than it could possibly acquire, if they were blended. This arises principally from three circumstances—

1st. The greater skill and dexterity naturally resulting from a constant and undivided application to a single object. . . .

2nd. The œconomy of time, by avoiding the loss of it, incident to a frequent transition from one operation to another of a different nature. . . .

3rd. An extension of the use of Machinery. A man occupied on a single object will have it more in his power, and will be more naturally led to exert his imagination in devising methods to facilitate and abrige labour, than if he were perplexed by a variety of independent and dissimilar operations. . . .

And from these causes united, the mere separation of the occupation of the cultivator, from that of the Artificer, has the effect of augmenting the *productive powers* of labour, and with them, the total mass of the produce or revenue of a Country. In this single view of the subject, therefore, the utility of Artificers of Manufacturers, towards promoting an increase of productive industry, is apparent.

II. As to an Extension of the Use of Machinery, a Point
Which, Though Partly Anticipated Requires To Be Placed in One or
Two Additional Lights

The employment of Machinery forms an item of great importance in the general mass of national industry. 'Tis an artificial force brought in aid of the natural force of man; and, to all the purposes of labour, is an increase of hands; an accession of strength, *unencumbered too by the expense of maintaining the laborer.* May it not therefore be fairly inferred, that those occupations, which give greatest scope to the use of this auxiliary, contribute most to the general Stock of industrious effort, and, in consequence, to the general product of industry? . . .

The Cotton Mill, invented in England, within the last twenty years, is a signal illustration of the general proposition, which has been just advanced. In consequence of it, all the different processes for spinning Cotton are performed by means of Machines, which are put in motion by water, and attended chiefly by women and Children; and by a smaller number of persons, in the whole, than are requisite in the ordinary mode of spinning. And it is an advantage of great moment, that the operations of this mill continue with convenience during the night as well as through the day. The prodigious effect of such a Machine is easily conceived. To this invention is to be attributed essentially the immense progress, which has been so suddenly made in Great Britain, in the various fabrics of cotton.

III. As to the Additional Employment of Classes of the Community, not Originally Engaged in the Particular Business

This is not among the least valuable of the means, by which manufacturing institutions contribute to augment the general stock of industry and production. In places where those institutions prevail, besides the persons regularly engaged in them, they afford occasional and extra employment to industrious individuals and families, who are willing to devote the leisure resulting from the intermissions of their ordinary pursuits to collateral labours, as a resource for multiplying their acquisitions or their enjoyments. The husbandman himself experiences a new source of profit and support from the increased industry of his wife and daughters; invited and stimulated by the demands of the neighboring manufactories. . . .

It is worthy of particular remark, that, in general, women and Children are rendered more useful, and the latter more early useful by manufacturing establishments, than they would otherwise be. Of the number of persons employed in the Cotton Manufactories of Great Britain, it is computed that four sevenths nearly are women and children; of whom the greatest proportion are children, and many of them of a very tender age. . . .

IV. As to the Promoting of Emigration from Foreign Countries

Men reluctantly quit one course of occupation and livelihood for another, unless invited to it by very apparent and proximate advantages. Many who would go from one country to another, if they had a prospect of continuing with more benefit the callings, to which they have been educated, will often not be tempted to change their situation, by the hope of doing better, in some other way. Manufacturers, who, listening to the powerful invitations of a better price for their fabrics, or their labour, of greater cheapness of provisions and raw materials, of an exemption from the chief part of the taxes, burthens and restraints, which they endure in the old world, of greater personal independence and consequence, under the operation of a more equal government, and of what is far more precious than mere religious toleration—a perfect equality of religious privileges; would probably flock from Europe to the United States to pursue their own trades or professions, if they were once made sensible of the advantages they would enjoy, and were inspired with an assurance of encouragement and employment, will, with difficulty, be induced to transplant themselves, with a view to becoming Cultivators of Land.

If it be true then, that it is the interest of the United States to open every possible avenue to emigration from abroad, it affords a weighty argument for the encouragement of manufactures; which, for the reasons just assigned, will have the strongest tendency to multiply the inducements to it. . . .

V. As to the Furnishing Greater Scope for the Diversity of Talents and Dispositions, which Discriminate Men from Each Other

If there be any thing in a remark often to be met with—namely that there is, in the genius of the people of this country, a peculiar aptitude for mechanic improvements, it would operate as a forcible reason for giving opportunities to the exercise of that species of talent, by the propagation of manufactures.

VI. As to the Affording a More Ample and Various Field for Enterprise

. . . The spirit of enterprise, useful and prolific as it is, must necessarily be contracted or expanded in proportion to the simplicity or variety of the occupations and productions, which are to be found in a Society. It must be less in a nation of mere cultivators, than in a nation of cultivators and merchants; less in a nation of cultivators and merchants, than in a nation of cultivators, artificers and merchants.

VII. As to the Creating, in Some Instances, a New, and Securing in All a More Certain and Steady Demand for Surplus Produce of the Soil

This is among the most important of the circumstances which have been indicated. It is a principal mean, by which the establishment of manufactures contributes to an augmentation of the produce or revenue of a country, and has an immediate and direct relation to the prosperity of Agriculture.

It is evident, that the exertions of the husbandman will be steady or fluctuating, vigorous or feeble, in proportion to the steadiness or fluctuation, adequateness or inadequateness, of the markets on which he must depend, for the vent of the surplus, which may be produced by his labor; and that such surplus in the ordinary course of things will be greater or less in the same proportion.

For the purpose of this vent, a domestic market is greatly to be preferred to a foreign one; because it is in the nature of things, far more to be relied upon. . . .

To secure such a market, there is no other expedient, than to promote manufacturing establishments. Manufacturers who constitute the most numerous class, after the Cultivators of land, are for that reason the principal consumers of the surplus of their labour.

This idea of an extensive domestic market for the surplus produce of the soil is of the first consequence. It is, of all things, that which most effectually conduces to a flourishing state of Agriculture. If the effect of manufactories should be to detach a portion of the hands, which would otherwise be engaged in Tillage, it might possibly cause a smaller quantity of lands to be under cultivation; but, by their tendency to procure a more certain demand for the surplus produce of the soil, they would, at the same time, cause the lands which were in cultivation to be better improved and more productive. And while, by their influence, the condition of each individual farmer would be meliorated, the total mass of Agricultural production would probably be increased. For this must evidently depend as much, if not more, upon the degree of improvement than upon the number of acres under culture. . . .

The foregoing considerations seem sufficient to establish, as general propositions, that it is the interest of nations to diversify the industrious pursuits of the individuals who compose them—that the establishment of manufactures is calculated not only to increase the general stock of useful and productive labour; but even to improve the state of Agriculture in particular, certainly to advance the interests of those who are engaged in it. . . .

The United States are to a certain extent in the situation of a country precluded from foreign Commerce. They can indeed, without difficulty obtain from abroad the manufactured supplies, of which they are in want; but they experience numerous and very injurious impediments to the emission and vent of their own commodities. Nor is this the case in reference to a single foreign nation only. The regulations of several countries, with which we have the most extensive intercourse, throw serious obstructions in the way of the principal staples of the United States.

In such a position of things, the United States cannot exchange with Europe on equal terms; and the want of reciprocity would render them the victim of a system which should induce them to confine their views to Agriculture, and refrain from Manufactures. A constant and increasing necessity, on their part, for the commodities of Europe, and only a partial and occasional demand for their own, in return, could not but expose them to a state of impoverishment, compared with the opulence to which their political and natural advantages authorise them to aspire. . . .

The objections to the pursuit of manufactures in the United States, which next present themselves to discussion, represent an impracticability of success, arising from three causes—scarcity of hands—dearness of labour—want of capital.

The two first circumstances, are to a certain extent real, and, within due limits, ought to be admitted as obstacles to the success of manufacturing enterprise in the United States. But there are various considerations, which lessen their force, and tend to afford an assurance that they are not sufficient to prevent the advantageous prosecution of many very useful and extensive manufactories. . . .

There are circumstances which have been already noticed with another view, that materially diminish, everywhere, the effect of a scarcity of hands. These circumstances are—the great use which can be made of women and children; on which point a very pregnant and instructive fact has been mentioned—the vast extension given by late improvements to the employment of Machines, which substituting the Agency of fire and water, had prodigiously lessened the necessity of manual labour—the employment of persons ordinarily engaged in other occupations, during the seasons, or hours of leisure; which, besides giving occasion to the exertion of a greater quantity of labour by the same number of persons, and thereby increasing the general stock of labour, as has been elsewhere remarked, may also be taken into the calculation, as a resource for obviating the scarcity of hands—lastly the attraction of foreign emigrants. Whoever inspects with a careful eye, the composition of our towns will be made sensible to what an extent this resource may be relied upon. This exhibits a large proportion of ingenious and valuable workmen, in different arts and trades, who, by expatriating from Europe, have improved their own condition, and added to the industry and wealth of the United States. It is a natural inference from the experience, we have already had, that as soon as the United States shall present the countenance of a serious prosecution of Manufactures—as soon as foreign artists shall be made sensible that the state of things here affords a moral certainty of employment and encouragement—competent numbers of European workmen will transplant themselves, effectually to insure the success of the design.

Ideas of a contrariety of interests between the Northern and southern regions of the Union, are in the Main as unfounded as they are mischievous. The diversity of Circumstances on which such contrariety is usually predicated, authorizes a directly contrary conclusion. Mutual wants constitute one of the strongest links of political connection, and the extent of these bears a natural proportion to the diversity in the means of mutual supply. . . .

But there are more particular considerations which serve to fortify the idea that the encouragement of manufactures is the interest of all parts of the Union. If the Northern and Middle states should be the principal scenes of such establishments, they would immediately benefit the More southern, by creating a demand for productions, some of which they have in common with the other states, and others of which, are either peculiar to them, or more abundant, or of better quality, than elsewhere. . . .

I. Protecting Duties—or Duties on Those Foreign Articles Which Are the Rivals of the Domestic Ones Intended To Be Encouraged

Duties of this nature evidently amount to a virtual bounty on the domestic fabrics since by enhancing the charges on foreign articles, they enable the National Manufacturers to undersell all their foreign Competitors. . . .

II. Prohibitions of Rival Articles, or Duties Equivalent to Prohibitions

This is another and an efficacious mean of encouraging national manufactures but in general it is only fit to be employed when a manufacture, has made such progress and is in so many hands as to insure a due competition, and an adequate supply on reasonable terms. Of duties equivalent to prohibitions, there are examples in the Laws of the United States. . . .

Considering a monopoly of the domestic market to its own manufacturers as the reigning policy of manufacturing Nations, a similar policy on the part of the United States in every proper instance, is dictated, it might almost be said, by the principles of distributive justice; certainly, by the duty of endeavoring to secure to their own Citizens a reciprocity of advantages.

III. Prohibitions of the Exportation of the Materials of Manufactures

The desire of securing a cheap and plentiful supply for the national workmen, and where the article is either peculiar to the Country, or of peculiar quality there, the jealousy of enabling foreign workmen to rival those of the nation with its own Materials, are the leading motives to this species of regulation. . . .

IV. Pecuniary Bounties

This has been found one of the most efficacious means of encouraging manufactures, and, is in some views, the best. . . .

It is a species of encouragement more positive and direct than any other, and for that very reason, has a more immediate tendency to stimulate and uphold new enterprises, increasing the chances of profit, and diminishing the risks of loss, in the first attempts. . . .

Bounties are sometimes not only the best, but the only proper expedient for uniting the encouragement of a new object of agriculture, with that of a new object of manufacture. It is the Interest of the farmer to have the production of the raw material promoted, by counteracting the interference of the foreign material of the same kind. It is the interest of the manufacturer to have the material abundant and cheap. . . .

The true way to conciliate these two interests is to lay a duty on foreign *manufactures* of the material, the growth of which is desired to be encouraged, and to apply the produce of that duty, by way of bounty, either upon the production of the material itself or upon its manufacture at home, or upon both. In this disposition of the thing, the Manufacturer commences his enterprise under every advantage which is attainable, as to quantity or price of the raw material: And the Farmer, if the bounty be immediately to him, is enabled by it to enter into a successful competition with the foreign material; if the bounty be to the manufacturer on so much of the domestic material as he consumes, the operation is nearly the same; he has a motive of interest to prefer the domestic Commodity, if of equal quality, even at a higher price than the foreign, so long as the difference of price is any thing short of the bounty which is allowed upon the article. . . .

The continuance of bounties on manufactures long established must almost always be of questionable policy: Because a presumption would arise, in every such Case, that there were natural and inherent impediments to success. But in new undertakings, they are as justifiable, as they are oftentimes necessary. . . .

There is no purpose to which public money can be more beneficially applied than to the acquisition of a new and useful branch of industry; no Consideration more valuable than a permanent addition to the general stock of productive labour. . . .

PART TWO

HAMILTON VIEWED BY HIS CONTEMPORARIES

6

Thomas Jefferson

In the following extracts, Jefferson tells us something of the hothouse political climate of the early 1790s and of Hamilton's character and beliefs. The first excerpt is drawn from Jefferson's celebrated Anas, *private memoranda made during this period; the second, from a letter to Washington, which offers a defense of his own actions as well as an arraignment of Hamilton's. This attack on a fellow cabinet member was partly responsive to immediately unfolding events, most pointedly to Hamilton's categorical assertions— as "American," "Amicus," "Catullus," "Metallus"—that the Secretary of State had placed Philip Freneau on the public payroll and that his intent was to slander and destroy his colleague in the Treasury Department. Hamilton, bolstered by John Jay's plea—"Resolve not to be driven from your station"—in turn determined to alienate Washington from Jefferson and drive the latter from government. He presented a bill of particulars to the chief executive: Jefferson was an enemy of funding; he was rude to the Secretary of the Treasury; he opposed the Constitution, etc. Jefferson's reply, which follows upon the* Anas *excerpt, was an effective defense of his policies and activities.*

THE ANAS[1]

. . . Nor was this an opposition to Genl. Washington. He was true to the republican charge confided to him; & has solemnly and repeatedly protested to me, in our private conversations, that he would lose the last drop of his blood in support of it, and he did this the oftener, and with the more earnestness, because he knew my suspicions of Hamilton's

[1] From Paul L. Ford, ed., *The Works of Thomas Jefferson* (New York: G. P. Putnam's Sons, 1904), vol. 1.

designs against it; & wished to quiet them. For he was not aware of the drift, or of the effect of Hamilton's schemes. Unversed in financial projects & calculations, & budgets, his approbation of them was bottomed on his confidence in the man. But Hamilton was not only a monarchist, but for a monarchy bottomed on corruption. In proof of this I will relate an anecdote, for the truth of which I attest the God who made me. Before the President set out on his Southern tour in April 1791. he addressed a letter of the 4th. of that month, from Mt. Vernon to the Secretaries of State, Treasury & War, desiring that, if any serious and important cases should arise during his absence, they would consult & act on them, and he requested that the Vice-president should also be consulted. This was the only occasion on which that officer was ever requested to take part in a cabinet question. Some occasion for consultation arising, I invited those gentlemen (and the Attorney genl. as well as I remember) to dine with me in order to confer on the subject. After the cloth was removed, and our question agreed & dismissed, conversation began on other matters and, by some circumstance, was led to the British constitution, on which Mr. Adams observed "purge that constitution of it's corruption, and give to it's popular branch equality of representation, and it would be the most perfect constitution ever devised by the wit of man." Hamilton paused and said, "purge it of it's corruption, and give to it's popular branch equality of representation, & it would become an *impracticable* government: as it stands at present, with all it's supposed defects, it is the most perfect government which ever existed." And this was assuredly the exact line which separated the political creeds of these two gentlemen. The one was for two hereditary branches and an honest elective one: the other for a hereditary king with a house of lords & commons, corrupted to his will, and standing between him and the people. Hamilton was indeed a singular character. Of acute understanding, disinterested, honest, and honorable in all private transactions, amiable in society, and duly valuing virtue in private life, yet so bewitched & perverted by the British example, as to be under thoro' conviction that corruption was essential to the government of a nation. . . . I told him that tho' the people were sound, there were a numerous sect who had monarchy in contempln. That the Secy of the Treasury was one of these. That I had heard him say that this constitution was a shilly shally thing of mere milk & water, which could not last, & was only good as a step to something better. That when we reflected that he had endeavored in the convention to make an English constn of it, and when failing in that we saw all his measures tending to bring it to the same thing it was natural for us to be jealous: and particular when we saw that these measures had established corruption in the legislature, where there was a squadron devoted to the nod of the treasury, doing whatever he had directed & ready to do what he should direct. That if the equilibrium of the three great bodies Legislative, Executive, & judiciary could be preserved, if the Legislature could be kept independant, I should never fear the result of such a government but that I could not but be uneasy when I saw that the Executive had swallowed up the legislative branch. He said that as to that interested spirit in the legislature, it was what could not be avoided in any government, unless we were to exclude particular descriptions of men, such as the holders of the funds from all office. I told him there was great difference between the little accidental schemes of self interest which would take place in every body of men & influence their votes, and a regular system for forming a corps of interested persons who should be steadily at the orders of the Treasury. He touched on the merits of the funding system, observed that [there?] was a difference of opinion about it some thinking it very bad, others very good. That experience was the only criterion of right which he knew & this alone would decide which opn was right. That for himself he had seen our affairs desperate & our credit lost, and that this was in a sudden & extraordinary degree raised to the highest pitch. I told him all that was ever necessary to establish our credit, was an efficient govmt & an honest one declaring it would sacredly pay our debts, laying taxes for this purpose & applying them to it. I avoided going further into the subject. He finished by another exhortation to me not to decide too positively on retirement, & here we were called to breakfast.

TO GEORGE WASHINGTON [2]

Monticello Sep 9, 1792.

I now take the liberty of proceeding to that part of your letter wherein you notice the internal dissentions which have taken place within our government, & their disagreeable effect on it's movements. That such dissentions have taken place is certain, & even among those who are nearest to you in the administration. To no one have they given deeper concern than myself; to no one equal mortification at being myself a part of them. Tho' I take to myself no more than my share of the general observations of your letter, yet I am so desirous ever that you should know the whole truth, & believe no more than the truth, that I am glad to seize every occasion of developing to you whatever I do or think relative to the government; & shall therefore ask permission to be more lengthy now than the occasion particularly calls for, or could otherwise perhaps justify.

When I embarked in the government, it was with a determination to intermeddle not at all with the legislature, & as little as possible with my co-departments. The first and only instance of variance from the former part of my resolution, I was duped into by the Secretary of the

[2] From Paul L. Ford, ed., *The Writings of Thomas Jefferson* (New York: G. P. Putnam's Sons, 1904), vol. 6.

Treasury and made a tool for forwarding his schemes, not then sufficiently understood by me; and of all the errors of my political life, this has occasioned me the deepest regret. It has ever been my purpose to explain this to you, when, from being actors on the scene, we shall have become uninterested spectators only. The second part of my resolution has been religiously observed with the war department; & as to that of the Treasury, has never been farther swerved from than by the mere enunciation of my sentiments in conversation, and chiefly among those who, expressing the same sentiments, drew mine from me. If it has been supposed that I have ever intrigued among the members of the legislatures to defeat the plans of the Secretary of the Treasury, it is contrary to all truth. As I never had the desire to influence the members, so neither had I any other means than my friendships, which I valued too highly to risk by usurpations on their freedom of judgment, & the conscientious pursuit of their own sense of duty. That I have utterly, in my private conversations, disapproved of the system of the Secretary of the treasury, I ackolege & avow: and this was not merely a speculative difference. His system flowed from principles adverse to liberty, & was calculated to undermine and demolish the republic, by creating an influence of his department over the members of the legislature. I saw this influence actually produced, & it's first fruits to be the establishment of the great outlines of his project by the votes of the very persons who, having swallowed his bait were laying themselves out to profit by his plans: & that had these persons withdrawn, as those interested in a question ever should, the vote of the disinterested majority was clearly the reverse of what they made it. These were no longer the votes then of the representatives of the people, but of deserters from the rights & interests of the people: & it was impossible to consider their decisions, which had nothing in view but to enrich themselves, as the measures of the fair majority, which ought always to be respected.—If what was actually doing begat uneasiness in those who wished for virtuous government, what was further proposed was not less threatening to the friends of the Constitution. For, in a Report on the subject of manufactures (still to be acted on) it was expressly assumed that the general government has a right to exercise all powers which may be for the *general welfare,* that is to say, all the legitimate powers of government: since no government has a legitimate right to do what is not for the welfare of the governed. There was indeed a sham-limitation of the universality of this power *to cases where money is to be employed.* But about what is it that money cannot be employed? Thus the object of these plans taken together is to draw all the powers of government into the hands of the general legislature, to establish means for corrupting a sufficient corps in that legislature to divide the honest votes & preponderate, by their own, the scale which suited, & to have that corps under the command of the Secretary of the Treasury for the purpose of subverting step by step the principles of the constitution, which he has so often declared to be a thing of nothing which must be changed. Such views might have justified something more than mere expressions of dissent, beyond which, nevertheless, I never went.—Has abstinence from the department committed to me been equally observed by him? To say nothing of other interferences equally known, in the case of the two nations with which we have the most intimate connections, France & England, my system was to give some satisfactory distinctions to the former, of little cost to us, in return for the solid advantages yielded us by them; & to have met the English with some restrictions which might induce them to abate their severities against our commerce. I have always supposed this coincided with your sentiments. Yet the Secretary of the treasury, by his cabals with members of the legislature, & by high-toned declamation on other occasions, has forced down his own system, which was exactly the reverse. He undertook, of his own authority, the conferences with the ministers of those two nations, & was, on every consultation, provided with some report of a conversation with the one or the other of them, adapted to his views. These views, thus made to prevail, their execution fell of course to me; & I can safely appeal to you, who have seen all my letters & proceedings, whether I have not carried them into execution as sincerely as if they had been my own, tho' I ever considered them as inconsistent with the honor & interest of our country. That they have been inconsistent with our interest is but too fatally proved by the stab to our navigation given by the French.—So that if the question be By whose fault is it that Colo Hamilton & myself have not drawn together? the answer will depend on that to two other questions; whose principles of administration best justify, by their purity, conscientious adherence? and which of us has, notwithstanding, stepped farthest into the control of the department of the other?

To this justification of opinions, expressed in the way of conversation, against the views of Colo Hamilton, I beg leave to add some notice of his late charges against me in Fenno's gazette; for neither the stile, matter, nor venom of the pieces alluded to can leave a doubt of their author. Spelling my name & character at full length to the public, while he conceals his own under the signature of "an American" he charges me 1. With having written letters from Europe to my friends to oppose the present constitution while depending. 2. With a desire of not paying the public debt. 3. With setting up a paper to decry & slander the government. 1st. The first charge is most false. No man in the U. S. I suppose approved of every title in the constitution: no one, I believe approved more of it than I did: and more of it was certainly disproved by my accuser than by me, and of it's parts most vitally republican. Of this the few letters I wrote on the subject (not half a dozen I believe) will be a proof: & for my own satisfaction & justification, I must tax you with the reading of them when I return to where they are. You will there see that my objection to the constitution was that it wanted a bill of rights securing freedom of religion, freedom of the press, freedom from standing armies, trial by jury, & a constant Habeas corpus act. Colo Hamilton's was that it wanted a king and house of lords. The sense of America has approved my objection & added the bill of rights, not the king and lords. I also thought a longer term of service, insusceptible of renewal, would have made a President more independent. My country has thought otherwise, & I have acquiesced implicitly. He wishes the general government should have power to make laws binding the states in all cases whatsoever. Our country has thought otherwise: has he acquiesced? Notwithstanding my wish for a bill of rights, my letters strongly urged the adoption of the constitution, by nine states at least, to secure the good it contained. I at first thought that the best method of securing the bill of rights would be for four states to hold off till such a bill should be agreed to. But the moment I saw Mr. Hancock's proposition to pass the constitution as it stood, and give perpetual instructions to the representatives of every state to insist on a bill of rights, I acknoleged the superiority of his plan, & advocated universal adoption. 2. The second charge is equally untrue. My whole correspondence while in France, & every word, letter, & act on the subject since my return, prove that no man is more ardently intent to see the public debt soon & sacredly paid off than I am. This exactly marks the difference between Colo Hamilton's views & mine, that I would wish the debt paid to morrow; he wishes it never to be paid, but always to be a thing where with to corrupt & manage the legislature. 3. I have never enquired what number of sons, relations & friends of Senators, representatives, printers or other useful partisans Colo Hamilton has provided for among the hundred clerks of his department, the thousand excisemen, customhouse officers, loan officers &c. &c. &c. appointed by him, or at his nod, and spread over the Union; nor could ever have imagined that the man who has the shuffling of millions backwards & forwards from paper into money & money into paper, from Europe to America, & America to Europe, the dealing out of Treasury-secrets among his friends in what time & measure he pleases, and who never slips an occasion of making friends with his means, that such an one I say would have brought forward a charge against me for having appointed the poet Freneau translating clerk to my office, with a salary of 250. dollars a year. That fact stands thus. While the government was at New York I was applied to on behalf of Freneau to know if there was any place within my department to which he could be appointed. I answered there were but four clerkships, all of which I found full, and continued without any change. When we removed to Philadelphia, Mr. Pintard the translating clerk, did not chuse to remove with us. His office then became vacant. I was again applied to there for Freneau, & had no hesitation to promise the clerkship for him. I cannot recollect whether it was at the same time, or afterwards, that I was told he had a thought of setting up a newspaper there. But whether then, or afterwards, I considered it as a circumstance of some value, as it might enable me to do, what I had long wished to have done, that is, to have the material parts of the Leyden gazette brought under your eye & that of the public, in order to possess yourself & them of a juster view of the affairs of Europe than could be obtained from any other public source. This I had ineffectually attempted through the press of Mr. Fenno while in New York, selecting & translating passages myself at first then having it done by Mr. Pintard the translating clerk, but they found their way too slowly into Mr. Fenno's papers. Mr. Bache essayed it for me in Philadelphia, but his being a daily paper, did not circulate sufficiently in the other states. He even tried, at my request, the plan of a weekly paper of recapitulation from his daily paper, in hopes that that might go into the other states, but in this too we failed. Freneau, as translating clerk, & the printer of a periodical paper likely to circulate thro' the states (uniting in one person the parts of Pintard & Fenno) revived my hopes that the thing could at length be effected. On the establishment of his paper therefore, I furnished him with the Leyden gazettes, with an expression of my wish that he could always translate & publish the material intelligence they contained; & have continued to furnish them from time to time, as regularly as I received them. But as to any other direction or indication of my wish how his press should be conducted, what sort of intelligence he should give, what essays encourage, I can protest in the presence of heaven, that I never did by myself or any other, directly or indirectly, say a syllable, nor attempt any kind of influence. I can further protest, in the same awful presence, that I never did by myself or any other, directly or indirectly, write, dictate or procure any one sentence or sentiment to be inserted *in his, or any other gazette,* to which my name was not affixed or that of my office.—I surely need not except here a thing so foreign to the present subject as a little paragraph about our Algerine captives, which I put once into Fenno's paper.—Freneau's proposition to publish a paper, having been about the time that the writings of Publicola, & the discourses on Davila had a good deal excited the public attention, I took for granted from Freneau's character, which had been marked as that of a good whig, that he would give free place to pieces written against the aristocratical & monarchical principles these papers had inculcated. This having been in my mind, it is likely enough I may have expressed it in conversation with others; tho' I do not recollect that I did. To Freneau I think I could not, because I had still seen him but once, & that was at a public table, at breakfast, at Mrs. Elsworth's, as I passed thro' New York the last year. And I can safely declare that my expectations looked only to the chastisement of the aristocratical & monarchical writers, & not to any criticisms on the proceedings of government: Colo Hamilton can see no motive for any appointment but that of making a convenient partizan. But you Sir, who have received from me recommendations of a Rittenhouse, Barlow, Paine, will believe that talents & science are sufficient motives with me in appointments to which they are fitted: & that Freneau, as a man of genius, might find a preference in my eye to be a translating clerk, & make good title to the little aids I could give him as the editor of a gazette, by procuring subscriptions to his paper, as I did some, before it appeared, & as I have with pleasure done for the labours of other men of genius. I hold it to be one of the distinguishing excellencies of elective over hereditary succesions, that the talents, which nature has provided in sufficient proportion, should be selected by the society for the government of their affairs, rather than that this should be transmitted through the loins of knaves & fools passing from the debauches of the table to those of the bed. Colo Hamilton, alias "Plain facts," says that Freneau's salary began before he resided in Philadelphia. I do not know what quibble he may have in reserve on the word "residence." He may mean to include under that idea the removal of his family; for I believe he removed, himself, before his family did, to Philadelphia. But no act of mine gave commencement to his salary before he so far took up his abode in Philadelphia as to be sufficiently in readiness for the duties of the office. As to the merits or demerits of his paper, they certainly concern me not. He & Fenno are rivals for the public favor. The one courts them by flattery, the other by censure, & I believe it will be admitted that the one has been as servile, as the other severe. But is not the dignity, & even decency of government committed, when one of it's principal ministers enlists himself as an anonymous writer or paragraphist for either the one or the other of them?—No government ought to be without censors: & where the press is free, no one ever will. If virtuous, it need not fear the fair operation of attack & defence. Nature has given to man no other means of sifting out the truth either in religion, law, or politics. I think it as honorable to the government neither to know, nor notice, it's sycophants or censors, as it would be undignified & criminal to pamper the former & persecute the latter.—So much for the past. . . .

7

Adams vs. Hamilton: The President and His Defenders

The Hamilton-Adams feud had been building for some years, and dates from the election year of 1796. Secretly nourishing presidential ambitions, Hamilton had been passed over by caucus chieftains in favor of Adams, with Thomas Pinckney of South Carolina selected as the vice presidential candidate—in the hope of carrying Southern as well as Northern voters. The Republicans competed with a full ticket, now that Washington successfully resisted a third term, and nominated Jefferson and Burr as their candidates. No distinction was made between presidential and vice presidential designations, however, since this election preceded the Twelfth Amendment which made it necessary to specify the office for which each candidate had been nominated. Taking advantage of this situation, Hamilton bent his energies to blocking Adams and worked almost as hard to deny him the prize as to defeat Jefferson. Pinckney, he claimed, was the better Federalist; possibly, reasoned Hamilton, South Carolina's delegates would be persuaded to vote for their favorite son for the highest office (rather than, as commonly understood, for the vice presidency). It was an audacious gamble and nearly gave the presidency to Jefferson. Certainly it helped to make him vice president, and ignited a bitter and long-lived dispute among Federalists.

But international crises, triggering nationalism, became a political solvent in the late 1790s, papering over the internal fissures in Federalist ranks. Both pro- and anti-Hamiltonians saw in overseas developments an opportunity to unite the country as well as to end the menace of Jacobinism once and for all. Hamilton, more than the chief executive, would have tolerated armed conflict; but, as a nationalist, he wanted it defensive in appearance lest it further divide his countrymen and, as a realpolitiker, he was in an even more ambiguous position, being aware that England, in serious distress herself, could not provide protection against a possible French invasion.

French actions in these recurrent foreign policy crises were characterized by duplicity and insufferable arrogance—what with the

XYZ affair and continuing violation of America's commercial rights by France's privateers. Presidential messages to Congress urged preparations for war and the legislators speedily passed a series of laws which would place the nation on a war footing. At Adams' request, George Washington agreed to come out of retirement and lead the new American army, providing Hamilton was appointed second in command.

Adams, needing Washington, backed away from his own choice of General Henry Knox, a fellow New Englander, and made the appointment; but he never forgave Washington for forcing Hamilton upon him and watched with justifiable bitterness while this "most restless, impatient, artful, indefatigable, unprincipled intriguer" solidified his influence upon Congress and the cabinet, where he already had the three department heads in his hip pocket. As inspector general, Hamilton turned to the routine chores of army commander with an enthusiasm that smacked of inspiration. He supervised the ordering of equipment and supplies; he reorganized many units; he established a fixed chain of command; and in idle moments he dreamed of conquest: he would seize Florida and Louisiana from Spain, and separate Venezuela and possibly the rest of Spanish possessions in South America from Madrid's control.

Much to Hamilton's disappointment, President Adams still determined upon a peaceful settlement of the Franco-American crisis. Holding out the olive branch, he nominated William Vans Murray as minister plenipotentiary to France, a development which fell like a bombshell upon the Hamiltonian camp. Being unable to turn the chief executive from his course, Party leaders made the best of the situation by persuading him to substitute a three-man commission. Hamilton tried a personal appeal but Adams, faced by internal financial difficulties, believed peace was best for the nation and remained unmoved. Indeed, he lamented that "this damned army will be the ruin of this country," a viewpoint shared by those who opposed a standing army. Second in command of a military force which apparently would never take the field, Hamilton's dreams of leading a conquering host south now suffered from presidential restrictions. He turned and twisted, but to no avail. Americans, supporting Adams, preferred getting their boys home to the expansionist option which he offered; and Congress obliged them in June 1800.

The frustration of Hamilton did not end matters. To the contrary, the rift between the two Federalist blocs was further widened by this development and, by the election year of 1800, their Party was cleaved in two as if by a battle axe. Hamilton's intemperate attack on John Adams—Letter . . . Concerning the Public Conduct and Character of John Adams, Esq., President of the United

States—caused some Federalists, such as John Marshall, Noah Webster, and Harrison Gray Otis, to rally to presidential colors. Webster, once one of Hamilton's warmest admirers, published a rebuttal accusing the New Yorker of Caesarism.

In the course of an 1800 tour of New England, ostensibly nonpartisan—to take leave of his disbanding troops—Hamilton also played the political game. He sought to build a bloc of supporters in behalf of C. C. Pinckney and against Adams' renomination. His activities reached the White House where Adams was already brooding over the "treachery" of Party leaders. The President reacted sharply, charging that Hamilton headed an "English party" in Federalist ranks. Such an assertion in effect threw down the gauntlet and Hamilton, never indecisive when so challenged, demanded verification or denial of this rumored presidential attack. But the chief executive chose to ignore his inquiry and Hamilton then resolved to speak out openly against him. The result was his indiscreet "public letter" which deeply bruised the reputation of author as well as subject, and which played into anti-Federalist (Republican) hands. That Hamilton could undertake this passionate arraignment and that Adams responded as vehemently as he did testifies to the intense animosity, virulent to the point of irrational, which moved both men. Hamilton, as a polemicist, was primus inter pares. *But Adams needed no defender, hardly taking a back seat to any man when it came to the rhetoric of political warfare. In these selections, in the course of defending the politics of his administration, he condemns Hamilton with a bitterness which suggests the irremediable animosity existing between them.*

JOHN ADAMS: "TO THE PRINTERS OF THE BOSTON *PATRIOT*" [1]

Mr. Hamilton's erroneous conceptions of the public opinion may be excused by the considerations that he was not a native of the United States; that he was born and bred in the West Indies till he went to Scotland for education, where he spent his time in a seminary of learning till seventeen years of age, after which no man ever perfectly acquired a national character; then entered a college at New York, from whence he issued into the army as an aid-de-camp. In these situations he could scarcely acquire the opinions, feelings, or principles of the American people. His error may be excused by the further consideration, that his time was chiefly spent in his pleasures, in his electioneering visits, conferences, and correspondences, in propagating prejudices against every man whom he thought his superior in the public estimation, and in com-

[1] From C. F. Adams, ed., *The Works of John Adams* (Boston, 1854), vol. 9.

posing ambitious reports upon finance, while the real business of the treasury was done by Duer, by Wolcott, and even, for some time and in part, by Tench Coxe.

His observation, that "France will never be without secret agents," is true, and it is equally true that England will always have secret agents and emissaries too. That her "partisans among our own citizens can much better promote her cause than any agents she can send," is also true; but it is at least equally true of the partisans of Great Britain. We have seen, in the foregoing papers, glaring and atrocious instances of the exertions of her public agents, secret emissaries, and partisans, among our citizens. But none have yet been mentioned that bear any comparison, in point of guilt and arrogance, with those of all kinds that have been exhibited within the last two or three years.

My worthy fellow-citizens! Our form of government, inestimable as it is, exposes us, more than any other, to the insidious intrigues and pestilent influence of foreign nations. Nothing but our inflexible neutrality can preserve us. The public negotiations and secret intrigues of the English and the French have been employed for centuries in every court and country of Europe. Look back to the history of Spain, Holland, Germany, Russia, Sweden, Denmark, Prussia, Italy, and Turkey, for the last hundred years. How many revolutions have been caused! How many emperors and kings have fallen victims to the alternate triumphs of parties, excited by Englishmen or Frenchmen! And can we expect to escape the vigilant attention of politicians so experienced, so keen-sighted, and so rich? If we convince them that our attachment to neutrality is unchangeable, they will let us alone; but as long as a hope remains, in either power, of seducing us to engage in war on his side and against his enemy, we shall be torn and convulsed by their manœuvers.

Never was there a grosser mistake of public opinion than that of Mr. Hamilton. The great alteration in public opinion had not then, nor has it yet, taken place. The French republic still existed. The French people were still considered as struggling for liberty, amidst all their internal revolutions, their conflicts of parties, and their bloody wars against the coalitions of European powers. Monarchy, empire, had not been suggested. Bonaparte had appeared only as a soldier; had acted on the public stage in no civil or political employment. A sense of gratitude for services rendered us in our revolution, by far more sincere and ardent than reason or justice could warrant, still remained on the minds, not only of our republicans, but of great numbers of our soundest federalists. Did Mr. Hamilton recollect the state of our presses; recollect the names and popular eloquence of the editors of the opposition papers; that scoffing, scorning wit, and that caustic malignity of soul, which appeared so remarkably in all the writings of Thomas Paine and Callender, which to the disgrace of human nature never fails to command attention and applause;

the members of the Senate and House who were decided against the administration, their continual intercourse and communications with French emissaries; the hideous clamor against the alien law and sedition law, both considered as levelled entirely against the French and their friends; and the surrender, according to the British treaty, of the Irish murderer Nash, imposed upon the public for Jonathan Robins? Did he recollect the insurrection in Pennsylvania, the universal and perpetual inflammatory publications against the land tax, stamp tax, coach tax, excise law, and eight per cent. loan? Did he never see nor hear of the circular letters of members of Congress from the middle and southern States? Did he know nothing of the biting sarcasms, the burning rage against himself and his own army? Did he know nothing of a kind of journal that was published, of every irregular act of any officer or soldier, of every military punishment that was inflicted, under the appellation of the Cannibal's Progress? Did he see nothing of the French cockades, ostentatiously exhibited against the American cockades?

Had a French minister been seen here with his suite, he would have been instantly informed of every source and symptom of discontent. Almost every Frenchman upon the continent, and they were then numerous in all the States, would have been employed in criminating the American Government, in applauding the condescension of the French Directory, and the friendly, conciliating disposition of the French nation. Nothing could have been kept secret. The popular clamor for peace on any terms would have been very difficult, if not impossible, to resist. The multitude in Philadelphia, as it was, were almost as ripe to pull me out of my house as they had been to dethrone Washington in the time of Genet. . . .

In these circumstances it was my opinion, and it is so still, it was infinitely better to conduct the negotiation at Paris than in Philadelphia. But if this was and is an error, it was certainly not of such consequence as Hamilton thought fit to represent it. If it was an error, I humbly conceive it would have better become Mr. Hamilton to have been silent than to endeavor to make it unpopular, since the step was taken and irrevocable when he wrote.

But the real truth is, he was in hopes, as well as Mr. Liston, that the French government would neither send a minister here nor receive one there—in short, that they would have gone to war with us. . . . Hamilton hoped that such provocations would produce an irreconcilable breach and a declaration of war. He was disappointed, and lost the command of his army. *Hinc illæ lacrimæ!*

There were other circumstances of more serious and solid importance, indicative of public opinion, which Mr. Hamilton, if he had been a vigilant and sagacious statesman, could not have overlooked. The venerable patriarchs, Pendleton and Wythe, of Virginia, openly declaimed for peace. . . . In New York, the great interest and vast bodies of the people, who are supposed to follow or direct the two great families of Clintons and Livingstons, aided by all the address and dexterity of Aaron Burr, was decidedly for peace with France. In Pennsylvania, Governor M'Kean, with his majority of thirty thousand votes, or in other words, at the head of the two vast bodies of Germans and Irish, reënforced by great numbers of English Presbyterians, Quakers and Anabaptists, were decidedly against a war with France.

After enumerating all these symptoms of the popular bias, it would be frivolous to enlarge upon the conversations, of which I was informed, at taverns and insurance offices, threatening violence to the President by pulling him out of his chair . . . if we went to war with France. . . .

In these circumstances, it was the height of folly to say, as Hamilton says, that it would have been safer to negotiate at Philadelphia than at Paris. . . . Our envoys were precisely instructed. Every article was prescribed that was to be insisted on as an ultimatum. In a treaty they could not depart from a punctilio. A convention they might make, as they did, at their own risk. But the President and Senate were under no obligation to ratify it. . . .

Where, then, was the danger of this negotiation? Nowhere but in the disturbed imagination of Alexander Hamilton. To me only it was dangerous. To me, as a public man, it was fatal, and that only because Alexander Hamilton was pleased to wield it as a poisoned weapon with the express purpose of destroying. Though I owe him no thanks for this, I most heartily rejoice in it, because it has given me eight years, incomparably the happiest of my life, whereas, had I been chosen President again, I am certain I could not have lived another year. It was utterly impossible that I could have lived through one year more of such labors and cares as were studiously and maliciously accumulated upon me by the French faction and the British faction, the former aided by the republicans, and the latter by Alexander Hamilton and his satellites. . . .

Mr. Tracy, of Connecticut, who indeed was always in my confidence, came to me, I believe, at the opening of the special session of Congress, which I called soon after my inauguration, and produced a long, elaborate letter from Mr. Hamilton, containing a whole system of instruction for the conduct of the President, the Senate, and the House of Representatives. I read it very deliberately, and really thought the man was in a delirium. It appeared to me a very extraordinary instance of volunteer empiricism thus to prescribe for a President, Senate, and House of Representatives, all desperately sick and in a state of deplorable debility, without being called. . . .

It began by a dissertation on the extraordinarily critical situation of the United States.

It recommended a new mission to France of three commissioners, Mr. Jefferson or Mr. Madison to be one.

It recommended the raising an army of fifty thousand men, ten thousand of them to be cavalry; an army of great importance in so extensive a country, vulnerable at so many points on the frontiers, and so accessible in so many places by sea.

It recommended an alien and sedition law.

It recommended an invigoration of the treasury, by seizing on all the taxable articles not yet taxed by the government. And lastly,

It recommended a national Fast, not only on account of the intrinsic propriety of it, but because we should be very unskilful if we neglected to avail ourselves of the religious feelings of the people in a crisis so difficult and dangerous.

There might be more, but these are all that I now recollect.

Mr. Hamilton's imagination was always haunted by that hideous monster or phantom, so often called a *crisis*, and which so often produces imprudent measures. . . .

The army of fifty thousand men, ten thousand of them to be horse, appeared to me to be one of the wildest extravagances of a knight-errant. It proved to me that Mr. Hamilton knew no more of the sentiments and feelings of the people of America, than he did of those of the inhabitants of one of the planets. Such an army without an enemy to combat, would have raised a rebellion in every State in the Union. The very idea of the expense of it would have turned President, Senate, and House out of doors. I adopted none of these chimeras into my speech, and only recommended the raising of a few regiments of artillery to garrison the fortifications of the most exposed places. Yet such was the influence of Mr. Hamilton in Congress, that, without any recommendation from the President, they passed a bill to raise an army, not a large one, indeed, but enough to overturn the then Federal government.

Nor did I adopt his idea of an alien or sedition law. I recommended no such thing in my speech. Congress, however, adopted both these measures. I knew there was need enough of both, and therefore I consented to them. . . .

Seizing on all the taxable articles not yet taxed, to support an army of fifty thousand men, at a time when so many tax laws, already enacted, were unexecuted in so many States, and when insurrections and rebellions had already been excited in Pennsylvania, on account of taxes, appeared to me altogether desperate, altogether delirious.

I wanted no admonition from Mr. Hamilton to institute a national fast. I had determined on this measure long enough before Mr. Hamilton's letter was written. And here let me say, with great sincerity, that I think there is nothing upon this earth more sublime and affecting than the idea of a great nation all on their knees at once before their God, acknowledging their faults and imploring his blessing and protection, when the prospect before them threatens great danger and calamity. . . .

In fine, Mr. Hamilton, in the passage I have been commenting upon, in this letter, has let out facts which, if he had possessed a grain of common sense, he would have wished should be forever concealed. I should never have revealed or explained them, if he and his partisans had not compelled me.

In page 26 [of Hamilton's *Letter . . . Concerning The Public Conduct and Character of John Adams*], is a strain of flimsy rant, as silly as it is indecent. "The supplement to the declaration was a blamable excess. It waved the point of honor, which after two rejections of our ministers required that the next mission should proceed from France." Where did he find this point of honor? If any such point had existed, it had its full force against the second mission; and its principal force consisted in the formal declaration of the Directory, that it "never would receive another minister plenipotentiary without apologies for the President's speeches and answers to addresses." If we had a right to wave this point of honor in one instance, we had in two. . . .

He argues the probability that France would have sent a minister here, from the fact that she did afterwards "stifle her resentment, and invite the renewal of negotiation." I know not whether this is an example of Mr. Hamilton's "analysis of investigation" or not. It is an argument *a posteriori*. It is reasoning upward or backward.

These invitations were not known nor made, when I pledged myself, by implication at least, to send a minister, when such invitations should be made. When they were made, I considered my own honor and the honor of the government committed. And I have not a doubt that Hamilton thought so too; and that one of his principal vexations was, that neither himself nor his privy counsellors could have influence enough with me to persuade or intimidate me to disgrace myself in the eyes of the people of America and the world by violating my parole. . . .

Mr. Hamilton acknowledges, that "the President had pledged himself in his speech" (he should have said in his message) "to send a minister, if satisfactory assurances of a proper reception were given." Notwithstanding this, Mr. Hamilton, and all his confidential friends, exerted their utmost art and most strenuous endeavors to prevail on the President to violate this pledge. What can any man think of the disposition of these men towards the personal or official character of the President, but that they were secretly, if not avowedly, his most determined and most venomous enemies? When the measure had been solemnly, irrevocably determined, and could not be recalled nor delayed without indelible dishonor, I own I was astonished, I was grieved, I was afflicted, to see such artificial schemes employed, such delays studied, such embarrassments thrown in the way, by men who were, or at least ought to have been, my bosom friends.

This was a point of honor indeed; not such a stupid, fantastical point of honor as that which Mr. Hamilton maintains with so much fanaticism and so much folly; but a point of honor in which my moral character was involved as well as the public faith of the nation. Hamilton's point of honor was such as one of those Irish duellists, who love fighting better than feasting, might have made a pretext for sending a challenge; and however conformable it might be to Hamilton's manner of thinking, it was altogether inconsistent with the moral, religious, and political character of the people of America. . . .

In page 26, Mr. Hamilton says, that the mission "could hardly fail to injure our interests with other countries."

This is another of those phantoms which he had conjured up to terrify minds and nerves as weak as his own. It was a commonplace theme of discourse, which, no doubt, the British faction very efficaciously assisted him in propagating. I know it made impression on some, from whose lips I too often heard it, and from whom I expected more sense and firmness. It appeared to me so mean, servile, and timorous, that I own I did not always hear it with patience. . . .

In page 37, another instance is given of my jealousy and suspicious disposition. The most open, unsuspicious man alive is accused of excessive suspicion!

I transiently asked one of the heads of departments, whether Ellsworth and Hamilton had come all the way from Windsor and New York to persuade me to countermand the mission. How came Mr. Hamilton to be informed of this?

I know of no motive of Mr. Ellsworth's journey. However, I have already acknowledged that Mr. Ellsworth's conduct was perfectly proper.[2] He urged no influence or argument for counteracting or postponing the missions.

Unsuspicious as I was, I could not resist the evidence of my senses. Hamilton, unasked, had volunteered his influence with all the arguments his genius could furnish, all the eloquence he possessed, and all the vehemence of action his feeble frame could exert. He had only betrayed his want of information, and his ardent zeal to induce me to break my word and violate the faith of the government. I know of no business he had at Trenton. Indeed I knew, that in strict propriety he had no right to come to Trenton at all without my leave. He was stationed at Newark, in the command of his division of the army, where he ought to have been employed in accommodating, disciplining, and teaching tactics to his troops, if he had been capable of it. He wisely left these things to another officer, who understood them better, but whom he hated for that very reason.

---

[2] In the first draught is the following addition,—

"Mr. Adams never suspected him to be in combination with Mr. Hamilton to endeavor to influence him in the affair of the mission."

There is reason to believe that he was in combination at least with Mr. Pickering and Mr. Wolcott, if not Mr. Hamilton.

I have no more to say upon this great subject. Indeed, I am weary of exposing puerilities that would disgrace the awkwardest boy at college.

Mr. Hamilton says, my "conduct in the office of President was a heterogeneous compound of right and wrong, of wisdom and error." As at that time, in my opinion, his principal rule of right and wrong, of wisdom and error, was his own ambition and indelicate pleasures, I despise his censure, and should consider his approbation as a satire on my administration.

"The outset," he says, "was distinguished by a speech which his friends lamented as temporizing. . . .

That address . . . sprung from a very serious apprehension of danger to our country, and a sense of injustice to individuals, from that arbitrary and exclusive principle of faction which confines all employments and promotions to its own favorites. . . .

But I soon found myself shackled. The heads of departments were exclusive patriots. I could not name a man who was not devoted to Hamilton, without kindling a fire. . . . When I was elected, . . . I soon found that if I had not the previous consent of the heads of departments, and the approbation of Mr. Hamilton, I run the utmost risk of a dead negative in the Senate. One such negative, at least, I had, after a very formal and a very uncivil remonstrance of one of their large, unconstitutional committees in secret. . . .

There is something in the 24th page . . . It is said, that "the session which ensued the promulgation of the despatches of our commissioners was about to commence." This was the session of 1798. "Mr. Adams arrived at Philadelphia. The tone of his mind seemed to have been raised."

Let me ask a candid public, how did Mr. Hamilton know any thing of the *tone* of Mr. Adams's mind, either before or at that conference? To make the comparison, he must have known the state of Mr. Adams's mind at both these periods. He had never conversed with Mr. Adams before, nor was he present at that conference. Who was the musician that took the pitch of Mr. Adams's mind, at the two moments here compared together? And what was the musical instrument, or whose exquisite ear was it, that ascertained so nicely the vibrations of the air, and Mr. Adams's sensibility to them? Had Mr. Hamilton a spy in the cabinet, who transmitted to him, from day to day, the confidential communications between the President and heads of department? If there existed such a spy, why might he not communicate these conferences to Mr. Liston, or the Marquis Yrujo, as well as to Mr. Hamilton? He had as clear a right. . . .

. . . It seemed to me, that they expected I should have proposed a declaration of war, and only asked their advice to sanction it. However, not a word was said.

That there was a disappointment, however, in Hamilton and his friends, is apparent enough from this consideration, that when it was known that a declaration of war was not to be recommended in the President's speech, a caucus was called of members of Congress, to see if they could not get a vote for a declaration of war, without any recommendation from the President, as they had voted the alien and sedition law, and the army. What passed in that caucus, and how much zeal there was in some, and who they were, Judge Sewall can tell better than I. All that I shall say is, that Mr. Hamilton's friends could not carry the vote.

My second proposition to the heads of departments was to consider, in case we should determine against a declaration of war, what was the state of our relations with France, and whether any further attempt at negotiation should be made.

Instead of the silence and reserve with which my first question was received, Mr. Hamilton shall relate what was said.

Mr. Hamilton says, "It was suggested to him (Mr. Adams) that it might be expedient to insert in the speech a sentiment of this import; that, after the repeatedly rejected advances of this country, its dignity required that it should be left with France in future to make the first overture; that if, desirous of reconciliation, she should evince the disposition by sending a minister to this government, he would be received with the respect due to his character, and treated with in the frankness of a sincere desire of accommodation. The suggestion was received in a manner both indignant and intemperate."

I demand again, how did Mr. Hamilton obtain this information? Had he a spy in the cabinet? If he had, I own I had rather that all the courts in Europe should have had spies there; for they could have done no harm by any true information they could have obtained there; whereas Hamilton has been able to do a great deal of mischief by the pretended information he has published.

It is very true, that I thought this proposition intended to close the avenues to peace, and to ensure a war with France; for I did believe that some of the heads of departments were confident, in their own minds, that France would not send a minister here.

From the intimate intercourse between Hamilton and some of the heads of departments, which is demonstrated to the world and to posterity by this pamphlet, I now appeal to every candid and impartial man, whether there is not reason to suspect and to believe, whether there is not a presumption, a violent presumption, that Hamilton himself had furnished this machine to his correspondent in the cabinet, for the very purpose of ensnaring me, at unawares, of ensuring a war with France, and enabling him to mount his hobby-horse, the command of an army of fifty thousand, ten thousand of them to be horse. . . .

. . . my message to Congress, of the 21st of June, 1798, . . . "I will never send another minister to France, without assurances that he will be received, respected, and honored, as the representative of a great, free, powerful, and independent nation." This declaration finally effected the peace. . . .

Mr. Hamilton calls the declaration that accomplished all this "a pernicious declaration!"

Pernicious it was to his views of ambition and domination. It extinguished his hopes of being at the head of a victorious army of fifty thousand men, without which, he used to say, he had no idea of having a head upon his shoulders for four years longer.

Thus it is, when self-sufficient ignorance impertinently obtrudes itself into offices and departments, in which it has no right, nor color, nor pretence to interfere.

Thus it is, when ambition undertakes to sacrifice all characters, and the peace of nations, to its own private interest.

I have now finished all I had to say on the negotiations and peace with France in 1800.

WEBSTER TO ALEXANDER HAMILTON [3]

New Haven, September, 1800

SIR,

It has long been known that you have attempted to direct the principal measures of our national councils, and this as essentially since your resignation as while a minister of the government. While General Washington administered the government, the influence of his *prime* minister was exerted in silence: the cautious maxims of that illustrious man led him to take counsel before he resolved; and when he decided, his decisions appeared to be, and probably were, his own.

But the character of his successor—the firmness of mind, self-confidence, and independence of Mr. Adams—have restrained your influence and called into *open* opposition the *secret* enmity which has long rankled in your breast. You boldly assail the conduct and character of Mr. Adams and endeavor to prove his vanity, self-sufficiency, jealousy, rashness, and *ungovernable temper* unfit him for the station of Chief Magistrate. The instances adduced in proof are mostly of a *private* and *trifling* nature, hardly worthy of being the subject of remark or refutation.

I will not here attempt to disguise or palliate the faults of Mr. Adams, but admit them for the present in the full extent that you describe, and endeavour to prove that *your policy* and *your conduct* have been the principal causes of the present decisions among Federal men, and that if these should result in the elevation of an Antifederal man to the chief magistracy, the fault will lie at *your* door and that of your supporters. . . .

Think not, Sir, that all the monstrous schemes of daring ambitious men

[3] From Harry Warfel, ed., *Letters of Noah Webster* (New York: Library Publishers, 1953). Reprinted by permission of Harry Warfel.

to overawe and control the constitutional powers of our government are either hidden or approved by Federal men. The writer of this letter has been too long the faithful servant of his country and too steady and uniform in the support of government and religion against the assaults of disorganizers to incur a suspicion of apostacy. But it is time to speak freely, to disclose the latent designs of some influential men, and arraign their schemes at the bar of public opinion. At this bar, Sir, your opinion and mine must be tried. I reprobate your policy. I know that most of the hardy sons of freedom in the northern states want no standing army to overawe domestic factions nor to resist foreign foes, unless under circumstances that do not now exist. They will cheerfuly submit to pay the necessary expences of defence; but the danger of invasion must *exist*—it must *appear*—before they will consent to pay soldiers. And I scruple not to say that, if it had been generally known that the executive did not recommend the raising of the 12 regiments and that you had been the father of the military system, no power in this country could have resisted the public indignation. And it is surprizing that your boasted wisdom and foresight should have, in this instance, yielded to the impulses of your military zeal. Indeed, it would be incredible, had not other instances occurred in which your passions had blinded your reason. But what can be expected from a man whose prominent talents have given him a confidence in his influence that disdains public opinion and overleaps all the ordinary maxims of prudence. To see Alexander Hamilton deliberately call together the most respectable citizens of New York to decide on the expediency of meeting a mob in the streets to vote on a question respecting the British treaty, much more, to see him haranguing that mob—surrounded by adherents who reprobated the measure, in which they joined to gratify their leader—surely this gives us no very high opinion of the correctness of his judgment.

But what shall we say to the conduct of a man who has borne some of the highest civil and military employments, who could deliberately write and publish a history of his private intrigues, degrade himself in the estimation of all good men, and scandalize a family to clear himself of charges which no man believed; to vindicate integrity which a legislative act had pronounced unimpeachable and which scarcely a man in America suspected! Sir, if Mr. Adams has ever been guilty of such glaring inconsistencies of conduct and indiscretions, I will join in declaring him unfit to administer the government.

But this is not all. . . . A great proportion of the people of America are satisfied that Mr. Adams has not made any sacrifices of public interest which clearly disqualify him for the station he holds. No other candidate clearly unites in himself a claim to universal suffrage—to be divided is to be ruined. Mr. Adams is advanced in life, and no person believes that his public services will extend beyond the end of the next period of Presidency. Under these circumstances what extreme indiscretion was it to undertake an opposition from which, in case of success, would inevitably result an irremediable division of the Federal interest and, in case of defeat, complete overthrow and ruin! Will not Federal men, as well as Antifederal, believe that your ambition, pride, and overbearing temper have destined you to be the evil genius of this country?

Besides, Sir, Mr. Adams has the credit of being the father of the navy, a system of defense vastly cheaper and more effectual, as well as more popular, than your military system. A navy is the natural protection of the United States: it meets our enemy before he arrives; it attacks him on the water, where alone in all probability this country will ever be assailed; it is less expensive than an army; it encourages the genius of our people which tends more to maritime affairs than to warfare on lands; it keeps the defenders of the country at a distance, where their vices will not infect the community; it limits the destrucion of war to those who fight, whereas land armies desolate fields and towns; it unites the protection of commerce and revenue with the defence of our independence.

Let me ask you, then, how your talents could be so misemployed as to depreciate the navy and give a preference to an army for defence, for in your remarks addressed to the people in 1798 you expressly declare a "considerable army to be an object of the *most* importance"! And how can the merchants be so insensible to their true interests as to join you in the clamor against Mr. Adams, *the father of that policy by which their business is protected!* . . .

It avails little that you accuse the President of *vanity,* for as to this there is less difference between men in the degree of the quality possessed than in the manner of showing it—and were it an issue between Mr. Adams and yourself which has the most, you could not rely on an unanimous verdict in your favor. The same remark is applicable to the charge of self-sufficiency. That the President is *unmanageable* is, in a degree, true; that is, you and your supporters cannot *manage* him, but this will not pass in this country for a crime. That he is unstable is alledged—pray, Sir, has he been fickle and wavering in his opposition to *your* policy? If he has, the sound part of the American people will join in reproaching him. Did he waver during the Revolutionary War? Did he waver at the negociations of 1783? There is a wide difference, Sir, between a hasty declaration in familiar conversation and instability in a system policy.

But it is an opinion formed on thirty years of public service that Mr. Adams is a man of pure morals, of firm attachment to republican government, of sound and inflexible integrity and patriotism, and by far the best read statesman that the late Revolution called into notice. Opposed to these qualifications for the station of Chief Magistrate, his occasional ill humour at unreasonable opposition and hasty expressions of his opinion are of little weight: and when to these considerations we add the extreme hazard of affording a triumph to the opposition, your conduct on this occasion will be deemed little short of insanity.

Whatever apologies you may make for this step and whatever apparent candour may be indicated by your declaration that you would not divert a vote from Mr. Adams, the world will duly appreciate the tendency of your letter and the views of the author. The world will find the difference between candor and Jesuitism—and in an attempt to defend the honor and interests of the United States by censuring the President for the embassy to France, the citizens of America will see the deep chagrin and disappointment of a military character *whose views of preserving a permanent military force on foot have been defeated by an embassy which has removed the pretext for such an establishment.*

RUSH TO ADAMS [4]

January 6, 1806

My venerable and dear Friend,

. . . General Miranda, whose name you have mentioned in your last letter, called upon me on his way to and from Washington. . . . He mentioned his intimacy with General Hamilton in his former visit to this country and surprised me very much by informing me that the General spoke with great contempt of the person whom he threatened with a pamphlet at Yorktown. Miranda told him his fame in Europe with posterity was placed beyond the reach of his hostility to him. "No, it is not," said H. "I have written a history of his battles, campaigns, &c., and I will undeceive them." This history I presume was destroyed after he became secretary of the treasury. . . .

ADAMS TO RUSH [5]

January 25, 1806

DEAR SIR,

I never had the good fortune to meet General Miranda nor the pleasure to see him. I have heard much of his abilities and the politeness of his manners. But who is he? What is he? Whence does he come? And whither does he go? What are his motives, views, and objects? Secrecy, mystery, and intrigue have a mighty effect on the world. You and I have seen it in Franklin, Washington, Burr, Hamilton, and Jefferson, and many others. The judgment of mankind in general is like that of Father Bouhours, who says, "For myself, I regard secret persons, like the great rivers, whose bottoms we cannot see, and which make no noise; or like those vast forests, whose silence fills the soul, with I know not what religious horror. I have for them the same admiration as men had for the oracles, which never suffered themselves to be understood, till after the event of things; or for

[4] From John Schutz and Douglass Adair, *The Spur of Fame* (San Marino, Cal.: Henry Huntington Library, 1966), p. 46. Reprinted by permission of the publisher.
[5] Ibid., p. 47.

the providence of God, whose conduct is impenetrable to the human mind." . . .

Miranda's anecdote of Hamilton's scorn of Washington is no surprise to me. Those who trumpeted Washington in the highest strains at some times spoke of him at others in the strongest terms of contempt. Indeed, I know of no character to which so much hypocritical adulation has been offered. Hamilton, Pickering, and many others have been known to indulge themselves in very contemptuous expressions, but very unjustly and ungratefully. His character as an able general, a wise statesman, and an honest man is justly established. . . . The history with which Hamilton threatened to destroy the character of Washington might diminish some of that enthusiastic exaggeration which represents him as the greatest general, the greatest legislator, and the most perfect character that ever lived but could never take from him the praise of talents and virtues, labors and exertions, which will command the esteem of the wisest and best men in all ages.

Although I read with tranquility and suffered to pass without animadversion in silent contempt the base insinuations of vanity and a hundred lies besides published in a pamphlet against me[6] by an insolent coxcomb who rarely dined in good company, where there was good wine, without getting silly and vaporing about his administration like a young girl about her brilliants and trinkets, yet I lose all patience when I think of a bastard brat of a Scotch pedlar daring to threaten to undeceive the world in their judgment of Washington by writing an history of his battles and campaigns. This creature was in a delirium of ambition; he had been blown up with vanity by the tories, had fixed his eyes on the highest station in America, and he hated every man, young or old, who stood in his way or could in any manner eclipse his laurels or rival his pretensions. . . .

ADAMS TO RUSH [7]

September, 1807

. . . Hamilton had great disadvantages. His origin was infamous; his place of birth and education were foreign countries; his fortune was poverty itself; the profligacy of his life—his fornications, adulteries, and his incests—were propagated far and wide. Nevertheless, he "affichéd" disinterestedness as boldly as Washington. His myrmidons asserted it with as little shame, tho' not a man of them believed it. All the rest of the world ridiculed and despised the pretext. He had not, therefore, the same success. Yet he found means to fascinate some and intimidate others. You and I know him also to have been an intriguer. . . .

[6] [A reference to Hamilton's *Letter . . . concerning the Public Conduct and Character of John Adams*.]

[7] Ibid., pp. 92–94.

8
Hail and Farewell

Whether men loved or loathed Hamilton, they could not deny his ability or fail to admire his resourceful intelligence. Witness, for instance, some relatively early and critical sketches of Hamilton by two French travellers, both of whom had been revolutionaries. Scholar, propagandist, and politician, Jean Pierre Brissot de Warville was a leader of the Gironde, the moderate wing of the French revolutionists. He had come to the United States in 1788 with two aims: to investigate possibilities for investments in American government securities for a French syndicate of bankers which wished to speculate in the United States public debt, and "to study men who had just acquired their liberty." Perhaps politically more palatable to Hamilton was the lawyer and judge, Moreau de Saint Méry. He had been an ardent revolutionist, to be sure, the presiding officer of the Paris commune; but in November 1793 he had fled from Robespierre and the guillotine into exile. His comments below suggest his gifts as diarist and critical observer.

Like Hamilton, Connecticut's Lieutenant Governor, Oliver Wolcott, Senior, had been a delegate to the Continental Congress and a Continental Army officer; and he expressed a similar attitude toward national affairs.

Washington's assessment of Hamilton should be understood in the context of the Adams-Hamilton contretemps noted above and of the ongoing Anglo-American crisis. Great Britain was scarcely less guilty than the French in violating neutral rights. She continued her policy of seizing American vessels—which seemed especially mindless and enigmatic given the low state of her military fortunes and the possibility that a relaxation of such a policy might encourage a military accord with the United States. Still consumed by warlike ambitions, Hamilton pressed for a strong posture toward both belligerents and rejected any thought of a senatorial race in favor of possible appointment as army commander. But Adams turned to Washington instead and it was the former chief executive who had insisted upon Hamilton—indeed he gave Adams a virtual ultimatum to this effect—rather than Henry Knox, whom the President had proposed as second in command. Washington here assesses Hamilton's character and the reasons for his support of the New Yorker as his chief aide.

Gouverneur Morris, Federalist Senator from New York, was hardly

*a detached commentator, being a long-time friend and admirer of
Hamilton. Nor is the funeral oration a vehicle noted for its accurate
rendering of a man. But this post-mortem tribute (one of a number:
e.g., Fisher Ames and Harrison Grey Otis were among those on record with posthumous accounts), if it does not shed any great illumi-
nation upon Hamilton's character, nonetheless tells us something of
the high esteem in which he was held by many publicly situated men.*

*Finally, John Marshall, in another posthumous sketch, gives us a
eulogy that is almost equally flattering, a benediction from one high
Federalist to another and significant for that reason alone.*

JEAN P. BRISSOT DE WARVILLE [1]

Mr. Hamilton is Mr. Madison's worthy rival as well as his collabora-
tor. He looks thirty-eight or forty years old, is not tall, and has a resolute,
frank, soldierly appearance. He was aide-de-camp to General Washington,
who had the greatest confidence in him, a confidence he deserved. Since
the war he has resumed the practice of law and has devoted himself mainly
to public life. Elected to Congress, he has distinguished himself by his
eloquence and by the soundness of his reasoning. Among the works which
have come from his pen the most distinguished are a large number of letters inserted in *The Federalist*, of which I shall speak hereafter, and the
Letters from Phocion, published in defense of the Loyalists. During the
war Mr. Hamilton fought the Loyalists with success, but when peace came
it was his opinion that they should not be driven to desperation by harsh
persecution, and he was fortunate enough to win over to clemency his
fellow citizens, who had been inspired by a justifiable resentment against
the Loyalists because of the damage they had done. This young orator's
moment of triumph came at the New York Convention. The antifederal-
ist party was strong in New York City, and three quarters of the members
of the convention when they left for Poughkeepsie were opposed to the
new Constitution. Mr. Hamilton, joining his efforts to those of the celebrated Mr. Jay, succeeded in convincing even the most obstinate among
them that the refusal of New York would have disastrous consequences for
the state and for the Confederation. Consequently they voted in favor of
the Constitution. The celebration in New York following the ratification
was magnificent. The ship *Federalist*, which took part in the festivities,
was renamed *Hamilton* in honor of this eloquent orator.

Hamilton married General Schuyler's daughter, a delightful woman
who combines both the charms and attractions and the candor and sim-

[1] Jean P. Brissot de Warville, *New Travels in the United States of America,* trans. and
ed. Durand Echeverria (Cambridge: The Belknap Press of Harvard University Press,
1964), pp. 147–48, 382–84. Copyright, 1964, by the President and Fellows of Harvard
College. Reprinted by permission of the publisher.

plicity typical of American womanhood. At the dinner to which he invited me I met General Mifflin, known for his distinguished record during the last war. He has the vivacity of a Frenchman, and is also extremely courteous.

Mr. King, whom I also saw at this dinner, is reputed to be the most eloquent man in the United States. What impressed me most about him was his modesty; he seemed completely unaware of his worth. Mr. Hamilton had the determined appearance of a republican; Mr. Madison, the thoughtful look of a wise statesman. . . .

Mr. Hamilton, let us admit it, has undervalued his country's potentialities, the probable income from taxes, and the men he is dealing with. The future is so brilliant and so secure that the nation could hope to retire a much larger debt. He has underestimated the revenue from taxes, as experience has already proved to him, for instead of the expected $1,800,- 000, he has collected in the first year, that is, from August 1, 1789, to September 30, 1790, $2,523,868.

As for his fellow citizens, Mr. Hamilton, with all his talents, all his logic and powers of reason, could have led them to do anything he wished. He could have easily persuaded everyone that it is in the public interest to pay the debt completely. All Americans know that without credit they cannot expand their commerce, and they all wish to trade on a large scale. They all feel that in order to achieve this kind of commercial activity they must give dignity and strength to their government. But such dignity is impossible if they do not pay their debts. They all know now that it is not money they lack or will lack, that the so-called shortage of money is due only to lack of confidence and to fluctuations of the public's faith in the government. They all know that the real way to re-establish this confidence and consequently to make money flow is to pay all their debts without any reduction and without any consideration of the price at which these obligations were purchased.

Even the farmers are convinced of this truth, although at first they favored a reduction of the debt. They are convinced of this twin truth: without public confidence, there is no trade: without trade, there is no agriculture and no industry. The farmers of the United States live well. They like to have their tea, coffee, sugar, etc., and they can pay for these only with what they produce; they therefore feel the need of an export trade, the need for credit to support this trade, and the need to create public confidence to maintain this credit. Such are the thoughts and feelings I found everywhere among all the citizens I met during my travels in the United States.

How is it possible that Mr. Hamilton has not consulted and obeyed this public opinion? Why was he frightened by the outcries of a few ill-informed men? Is it worthy of such an enlightened statesman to yield to the forces of ignorance and to compromise principles which should always be inflexible?

The celebrated D'Avenant indicated the road to be followed when he wrote that credit is acquired only by uninterrupted and certain payments and by strict fulfillment of the conditions of the loan:

> We give over trusting the public, or private persons, then only when we perceive fraud or evil faith in their proceedings, or when we judge their affairs to be desperate; but when the interruption in common payments is occasioned only by some accidents in the state, when both the government and particular persons take the utmost care to disengage themselves, and when it can be made to appear there is a fund sufficient to satisfy all pretensions, men's minds will become quiet and appeased; mutual convenience will lead them into a desire of helping one another . . . The huge engine of credit [. . .] is not to be put in order by patching here and there; and you can never have true motion till the legislative power interpose in setting all the springs right.

Mr. Hamilton is far from unfamiliar with these principles, for they all appear in his report. He recognizes throughout it the need to fulfill faithfully the nation's obligations in order to acquire credit, to make America respected, and to restore value to government stocks, public lands, etc. But unfortunately, Mr. Hamilton also believed that there are situations when states may fail to meet their obligations, provided they plan to repair in the future the harm done, and he seemed to believe that the United States was somewhat in that position. This was an error. Mr. Hamilton did not have enough trust in his own strength or in that of his country to dare attempt a large operation based on respect for good faith, which would have necessarily produced excellent credit and opened up vast resources to Americans.

In addition to the plan adopted by Congress he had proposed several others, for instance, that of giving to subscribers one third of their loan in land, an operation which would have looked less like bankruptcy since the debtor would have acquitted himself of his debt by surrendering the property pledged as security. But it would have been unworthy of the United States to impose such an arrangement on its creditors. Also, he suggested a tontine. This was a much more suitable idea, but perhaps Americans are too unfamiliar with this type of speculation for it to have been a success.

MOREAU DE SAINT MÉRY [2]

August 26. [1794] Same rounds, and in addition I called upon Minister Hamilton with Talleyrand's letter of introducion. I arrived at the

[2] Kenneth Roberts and Anna Roberts, *Moreau de Saint Méry's American Journey* (Garden City: Doubleday & Company, Inc., 1947), pp. 135–38. Copyright 1947 by Kenneth Roberts and Anna M. Roberts. Reprinted by permission of Doubleday & Company, Inc., and the Society of Authors as literary representative of the Estate of Kenneth Roberts.

house where his office was. A man in a long gray linen jacket, whom I found in the corridor of the ground floor, told me he was not in. I came out again from this house, which had little to recommend it, and went away astounded that the official lodgings of a minister could be so poor.

I had gone only a few feet when I saw a person pass me, who, for some reason unknown to me, I was sure was M. Hamilton. I turned and followed him, and we entered the corridor almost together. The same man was still there. He inserted a key, opened a room where M. Hamilton was (for it was he), and to my pleasure ushered me in.

I had been told to avoid seeming inquisitive, and particularly not to question him; but he showed great trust in me, and spoke to me frankly about France and America.

He advised me to set up my wife as head of a school for young ladies, but I told him of my arrangement with M. de la Roche.

I could not help noticing that the furnishings and equipment of his ministerial office were not worth fifty French livres. His desk was a plain pine table covered with a green cloth. Planks on trestles held records and paper, and at one end was a little imitation Chinese vase and a plate with glasses on it.

His usher, or the man who served him in his office, had, with the gray linen jacket of which I have spoken, trousers of the same material, and his bare legs showed below them. In a word, I felt I saw Spartan customs all about me.

Here are some very important details about M. Hamilton. He was a creole from St. Kitts, one of the English Antilles, and a love child. He went to the North American continent and lived in New York. He was destined for the bar when the first troubles of this country showed themselves. Then he wrote and frequently published his opinions under various fictitious names.

These marks of patriotism caused him to be appointed captain of artillery. Then General Washington, impressed by his opinions, took him as his secretary, made him a colonel and his first aide-de-camp.

Consumed by ambition, he wished to have it believed that he was the master mind in everything, and this determined Washington to part with him.

Then Hamilton was given a battalion. Endowed with true courage, he served with the grenadiers and the chasseurs of the French army. He commanded this battalion in the attack at Yorktown; but dissatisfied because he was not given all the glory for the capture of a redoubt, he retired and took up the practice of law in New York.

When the independence of the Americans was recognized, each state regarded itself as independent and wished to proceed according to its own particuar interest. Trouble promptly developed everywhere. Acts of violence even started a civil war,[3] whereupon several people had the idea

[3] Shays' Rebellion.

of announcing publicly that business would be destroyed if each state persisted in obstructing and burdening it. It was then wisely suggested that each state should send commissioners to decide on ways to obviate such a disaster, and New York was designated as the most central meeting place.

Among the number of the zealots for the common good was Hamilton, who had married General Schuyler's daughter and thus had acquired the support and help of his brothers-in-law, Renslaer and Church, members of the Commons of England, and their families.

The commissioners declared that it would be absurd to consider any general rule for business, without some central authority to see that the rules were executed.

As a result they planned to authorize the organization of a central power capable of forcing each state to obey.

This authority was obtained, whereupon they produced the federal Constitution, of which Hamilton is known to have been one of the greatest apostles.

Washington remembered him and made him Minister. For the second time Hamilton in 1794 (the period when I knew him) wished everyone to think that in him alone lay the salvation of America, and for the second time Washington replied by dismissing him.

Hamilton, who had never known anything but the American continent, and who judged Europe from books, was, I repeat, enamored of the kind of great power which makes itself obeyed without argument. Civil War did not frighten him because he was a man of great courage with a natural military talent, and because he believed and said that America could only have a real and stable government after it had been created and consolidated by internal dissensions.

Rather than succeed Washington immediately in the presidency, Hamilton groomed Jay for the position. His reasons were that the very name of Washington had given too great a delicacy to the scales in which his successors would be weighed, and that Jefferson's party, which would be displeased to see him, Hamilton, President, would make Jay regret his success, because he lacked character, and therefore Jay would not have a prolonged presidency.

But it was John Adams who succeeded Washington. When the question of a successor to this second President arose, the electors put up Jefferson and Burr. The first became President, and the second Vice-President.

When it came time to elect a successor to Jefferson, the resulting political quarrel agitated the entire United States. This gave rise to a duel between Burr and Hamilton, in which the latter was killed. Thus Hamilton's ambition was ended.

He was small, with an extremely composed bearing, unusually small eyes, and something a little furtive in his glance. He spoke French, but quite incorrectly. He had a great deal of ready wit, kept a close watch over himself, and was, I repeat, extremely brave. He had no desire for private gain, but was eaten up with ambition, and ardently admired the laws and government of England, and its financial system. Personally he was very much of an autocrat, and an ardent guardian of the prerogatives of the Executive.

The death of Hamilton aroused widespread regrets, and it can be said that he was one of the most outstanding statesmen which the United States of America had developed.

FROM OLIVER WOLCOTT, SEN. [4]

Litchfield, June 17th, 1793.

Sir,

I have examined the statement of the Secretary of the Treasury which you sent me, and although I am not able to judge of this business in the detail, yet the energetic reasons which he has assigned for his own conduct, cannot, I believe, fail of making the most convincing impressions, and fix his adversaries in a state of despondence. I never had the least doubt, both as to the abilities and recitude of Mr. Hamilton. Indeed a man must be uncommonly stupid, not to know that the national fiscal department must be conducted not only with regard to every species of property within the United States, but to the whole system of commerce, and whatever has the name of property, which can have any connection with this country. The man who can take so comprehensive a view, unaided by any former national experience, as to be able to establish a system of public credit after it was by abuse of all public faith and confidence nearly annihilated, so as within the short term of four years fully to restore and establish it upon a stable basis, and by his provident care to guard against all contingencies which might do it an injury, and by the same operation raise a people from the most torpid indolence and despondency, to a state of the most vigorous enterprise, industry and cheerfulness, and increase the value of property within the same period one third more than it before was, (which I believe has been the case within this state, notwithstanding our vast emigrations) he who can effect all this without imposing a sensible burden upon any one, or deranging one useful occupation or business, must possess talents and industry and a species of intuition, which will ever insure him respect and the highest esteem from all but such only as are infected by that basest and vilest of human affections, envy. In this state I never heard any one speak of Mr. Hamilton but in terms of respect, and the same of the officers of his department. I shall furnish a number of gentlemen in this part of the state with the reading of the fiscal statement which you sent me, for although we are very quiet and confiding in the rectitude of

[4] George Gibbs, *Memoirs of the Administrations of Washington and John Adams* (New York, 1846), pp. 101–2.

the national administration; yet there are some who wish to have it otherwise (or I am mistaken) if they dare make the attempt—at present they dare not.

WASHINGTON TO ADAMS, SEPTEMBER 25, 1798 [5]

. . . I have no hesitation in declaring, that, if the public is to be deprived of the services of Colo. Hamilton in the military line, that the post he was destined to fill will not be easily supplied; and that this is the sentiment of the public, I think I can venture to pronounce. Although Colonel Hamilton has never acted in the character of a General Officer, yet his opportunities, as the principal and most confidential aid of the commander-in-chief, afforded him the means of viewing every thing on a larger scale than those, whose attentions were confined to Divisions or Brigades, who knew nothing of the correspondences of the commander-in-Chief, or of the various orders to, or transactions with, the General Staff of the Army. These advantages, and his having served with usefulness in the Old Congress, in the General convention, and having filled one of the most important departments of government with acknowledged abilities and integrity, have placed him on high ground, and made him a conspicuous character in the United States, and even in Europe.

To these, as a matter of no small consideration, may be added, that, as a lucrative practice in the line of his profession is his *most certain* dependence, the inducement to relinquish it must in some degree be commensurate. By some he is considered as an ambitious man, and therefore a dangerous one. That he is ambitious, I shall readily grant, but it is of that laudable kind, which prompts a man to excel in whatever he takes in hand. He is enterprising, quick in his perceptions, and his judgment intuitively great; qualities essential to a military character, and therefore I repeat, that his loss will be irreparable.

With respect to General Knox, I can say with truth, there is no man in the United States with whom I have been in habits of greater intimacy, no one whom I have loved more sincerely, nor any for whom I have had a greater friendship. But esteem, love, and friendship can have no influence on my mind, when I conceive that the subjugation of our government and independence are the objects aimed at by the enemies of our Peace, and when possibly our all is at stake.

In the first moments of leisure, after the Secretary of War left this place, I wrote a friendly letter to General Knox, stating my firm belief, that, if the French should invade this country with a view to the conquest or the division of it, their operations would commence at the southward, and endeavored to show him, in that case, how all-important it was to engage

[5] P. L. Ford, ed., *The Writings of George Washington* (New York and London: G. P. Putnam's Sons), vol. 14, pp. 101–2.

General Pinckney, his numerous family, friends, and influential acquaintance *heartily* in the cause; sending him at the same time a copy of the arrangement, which I supposed *to be final;* and, in a subsequent letter, I gave him my opinion fully with respect to the relative situation of himself and Colonel Hamilton, not expecting, I confess, the difficulties which have occurred.

FUNERAL ORATION [6]

On a stage erected in the portico of Trinity Church, Mr. Gouverneur Morris, having four of General Hamilton's sons, the eldest about sixteen and the youngest about six years of age, with him, rose and delivered to the immense concourse in front an extemporary Oration, which, being pronounced slowly and impressively, was easily committed to memory, and being very soon afterwards placed on paper, is presumed to be correct even to the language.

Fellow-Citizens,

If on this sad, this solemn occasion, I should endeavour to move your commiseration, it would be doing injustice to that sensibility which has been so generally and so justly manifested. Far from attempting to excite your emotions, I must try to repress my own, and yet I fear that instead of the language of a public speaker, you will hear only the lamentations of a bewailing friend. But I will struggle with my bursting heart, to pourtray that Heroic Spirit, which has flown to the mansions of bliss.

Students of Columbia—he was in the ardent pursuit of knowledge in your academic shades, when the first sound of the American war called him to the field—A young and unprotected volunteer, such was his zeal and so brilliant his service, that we heard his name before we knew his person.—It seemed as if God had called him suddenly into existence, that he might assist to save a world.

The penetrating eye of Washington soon perceived the manly spirit which animated his youthful bosom. By that excellent judge of men he was selected as an Aid, and thus he became early acquainted with, and was a principal actor in, the most important scenes of our Revolution.

At the siege of York, he pertinaciously insisted, and he obtained the command of a Forlorn Hope. He stormed the redoubt; but let it be recorded, that not one single man of the enemy perished. His gallant troops, emulating the heroism of their chief, checked the uplifted arm, and spared a foe no longer resisting. Here closed his military career.

Shortly after the war, your favour—no, your discernment, called him to public office. You sent him to the convention at Philadelphia: he there as-

[6] *New York Evening Post,* July 16, 1804, as reprinted in [William Coleman, ed.], *A Collection of the Facts and Documents Relative to the Death of Major General Alexander Hamilton* (New York, 1804), pp. 42–47.

sisted in forming that constitution which is now the bond of our union, the shield of our defence, and the source of our prosperity. In signing that compact he exprest his apprehension that it did not contain sufficient means of strength for its own preservation; and that in consequence we should share the fate of many other republics, and pass through Anarchy to Despotism. We hoped better things. We confided in the good sense of the American people; and above all we trusted in the protecting Providence of the Almighty. On this important subject he never concealed his opinion. He disdained concealment. Knowing the purity of his heart, he bore it as it were in his hand, exposing to every passenger its inmost recesses. This generous indiscretion subjected him to censure from misrepresentation. His speculative opinions were treated as deliberate designs; and yet you all know how strenuous, how unremitting were his efforts to establish and to preserve the constitution. If then his opinion was wrong, pardon, oh! pardon that single error, in a life devoted to your service.

At the time when our government was organized, we were without funds, though not without resources. To call them into action, and establish order in the finances, Washington sought for splendid talents, for extensive information, and, above all, he sought for sterling, incorruptible integrity—All these he found in Hamilton.—The system then adopted has been the subject of much animadversion. If it be not without a fault, let it be remembered that nothing human is perfect—Recollect the circumstances of the moment—recollect the conflict of opinion—and above all, remember that *the minister of a republic must bend to the will of the people.* The administration which Washington formed, was one of the best that any country was ever blest with. And the result was a rapid advance in power and prosperity, of which there is no example in any other age or nation. The part which Hamilton bore is universally known.

His unsuspecting confidence in professions which he believed to be sincere, led him to trust too much to the undeserving. This exposed him to misrepresentation. He felt himself obliged to resign—The care of a rising family, and the narrowness of his fortune, made it a duty to return to his profession of their support. But though he was compelled to abandon public life, never, no, never for a moment did he abandon the public service. He never lost sight of your interests——I declare to you, before that God in whose presence we are now so especially assembled, that in his most private and confidential conversations, the single objects of discussion and consideration were your freedom and happiness.

You well remember the state of things which again called forth Washing from his retreat to lead your armies. You know that he asked for Hamilton to be his second in command. That venerable sage well knew the dangerous incidents of a military profession, and he felt the hand of time pinching life at its source. It was probable that he would soon be removed from the scene, and that his second would succeed to the command. He knew, by experience, the importance of that place—and he thought the sword of America might safely be confided to the hand which now lies cold in that coffin. Oh! my fellow-citizens, remember this solemn testimonial, that he was not ambitious. Yet he was charged with ambition; and wounded by the imputation, when he laid down his command, he declared, in the proud independence of his soul, that he never would accept of any office, unless in a foreign war he should be called on to expose his life in defence of his country. This determination was immovable. It was his fault that his opinions and his resolutions could not be changed. Knowing his own firm purpose, he was indignant at the charge that he sought for place or power. He was ambitious only of glory, but he was deeply solicitous for you. For himself he feared nothing, but he feared that bad men might, by false professions, acquire your confidence, and abuse it to your ruin.

Brethren of the Cincinnati—There lies our chief! Let him still be our model. Like him, after long and faithful public service, let us cheerfully perform the social duties of private life. Oh! he was mild and gentle. In him there was no offence; no guile—his generous hand and heart were open to all.

Gentlemen of the Bar—You have lost your brightest ornament. Cherish and imitate his example. While, like him, with justifiable, with laudable zeal, you pursue the interests of your clients, remember, like him, the eternal principles of justice.

Fellow-Citizens—You have long witnessed his professional conduct, and felt his unrivalled eloquence. You know how well he performed the duties of a Citizen—you know that he never courted your favour by adulation, or the sacrifice of his own judgment. You have seen him contending against you, and saving your dearest interests, as it were, in spite of yourselves. And you now feel and enjoy the benefits resulting from the firm energy of his conduct. Bear this testimony to the memory of my departed friend. I CHARGE YOU TO PROTECT HIS FAME—It is all he has left—all that these poor orphan children will inherit from their father. But, my countrymen, that Fame may be a rich treasure to you also. Let it be the test by which to examine those who solicit your favour. Disregarding professions, view their conduct, and on a doubtful occasion, ask, *Would Hamilton have done this thing?*

You all know how he perished. On this last scene, I cannot, I must not dwell. It might excite emotions too strong for your better judgment. Suffer not your indignation to lead to any act which might again offend the insulted majesty of the law; on his part, as from his lips, though with my voice—for his voice you will hear no more,—let me entreat you to respect yourselves.

And now, ye ministers of the everlasting God, perform your holy office, and commit these ashes of our departed brother to the bosom of the Grave!

JOHN MARSHALL [7]

This gentleman [Alexander Hamilton] was a native of the island of St. Croix, and, at a very early period of life, had been placed by his friends, in New York. Possessing an ardent temper, he caught fire from the concussions of the moment, and, with all the enthusiasm of youth, engaged first his pen, and afterwards his sword, in the stern contest between the American colonies and their parent state. Among the first troops raised by New York was a corps of artillery, in which he was appointed a captain. Soon after the war was transferred to the Hudson, his superior endowments recommended him to the attention of the Commander-in-chief, into whose family, before completing his twenty-first year, he was invited to enter. Equally brave and intelligent, he continued, in this situation, to display a degree of firmness and capacity which commanded the confidence and esteem of his general, and of the principal officers in the army.

After the capitulation at Yorktown, the war languished throughout the American continent, and the probability that its termination was approaching daily increased.

The critical circumstances of the existing government rendered the events of the civil, more interesting than those of the military department; and Colonel Hamilton accepted a seat in the congress of the United States. In all the important acts of the day, he performed a conspicuous part; and was greatly distinguished among those distinguished men whom the crisis had attracted to the councils of their country. He had afterwards been active in promoting those measures which led to the convention at Philadelphia, of which he was a member, and had greatly contributed to the adoption of the constitution by the state of New York. In the pre-eminent part he had performed, both in the military and civil transactions of his country, he had acquired a great degree of well merited fame; and the frankness of his manners, the openness of his temper, the warmth of his feelings, and the sincerity of his heart, had secured him many valuable friends.

To talents equally splendid and useful, he united a patient industry, not always the companion of genius, which fitted him, in a peculiar manner, for subduing the difficulties to be encountered by the man who should be placed at the head of the American finances. . . .

Seldom has any minister excited the opposite passions of love and hate in a higher degree than Colonel Hamilton. His talents were too pre-eminent not to receive from all the tribute of profound respect; and his integrity and honour as a man, not less than his official rectitude, though slandered at a distance, were admitted to be superior to reproach, by those enemies who knew him.

---

[7] John Marshall, *The Life of George Washington*, 2nd ed., abridged (Philadelphia, 1833), vol. 2, pp. 168, 356–58.

But with respect to his political principles and designs, the most contradictory opinions were entertained. While one party sincerely believed his object to be the preservation of the constitution of the United States in its original purity; the other, with perhaps equal sincerity, imputed to him the insidious intention of subverting it. While his friends were persuaded, that as a statesman, he viewed all foreign nations with an equal eye; his enemies could perceive in his conduct, only hostility to France and attachment to her rival.

It was his fortune to hold a conspicuous station in times which were peculiarly tempestuous, and under circumstances peculiarly unfavorable to the fair action of the judgment. In the midst of prejudices against the national debt, which had taken deep root, and had long been nourished, he was called to the head of a department, whose duty it was to contend with those prejudices, and to offer a system which, in doing justice to the creditor of the public, might retrieve the reputation of his country. While the passions were inflamed by a stern contest between the advocates of a national, and of state governments, duties were assigned to him, in the execution of which there were frequent occasions to manifest his devotion to the former. When a raging fever, caught from that which was desolating France, and exhibiting some of its symptoms, had seized the public mind, and reached its understanding, it was unfavourable to his quiet, and perhaps to his fame, that he remained uninfected by the disease. He judged the French revolution without prejudice; and had the courage to predict that it could not terminate in a free and popular government.

Such opinions, at such a time, could not fail to draw a load of obloquy upon a man whose frankness gave them publicity, and whose boldness and decision of character insured them an able and steady support. The suspicions they were calculated to generate, derived great additional force from the political theories he was understood to hold. It was known that, in his judgment, the constitution of the United States was rather chargeable with imbecility, than censurable for its too great strength; and that the real sources of danger to American happiness and liberty, were to be found in its want of the means to effect the objects of its institution;—in its being exposed to the encroachments of the states,—not in the magnitude of its powers. Without attempting to conceal these opinions, he declared his perfect acquiescence in the decision of his country; his hope that the issue would be fortunate; and his firm determination, in whatever might depend upon his exertions, to give the experiment the fairest chance for success. No part of his political conduct has been perceived, which would inspire doubts of the sincerity of these declarations. His friends may appeal with confidence to his official acts, to all his public conduct, for the refutation of those charges which were made against him while at the head of the treasury department, and were continued, without interruption, till he ceased to be the object of jealousy.

In the esteem and good opinion of the President, to whom he was best known, Colonel Hamilton at all times maintained a high place. While balancing on the mission to England, and searching for a person to whom the interesting negotiation with that government should be confided, the mind of the chief magistrate was directed, among others, to this gentleman. He carried with him out of office, the same cordial esteem for his character, and respect for his talents, which had induced his appointment.

PART THREE

HAMILTON IN HISTORY

Of all the founding fathers, Hamilton remains the most enigmatic and highly controversial. His name evokes sharply contrasting reactions. It always has. More often than not these reactions take the form of a rivalry between disciples of Hamilton and Jefferson. As J. L. Garvin, an English observer, declared in the 1920s, Hamilton and Jefferson "present to the whole world those opposite types of faculty and desire which sway the workings of all free government, and revive again and again the full strength of party conflict." The work of the historian-ambassador Claude Bowers, though not the most recent, is typical of this pro-Jeffersonian school; so, too, are studies by Vernon Louis Parrington, Henry Bamford Parkes and closer to our own times, by Joseph Charles, who sees Hamilton as an eighteenth-century wheeler-dealer, manipulating early national period finances in order to favor a select "moneyed interest."

Such a view has its direct lineage from the Jacksonian era when Hamilton's posthumous reputation was cast in the mode which would endure, with two notable exceptions (post–Civil War and Progressive period rehabilitations), until the mid-twentieth century. The party of Andrew Jackson accepted the view of Hamilton and of the Federalists set forth in 1828 by Martin Van Buren; namely, that the New Yorker was elitist in inclination, hostile to the average man, partial toward monarchy. This proposition persisted through the New Deal period, which is surprising since Franklin D. Roosevelt's policy in practice represented the triumph of Hamiltonian principles.

A conflicting estimate has also characterized the Hamiltonian literature, one which has become increasingly fashionable. For example, a highly popular college textbook has a subchapter entitled, "Hamilton Wins," which describes how the post–Civil War years conform more to Hamilton's ideals than to Jefferson's. More recently, Bray Hammond has abrasively commented that, "Americans still maintain a pharisaical reverence for Thomas Jefferson, but they have in reality little use for what he said and believed—save when, on occasion and out of context, it appears to be of political expediency. What they really admire is what Alexander Hamilton stood for, and his are the hopes they have fulfilled."

If one accepts this statement as accurate, it makes the failure to honor Hamilton all the more striking. For there are no Hamilton Day dinners sponsored by Republicans. Nor are there any proposals to erect a Hamiltonian Memorial near the Potomac. To the contrary, Hamilton still suffers from the apparently immutable indictment that he was a monarchist and an elitist. He is forever the man who was uncivil to Washington in 1781; who tolerated that outburst of speculation attendant upon his first financial measures; who manipulated members of Adams' cabinet; who subverted and gratuitously attacked the second president; who had a tasteless affair with Mrs. Reynolds; who exhibited impatience, immoderation, inordinate ambition; who had a tendency to glorify the military, to exalt the wealthy, and to affect an unpardonable hubris. So fixed is this image that most conservatives no longer pay homage to his name, eschewing the trend of the 1920s when books extolling Hamilton as the founder of American capitalism made their appearance and when the Republican orthodox—such as Arthur Vandenberg and Andrew Mellon, along with presidents Warren G. Harding and Calvin Coolidge—flocked to the Hamiltonian colors. But Hamilton would be forgotten with the Depression and his total eclipse from the mainstream became complete.

Or almost so. Hamilton's position today remains more often than not as foil to Jefferson. He is, therefore, hardly about to be canonized as a hero of democracy. But some recent studies have tried to incorporate Hamilton into the American liberal tradition, even to see him—as Broadus Mitchell has—as our first economic planner. Certainly, in a world of increased national planning, of quickening interest in statecraft, of real-politik as the star to steer by in foreign affairs, there is a renewed interest in and appreciation of Hamilton's brilliance. Recent historians have sought to correct to balance. They have observed that his taste for power should be set against his use of power in an instrumental sense—for a grand end and not as an end in itself. They have emphasized his enlightened view of the Black man, his advocacy of manumission and (in 1802) of Toussaint l'Ouverture, "the Napoleon of the Antilles"—unlike Jefferson who drew the color line and reversed Hamilton's and Adams' views on Santo Domingo. They have found that the New Yorker, unlike Jefferson, was less prepared to tolerate an Anglo-American alliance. They have contrasted pejorative qualities with commentary on Hamilton's courage, enthusiasm, resourcefulness. They have noted his vision and boldness, opposing his admittedly anti-democratic sympathies with his vision of the vast potential for American capitalism and the American political scheme.

All four selections below approach Hamilton and his achievements differently, but they are nonetheless complementary; they offer a corrective enabling us to distinguish the essential Hamilton, and they suggest something of the high esteem in which he is now held by contemporary practitioners of the historian's craft.

9

Richard B. Morris: Alexander Hamilton after Two Centuries[1]

As he was about to assume the office of the Presidency George Washington remarked to a friend: "My movements to the chair of government will be accompanied by feelings not unlike those of a culprit who is going to the place of his execution." Washington's observation was indeed prophetic. Since the days of the Founding Fathers America's great public figures have been the recipients of much uncritical adulation and the targets of fierce vilification. They have been placed on a pedestal or kicked in the gutter. They have become transfigured into mythological heroes with saintlike attributes or into rascals whose motives have been impugned, whose personal lives have been invaded, and whose achievements belittled and distorted.

The career of Alexander Hamilton is an outstanding illustration of this ironic phenomenon of American politics. Endowed with exceptional precocity, consuming energy, and high ambition, Hamilton stood in the center of events from the earliest days of the Revolution until the late years of President Adams' administration. In the course of his public career he accumulated a wide variety of enemies. John Adams called him "the bastard brat of a Scots peddler." Jefferson charged him with being "not only a monarchist, but for a monarchy bottomed on corruption." The hired scribbler, Callender, defamed him as a Caligula, and Senator Maclay called him a crook. Since his own day he has been assailed as an enemy of democracy, a friend of reaction, an ally of the special interests, a High Tory who sought to erect a leviathan state, and an arch-plotter against the life of the republic.

That such charges were groundless was the sober judgment of many of Hamilton's contemporaries. Washington, perhaps Hamilton's greatest admirer and certainly his chief disciple, paid tribute to his enterprise, his quick perception, and "his judgment intuitively great." Granted that Hamilton was ambitious, Washington considered that his ambition was "of that laudable kind, which prompts a man to excel in whatever he takes in hand." The worldly Talleyrand, who knew him well, bracketed

[1] From Richard B. Morris, ed., *Alexander Hamilton and the Founding of the Nation* (New York: The Dial Press, 1957), pp. vii–xiv. Copyright © 1956 by Richard B. Morris. Reprinted by permission of Richard B. Morris.

Hamilton with Napoleon and Fox. These three he considered the outstanding figures of that epoch. One political opponent conceded that Hamilton, "more than any other man, did the thinking of the time."

That Hamilton should have become a symbol of party, class, and faction is one of the ironies of American history. No man of his generation accomplished more to break down local barriers and sectional prejudices which had hampered the formation of a strong union. Save Washington, no man was more opposed to the spirit of party and faction. Yet, the Hamiltonian program fomented both the party spirit and partisanship. Hamilton did not foresee that the two-party system would prove a stabilizing force in American government. To him party was synonymous with disorder and instability.

Hamilton was one of our first great nationalists. "Think continentally," he counseled the young nation. He believed in the destiny of America and wished to confer upon the national government powers appropriate to its needs and opportunities. In *The Federalist* he shows how such national unity could be achieved without sacrificing states' rights and without jeopardizing individual liberties. His interpretation of the Constitution was both audacious and masterly. His enunciation of the doctrine of implied powers gave the nationalist Supreme Court the arguments for that broad construction which they put upon the Constitution. His interpretation of the taxing power opened up to the federal government sources of revenue essential to its needs prior to the adoption of the income tax amendment. A staunch advocate of separation of powers and checks and balances, Hamilton asserted the independence of the judiciary, and, of all the Founding Fathers, was most forceful in arguing for the right of the Supreme Court to declare laws of Congress unconstitutional. He believed that the courts were the safeguard of minority rights, and was confident that curbs upon judicial usurpation existed in the Constitution.

Hamilton was an administrative genius, perhaps the greatest America has yet produced. He believed in a strong executive, guarded the Presidency from encroachments upon its power by the legislative branch of the government, and assumed an influence in Washington's cabinet which is unmatched in the annals of the American cabinet system. Concerning himself with every phase of public policy, he was more than merely Secretary of the Treasury. He was in fact Washington's prime minister.

Hamilton's inventive mind grasped an extraordinary range of governmental problems—constitutional, economic, diplomatic, and military. His fiscal program was bold, original, and constructive, and firmly established American credit at home and abroad. To do so, he created a national debt and made effective use of the government's taxing power. With pardonable rhetoric Daniel Webster spoke of Hamilton's achievements: "He smote the rock of national resources and abundant streams of revenue gushed forth; he touched the dead corpse of public credit and it sprang upon its feet." The program injected confidence and buoyancy into the business community, but was received with less enthusiasm in other quarters. Farmers, small shopkeepers, and craftsmen saw little immediate advantage to them in the funding operations and rallied to Jefferson's opposition standard.

Hamilton was the friend of business enterprise, but he believed that business should be regulated in the interest of the general welfare, that competition should be fostered and monopoly discouraged. He did not subscribe to the view that business was not the business of government. Believing as he did in a government possessed with energy and initiative, he could scarcely be expected to allow the government to stand inert while the economy stagnated or was stifled by foreign competition. Hamilton advocated a nationally directed and controlled economy in the interest of private enterprise. He believed that the economy should be invigorated and protected by bounties and tariffs, by canals, roads, and other public improvements built by the federal government, and "by opening an asylum" to the poor and oppressed of other lands. He believed in maintaining a sound credit, in keeping the national debt within bounds, but he could scarcely be called a hard-money man, and would today be considered an advocate of a managed currency. He recognized that private enterprise was subject to abuse. He castigated bank abuses as "pernicious," and insisted that "public utility" was "more truly the object of public banks than private profit."

Hamilton's remarkable grasp of national interest was evident in the direction he gave to the foreign policy of the Washington administration. He was a realist. He saw nothing "absurd" or "impracticable" in a league or alliance of nations, but cautioned Americans against becoming "the instruments of European greatness." He believed that a power friendly today could become an enemy tomorrow, "that peace or war will not always be left to our option." At the time of Jay's treaty he opposed war with Great Britain because in his judgment a cessation of trade would "cut up credit by the roots," and above all because America needed time. It was too young and weak to involve itself in European wars. These ideas were given expression in Washington's Farewell Address, which in final form drew substantially upon Hamilton's "original draft." Hamilton's guiding principles were prudence, realism, discretion in speech, moderation in action, concern for the national interest. "Real firmness is good for every thing," he once counseled. "Strut is good for nothing."

Hamilton was an extraordinary advocate. As a speaker he was less effective with crowds than with assemblies and in the courtroom. He was an orator in the tradition of Pitt, Fox, and Burke. It was the kind of oratory that changed votes and persuaded judges. But it was as an essayist rather than an orator that Hamilton was most persuasive. *The Federalist* has justly become the classic of constitutional analysis and reasoning. Hamilton's "Phocion," "Camillus," and "Pacificus" letters are other powerful examples of a form of polemical writing that has unfortunately vanished from the literary scene. Flattering his readers by his appeal to logic and reason, Hamilton moved them to action by powerful emotional arguments. It need hardly be added that Hamilton wrote his own speeches and state papers. He did not need other men to fabricate ideas for him or ghost writers to dress them in literary garb.

It has been the fashion to pin the label of conservatism upon Hamilton, and in many respects he was profoundly conservative. But the program he, along with Madison, advocated in the Confederation period—the establishment of a strong national government, the creation of a new kind of republican federalism—was profoundly radical. It constituted a sharp break with the political ways of the past to which his opponents, the die-hard states'-rights particularists, wished to adhere.

Hamilton's brand of conservatism meant holding on to the tried and proven values of the past, but not standing still. He was not afraid of the new and the experimental. "There are epochs in human affairs when *novelty* even is useful," when "a change is necessary, if it be but for the sake of change," he wrote in advocating his program of Continental reforms as early as 1780. Hamilton believed in change and progress, but he hoped change would come by evolution rather than by volcanic eruption. There was, then, nothing paradoxical about the fact that Hamilton was an ardent defender of the American Revolution and an equally ardent foe of the French Revolution. The former, in Hamilton's eyes, was a political revolution actuated by principles of law, justice, and moderation, whereas the French Revolution, as he saw it, became a class struggle, employing violence and terror, and seeking imperialist ends through military aggrandizement.

Hamilton's enlightened conservatism, his devotion to "the mild reign of rational liberty," is perhaps best exemplified by his desire to conserve civil liberties, by his attachment to due process, to trial by jury, to the freedom of the press, and to the rights of minorities. He opposed loyalty oaths, indiscriminate confiscation of property, and religious tests for voting. "Let us not establish a tyranny," he warned at the time the Sedition Act was being considered by Congress.

In the last analysis it is the enduring quality of Hamilton's program which provides the true measure of his greatness as a statesman. Hamilton's successors in office found that his fiscal policies could not be rudely dethroned. "We can pay off his debts in fifteen years, but we can never get rid of his financial system," Jefferson grimly confessed on ascending to the Presidency. To justify the most significant acomplishment of his administration—the purchase of Louisiana—Jefferson had to adopt Hamilton's broad construction of the Constitution. Since that day the difference between the broad and the strict constructionists, between the Hamiltonians and the Jeffersonians, has been in large measure a difference between the party *in* power with responsibility and the party *out* of power and in opposition. Jefferson might have explained this philo-sophically by reminding us that "every difference of opinion is not a difference of principle."

Jefferson wanted "a wise and frugal government." Hamilton wanted a government that could act. Wars, unemployment, and the complexities and tensions of modern civilization have steadily foisted upon govern-ment new and awesome responsibilities. Woodrow Wilson once put the issue quite succinctly:

> We used to think in the old-fashioned days when life was very simple that all government had to do was to put on a policeman's uniform, and say, "Now don't anybody hurt anybody else." We used to say that the ideal of government was for every man to be left alone and not inter-fered with, except when he interfered with somebody else; and that the best government was the government that did as little governing as pos-sible. That was the idea that obtained in Jefferson's time. But we are coming now to realize that life is so complicated that we are not dealing with the old conditions, and that the law has to step in and create new conditions under which we may live, the conditions which will make it tolerable for us to live.

The ends of government to which Wilson was pointing have in the course of time ranged beyond the vision of the Founding Fathers, but the means of achieving them are orthodox Hamiltonian means. Today neither of the two great parties would venture to challenge the effective exercise of political power for the general welfare. Were Alexander Hamilton alive in the mid-twentieth century he would find that both parties accept as axiomatic the Hamiltonian proposition that the central government must have effective powers.

In his army paybook Hamilton, as a young Revolutionary officer, made various notes and jotted down a variety of quotations. One of them is surprisingly self-revealing. It is from an oration of Demosthenes, and, as entered by Hamilton, reads: "As a general marches at the head of his troops, so ought wise politicians, if I dare use the expression, to march at the head of affairs; insomuch that they ought not to wait the *event*, to know what measures to take; but the measures which they have taken ought to produce the *event*."

Truly it may be said that Hamilton constantly seized the initiative and kept ahead of events. Talleyrand said of Hamilton, "he has antici-pated Europe." It may with as much accuracy be asserted that he antici-pated America. The prophetic nature of much of Hamilton's thinking seems positively uncanny. It was Richard Rush, a Secretary of the Treasury from the opposition party, who paid tribute to Hamilton's direction of operations of the Treasury "with a forecast so luminous as still to throw a guiding light over the path of his successors." Hamilton envisioned America as a great industrial giant, whose manufacturing output would raise the general standard of living and stimulate both commerce and agriculture. Hamilton believed that the nation must be put into a strong posture of defense, that we could not rely upon the long-range peaceful intentions of foreign powers or count upon permanent alliances. He even warned of wars starting by surprise attacks without the formality of a declaration. Hamilton's alertness to the dangers of nullification, interposition, and secession take on somber overtones in the light of later history. An advocate of the supremacy of the Union, his views were to be upheld by Jackson and vindicated by Lincoln. Hamilton anticipated the later assumption by the Supreme Court of powers for the federal government on the basis of three clauses in the Constitution—the necessary and proper clause, the general welfare clause, and the commerce clause. These three clauses, as Hamilton interpreted them, have provided the constitutional foundation for much of the activity of our modern federal government in the fields of taxation, finance, business regulation, and social welfare, activities undreamed of when the nation was in its infancy. To Hamilton the enormous expansion of the power of the Presidency by the mid-twentieth century would have been less a surprise than a vindication of his notions of the need for administrative power, energy, and efficiency.

Hamilton's failures as a statesman are attributable more to personality and tactics than to basic principles. Hamilton carried courage in politics to the point of self-immolation. If there was any attacking to be done, he did not assign the task to someone else, but took it on himself. As Jefferson put it, he was truly the "Colossus of the Federalists," and the standing No. 1 target for the shafts of the opposition. Opinionated and self-assured, he lacked that understanding of the art of compromise, the mastery of which is so essential to the aspiring politician. Thus, he was inflexible when a little yielding would have made all the difference. The best example of this was his break with Madison over the question of discriminating between original and subsequent holders of public securities. Though probably impractical in operation, some sort of discrimination would have seemed fair and equitable and would certainly have been good politics. Hamilton lacked terminal facilities. He was candid, but he was also indiscreet. He wrote brilliantly, but he wrote too much and too often. His astonishing attack on President John Adams left Hamilton a party leader without a following.

With some justice it has been said that Hamilton loved his country more than he did his countrymen. He would not bow to what he called "the majesty of the multitude." Direct democracy, he felt, was unsuitable to a large nation like America. It would, he feared, prove tumultuous and fickle. But he was reconciled to the system of representative democracy set up in the Constitution. Although an admirer of the British constitution, he realized that only a republic was suited to the American temper. While Hamilton was often portrayed by his opponents as an enemy of the people, the fact is that he was less afraid of the people than he was of state political machines and state legislatures. In Hamilton's thinking the loyalty of the people to the national government was an essential weapon to counteract the separatist and divisive tactics of the Antifederalists. It must be confessed that there were times when Hamilton had his doubts about the way democracy was working out, and that he was understandably less enthusiastic about democracy when his party was voted out of office than when it was in power. But he believed in the power of reason founded upon full disclosure of the facts, and he had faith in the force of an enlightened public opinion. "I desire above all things," he wrote, "to see the equality of political rights, exclusive of hereditary distinction, firmly established by a positive demonstration of its being consistent with the order and happiness of society." . . .

Some of [Hamilton's] writings go back almost two centuries, but they pose problems and suggest solutions which have as much significance today as when the nation was founded. These are times of challenge for America, a time anticipated by Hamilton, when this country at long last has assumed "an attitude correspondent with its great destinies." We can ill afford to ignore Hamiltonian means any more than we can neglect Jeffersonian ends if we wish to attain that delicate balance between liberty and security which will keep us free and secure peace in our time.

10

Broadus Mitchell: Continentalist[1]

In this summary treatment, in comment on Hamilton's beginnings, we are tempted to take too long a run for our leap. And yet the little known first third of his life, in the West Indies, held features powerful in his later career. It is a dramatic reflection that this child, who was to comprehend the promise of an imperial continent, was born, to the best of our belief, on the merest speck of an island in the blue Caribbean, miles from our mainland and thirteen hundred miles from New York. Nevis is a volcanic cone, only five miles in diameter at the gently sloping shores. Its lofty crater, no longer belching brimstone, is generally enveloped in its own clinging, snowy cloud. The modest settlement of Charles Town, behind the western crescent beach, is unchanged in two hundred years, except that the stone fort and some of the houses, hardly less somber and substantial, have yielded to hurricane or neglect. On the front street is the reputed birthplace of our hero. The double flight of steps gives entrance to vacancy, and the garden wall encloses only weeds. This is the empty shell in the silent nest.

It would be quite possible for a parson or storekeeper, in Hamilton's childhood or since, to know every man, woman, child, donkey, and goat on the island. Its minute life, vastly detached from all but the neighboring St. Kitts, made Nevis, for these very reasons, a fortunate point of origin for one who was to help create American dominion. He came to the Continent a visitor, without roots in any part of it, and hence could adopt all of it.

Also this boy, whose passion was to be organization, came from a completely broken home and kindred. Born out of wedlock, he was left an orphan at thirteen by the death of his mother, following the earlier permanent departure of his father on island wanderings. By this time, doubtless through several transfers which we cannot trace, Alexander had been taken from British Nevis to Danish St. Croix (Christiansted). Here his mother's relatives, formerly notably prosperous, suddenly disintegrated in estate, physical and moral, at just the time when he was most in need of their rescue. Causes are unimportant for us; they embraced sale of the uncle's home plantation to an incompetent debtor, the absconding of one cousin, suicide of another, and a succession of disappointing marriages by a third. This last, however, though clutching at

---

[1] From Broadus Mitchell, *Heritage from Hamilton* (New York: Columbia University Press, 1957), pp. 3–32. Reprinted by permission of the publisher.

remnants, was the only one of the clan in fact eager to share with Alexander.

This explosion of fortunes put a cap to earlier mischiefs in his family history. His mother, Rachael Faucette (Anglicized from the French form to Fawcett), before his birth had been imprisoned by her husband on scandalous charges which ended in his divorcing her. The court forbade her to remarry. In a few years, still young and spirited, her affections were for the first time engaged, by a Scotsman, James Hamilton, offshoot of an ancient house in Ayrshire. Among his endearing qualities, ability to make a living for his common-law wife and two sons, James, the elder, and Alexander, was not numbered. Still, somehow they rubbed along, defying convention with mutual affection for a decade before he passed, to all intents, from the picture. Rachael, with a small inheritance from her mother, bravely made the best of a hard lot by opening a little store in the principal town of St. Croix, where the boys may have helped her measure out homely staple provisions. This for a few years until she died of a fever, and her sons, in heavy veils, watched her body interred in a grave long lost to memory.

Incidentally, in the aftermath of inventory of her pathetic effects, it came out, before the probate judge, that Alexander was born, if we may believe the evidence, two years earlier than has hitherto been supposed, that is, in 1755 instead of 1757. We have some corroborative testimony in his own chary allusions to his history. If true, his precociousness is turned only from the astonishing to the credible; it helps us to understand his early maturity, as aide to Washington at twenty-two, not twenty, and his appointment to the United States Treasury at thirty-four, not thirty-two.

Several biographers have inevitably been busy with the ready-made certainty that Alexander Hamilton had his happy combination of traits from the quick French blood of his mother and the calculating Caledonian derivation of his father. Animation and perception were surely joined in him with the prudent habit of second thoughts, but attributing this blend of endowments to racial strains seems conjectural.

In any case, with verve and system, he promptly overcame obstacles. Perhaps his zeal was spurred beyond the ordinary by the lapses of his relatives. His performance as clerk, at desk and counter, in the trading post of Nicholas Cruger in St. Croix led to a new prospect. And well it might, for what other teen-ager showed such eager discharge of responsibilities beyond his years? We have a sheaf of his business letters written in a period of months as proxy for his absent employer. They show grown-up judgment added to youthful exultant energy. This experience of import-export traffic by the little sloops of the time, shuttling to Boston, New York, Philadelphia, and the Spanish Main, informed him on the economy of the island of St. Croix. The main export was muscovado sugar; most provisions and all manufactures must be brought in from Denmark or the Continent. Thus the society was a dependent one with the inevitable hazards of staple agriculture. The basis of all was sun and slavery. A small minority of elegant planters, and the merchants, ship captains, officials, and soldiers who did their bidding, ground the black work force overwhelmingly outnumbering all whites. The severity of labor and cruelties of discipline shock the modern reader of abundant records. Driven to desperation but unable to escape the island, slaves recurrently revolted, burning canefields, murdering overseers and masters. Torpor of the economy was matched by terror of the mind.

These effects could not have escaped Alexander's reflection. If afterward, in a new setting and called to act a public part, he made himself the engine of a varied, balanced economy, and the constant foe of slavery, he was improving lessons learned in the predatory paradise of his youth.

From St. Croix, at seventeen, by pluck and luck Alexander was whisked to New York for an education. Cruger, admiring and generous, was a younger son of a great New York merchant family. His partner, Cornelius Kortright, was another. Alexander's cousin Ann (née Lytton) lent what she could wangle from her inheritance. What sparked this cooperation of his friends was doubtless the pleas of Hugh Knox, Presbyterian clergyman and perceptive patron. Native of northern Ireland, teacher in Delaware, graduate of Princeton, for twenty years his spirit had survived island isolation. Newly arrived on St. Croix, he discovered Alexander, fed his mind, and espoused his ambition. Here Knox found the complete little man of business, who yet devoured books, wrote verses (sacred and profane) for the local newspaper, absorbed sermons and more potent private exhortations. The pupil's faculties were confined only by his narrow opportunities. His avidity reached to the cynical monitions of Machiavelli, not offset by the couplets of Pope or the classic histories of Plutarch. He pondered and praised the British constitution. Shouldn't there be something for this surprising youngster beyond the mongering of molasses and salt cod, mules and human workstock?

The story, maybe authentic because first printed by Hamilton's son, is that, in the words of Mrs. Atherton's biographical novel *The Conqueror*, a hurricane of August, 1772, "blew him into history." Warmed by Knox's public sermon, Alexander described the wreck of the island in a letter to his father. The preacher showed it around for its florid picture and piety. Over Alexander's protest, Knox inserted it in the island newspaper. Whether or not, the catastrophe arousing charity, this letter turned the trick, Alexander's friends rallied and dispatched him to the Continent with the promise of consignments of sugar to defray his schooling.

He landed at Boston, perhaps in the autumn of 1772, where Sam Adams was damning Parliament and Hancock was parading the city militia. But the young visitor's preference for British authority did not yield then nor for some months afterward. He posted to New York, bearing letters from Knox to Presbyterian worthies, and was received by Cruger's merchant correspondents, Kortright & Co. (It chanced, by the by, that Kortright land embraced the site of the present Columbia University.) In preparation for college, Alexander was handed over to the tutelage of Francis Barber at his academy at Elizabethtown, New Jersey, where he seems to have spent the better part of a year under the patronage of William Livingston and Elias Boudinot and part of the time lived in the effulgent home of the latter. Swiftly repairing his deficiencies in the classics, and by now won to republican hopes, Alexander was presented to President Witherspoon with every academic and sectarian entitlement for admission. He preferred Princeton because it was politically more dissentient than loyal King's College in New York. After oral quiz, Witherspoon highly approved him, but the rules, it turned out, could not be bent to Alexander's insistence that he be allowed to pass through the courses as rapidly as he could dispatch them, without regard to class years. Thence perforce to King's, where aristocratic leniency made exception in his case, setting an example of discretion which registrars, beset as they doubtless are, may well remember.

So New York became his home for life. Hamilton's Continental outlook, predisposed by his arrival from a distant island, could not have been preserved so faithfully through crowded years of legislature, Congress, conventions, and cabinet had fortune cast his lot elsewhere. Had he remained in Boston he would not have found himself at the hub of the American universe. New England was earlier fervid in the colonies' cause than New York, and continued Federalist longer, but with all its influence it was at a geographic extreme. The West Indies had contacts with the Carolinas; Knox's brother was at Edenton and Alexander's half-brother was making a tidy fortune near Charleston. But that was at the other end of the country and would have identified our hero with the fiercest localism of all. To Virginia he had no introduction, but with all the Old Dominion's national contribution, later political developments, had he located there, would have put him at a sectional disadvantage as a Continental advocate. Good men grew in New Jersey, those who befriended Alexander Hamilton foremost among them, but the short sail from Elizabethtown Point to the Battery was, for Hamilton's future, a transfer of immense consequence.

As New Yorker, Hamilton was in mid-position. Increasingly, from harbor and hinterland, New York City drew economic resources which recommended its political counsel. Hamilton the better used this fulcrum to pry other parts into national compliance because his pride in New York never made him, like George Clinton, its proprietary champion. His marriage, while yet in the army, to Elizabeth, daughter of General Philip Schuyler of Albany, aided and abetted his Continental viewpoint and urgings, for Schuyler's penchant was all of that sort, and each gave to the other's enthusiasm and designs. Further, embraced in trust and affection into the Schuyler family and following, Hamilton had an upstate as well as southern counties influence, without which his Federalist pretensions would have been dishonored at home.

In reaction to pro-British preceptors at King's, especially President Myles Cooper and his Anglican supporters, the young collegian began contributing to the patriot newspaper of John Holt. For the likely identification of these anonymous pieces we have much to hope from researches of the editors of a comprehensive collection of Hamilton's writings, now in progress in Columbia University.

These pieces in the press led on to his impetuous speech at the meeting in the Fields (now City Hall Park) in July, 1774, in support of democratically chosen delegates to the Continental Congress. This was his first public identification with resistance. More deliberate were his two long pamphlets answering the Tory "Westchester Farmer," the doughty Samuel Seabury. While the apologist of Parliament had addressed himself to New Yorkers, our collegian's replies embraced all of the colonies. He had come to know McDougall, Lamb, Sears, Willett, and others of the Liberty Boys who were not squeamish about a little mob violence. Hamilton would have none of this. He protested when Rivington's types were destroyed, and saved President Cooper from a coat of tar and feathers by hastening him over the back fence of the College when his would-be punishers had broken down the gate. Hamilton harangued the ugly crowd, and later, with characteristic thoroughness, he joined Cooper, wandering on the river bank, and escorted him to a place of refuge.

By stages of student drill, and then membership in the militia, Hamilton left college in the spring of 1776 when he obtained the captaincy of the New York Artillery Company. Before the Battle of Long Island this was mustered into Continental service, shared Washington's retreat to Pennsylvania, blasted away at the British in the surprise attacks on Trenton and Princeton, and wound up in winter quarters at Morristown. Soon (March 1, 1777) he was appointed one of the aides of the commander in chief, with the rank of lieutenant colonel. We may choose between several stories, all honorific, of how Alexander Hamilton came to the notice of Washington. He had refused staff invitations from two general officers earlier, preferring field command. Though later, momentarily, he regretted leaving the line for the headquarters "military family," his service of four years (nearly the longest of all of the aides) in closest association with Washington probably determined his after career. He was hourly with the commander in chief in battle, bivouac, and camp —dispatching orders, preparing reports, and corresponding, under Washington's direction, with Congress and all commanders. He became Washington's other self, which could not have been without a deal of originality in the young aide. In this confidential association Hamilton knew the whole problem of Revolutionary America, military, political, economic. His deep concern prompted him to his own proposals to Robert Morris and others for solution, without in any way committing Washington. A tiff with Washington, when nerves of both were frayed, was quickly followed by renewed understanding between them and entrusting of Colonel Hamilton with capture of the last British redoubt at Yorktown.

Notable figures who served during the Revolution in legislature, executive office, and diplomatic assignment complained that the Society of the Cincinnati set up a presumed preference of patriotism for those in the army. No moral distinction was implied by the Cincinnati and yet, in the sequel of political developments, ex-officers of the army had a genuine advantage. Veterans, in the eyes of the country, have been clothed with special gratitude, though sometimes they have been treated to empty praise and pity. Chief army officers had acquired intimate knowledge of each other under trying circumstances. They had acted together for the whole country, many of them in every theater of the war. They shared a personal attachment to Washington which translated itself into national action as civilians. This common experience by no means barred political differences, but the bond was material, particularly in the formative stages of establishing the independent government. Further, army men saw the weaknesses of wartime government from the most critical angle, and they were ready to condemn the same symptoms after the peace. Many of them, therefore, like Hamilton, in putting off the tunic felt a special call to don the toga.

Hamilton, at Washington's headquarters, had been at the operative center of the national struggle. He had come to know and could estimate principal men from all parts of the country. His service as aide to Washington had been as much political and diplomatic as military, though the commander in chief deferred perhaps too scrupulously to the civil authority. Hamilton early saw that to win the war, government must be drawn to a focus and economic resources must be marshaled. His later work was an extension of these earlier, partial, disappointed pleas. His lengthy arguments to Duane and Morris, begging for responsible administration and a publicly sponsored bank, in the course of a decade took on sharper definition, but they remained the same in scope and purpose. All was for strengthening the central authority, *de facto,* in what could not yet be a nation in the sense of political organization. Others were disgusted with Congress and alarmed by disorder in the finances, but nobody else, at least in the army, analyzed with such vigor or formulated remedies with such documentation.

Like Tom Paine, Hamilton wrote on a drumhead. However, Paine's patriotic exhortation, the most moving of its kind, did not involve the distraction of devising institutional remedies. Hamilton reviewed history, invoked the experience of other countries, cited figures, drew up detailed instruments. A clue to his means is in the last paybook of his

New York Artillery Company. His command was handed over when he joined Washington's staff, and the book remained with him as a receipt; he used blank pages at the back for notes of his reading in Postlethwayt's *Dictionary* and other compendia. Similar memoranda of the war years exist, though probably more have been lost except as they appeared in his advocacies. How he found time for economic logistics we may only guess. We know from his whole life that his industry and faculty of concentration were phenomenal. He turned from one task to another in rapid succession and executed each with thoroughness and finish. Distinguished contemporaries were obliged to clear away and square off for a new project. They waited for favorable intervals. Hamilton kept several undertakings in the works at once. Hamilton College treasures his camp writing desk, a speaking memorial of the many kinds of papers he prepared. Later others collaborated with him in objects that taxed overtime effort, notably Madison and Jay in *The Federalist*. But their contributions were fewer and had the benefit of more leisure. In spite of a demanding law practice, in a prodigious spurt he supplied eighteen numbers of this series in a block.

After Yorktown he repaired to Albany for what was almost his only period of absorption in a single object, brief study for admission to the bar. For once he had to ask for a short extension of time, for the examination. But even so he rocked his son's cradle while mastering basic texts and manuals and, as a by-product, made his own handbook of practice in the Supreme Court of New York. A copy of this, one of several known to have been made by other students and young practitioners, has recently turned up, and testifies to his penchant for reducing vexing detail to system. He was still walking the floor with Blackstone and the baby when he yielded to the repeated plea of the Superintendent of Finance that he become Receiver of Continental Revenue for New York, in the summer of 1782. This sounds passive. In fact, he had to devise a tax system for his state if proceeds were to flow to the central treasury. He must meet with committees of the legislature to inform and persuade, must make himself mustermaster for whatever resources could be wrung for the nation from reluctant governor and counties not still occupied by the enemy. He was not only Morris' energetic local lieutenant, but cooperated in his chief's plans for the country's currency and credit. His work was preparatory. This apprenticeship helped to place him in the United States Treasury seven years later, for it was introduction to the practice of public finance and earned him the recommendation of Robert Morris. He relinquished his post because the legislature, admiring his zeal (though not responding with funds), elected him to Congress.

Here commenced a new phase of Hamilton's service to the country. It was a parlous period in which, pending the treaties of peace, economic and political wreckage of the war was to undergo emergency repair. More foreign loans could be wheedled only if supported by establishment of unquestioned revenue under the sole control of Congress. Ham-ilton threw his whole force into improving and pressing the proposal of a federal import duty collected by loyal agents. Every objection was raised, every footless delay was devised, every exasperating reversal of consent was practiced by inhibited colleagues reflecting the exhaustion and jealousies in their states. When at length all seemed in train except recalcitrant Rhode Island, and Hamilton had prepared a last remon-strance and persuasion to Newport, Virginia blackslid and his own New York attached unacceptable conditions to compliance. This was in the face of a clamorous army at Newburgh which could not be disbanded—if indeed that was militarily safe—without being paid. Hamilton was desperate. While, on the one hand, he joined with his father-in-law, Schuyler, in a noble call, adopted by the New York legislature, for a con-stitutional convention to enable a new start, he briefly toyed with the notion that aggrieved soldiers might collect their arrears at bayonet-point and also assist to recruit the general credit. He promptly dropped this dangerous idea and aided Washington in reproving incipient rebellion of officers in the encampment.

The incident, happily got over, requires a pause. Certain critics have ventured that Hamilton, in his vehement nationalism, was ever impatient with constitutional limitations and, had opportunity offered in the course of developments, would have become, in modern terms, fascist. They have supported this contention by pointing to his later furious disap-pointment when the provisional army, of which he was chief organizer, was dissolved because President Adams, after warlike threats, composed differences with France. The allegation is that Hamilton had reached the stage of wanting to subvert political government and employ large armed forces under his command for domination at home and conquest abroad, à la Napoleon. We shall come to that question in course. Here we must note that his indulgence in the conjecture of military rule, or extempore military assistance to civil authority, in 1783, though swiftly put by, betrays a contrast to the steady wisdom of Washington. Washing-ton, too, more than a decade later, not a little abetted by Hamilton, was eager to discountenance dissenting political societies and to punish their leaders, especially if believed to be under foreign influence. But, with-out doubt, Washington's political prudence and patience were superior to Hamilton's. In their collaboration of many years Hamilton was the quicker and more fertile in expedients and of unexampled service in executing agreed policy. But his direction needle did not point to the lodestar as unwaveringly as did Washington's. The temperamental and moral difference argues a defect in Hamilton, though all additional acquaintance with the period confirms the popular conviction, then and since, that Washington set a standard not matched by any of his con-temporaries.

Hardly was the Newburgh crisis overcome when Hamilton played a chief part, as spokesman of Congress, in suppressing mutinous troops who menaced its meetings. Further, he characteristically protested against the failure of the Pennsylvania authorities to support the safety and dignity of the national body. As chairman of a committee he reported to President Boudinot that Congress should be moved to the rural protection of Princeton. This incident helped produce the demand for a federal district over which Congress could exercise complete sway, and the eventual choice of location, as we shall see, became a bargaining point in adoption of Hamilton's fiscal system.

He lingered in Congress during the summer of 1783 vainly hoping the preliminary treaty of peace would arrive, but finally put out for New York to establish his home and law office (in Wall Street). He found the city in no peaceful mood. Already, in advance of evacuation, British merchants were fleeing from threats of vindictive patriots. Right at the start Hamilton protested against the rashness of depriving the community of men of capital and enterprise who would be sorely needed in reconstructing the economy. In the coming months he broadened his appeal for fair treatment of Tories and their sympathizers. He published his "Phocion" articles, begging that former enemies, where they wished to remain as useful citizens or residents, should be protected in their civil and property rights. As a practical matter, why drive off competent persons to strengthen Canada, likely to become a competitor or even a foe? His sensible arguments might well have been reverted to when we deported enemy aliens and other suspected residents after World War I. They apply with greater force to the recent, or current, frenzy for denying civil liberties in the name of national security. Later, when he had chief responsibility for girding for war with France, he too far consented in the Alien and Sedition Acts, which makes it the more suitable to dwell on his advice when he was calmer.

Hamilton's remonstrances were without effect. The legislature was zestful, under Governor George Clinton's command, to banish and expropriate. War measures to these ends of punishing former enemies, foreign and domestic, were confirmed and extended in rapid succession. The notorious Trespass Act gave patriots the right to sue for recovery of the rents of their property enjoyed by the British during the occupation. This, Hamilton declared, was an infraction of the treaty of peace which was the supreme law of the land. No state, under whatever provocation, could defy this national engagement. Our new independence must not be smirched with dishonor. He did put a check to this rampage by winning the most celebrated of his early law cases, in which he appeared for the defendant Waddington against the Widow Rutgers.

Waddington, a British merchant, had used a brewhouse and some other property of Mrs. Rutgers under authority of the military commander of the city to whom he paid his rent. Braving almost unanimous public hostility, Hamilton secured a judgment from the mayor's court (from which there was no legal appeal) freeing Waddington of liability under the charge of trespass. The state law, Hamilton maintained, however explicit, was null and void in face of the treaty which was national sovereignty. Organized city protest demanded that the legislature displace the members of the court, but in vain. After this success, Hamilton was flooded with other cases of similar sort, and the professional harvest he now reaped was an early count in the accusation which followed him in one way and another during the remainder of the life, namely, that he was pro-British. The passionate, goaded by the inescapable injuries of war, failed to see that he was truly pro-American, for the sake of legal integrity, political comity, and economic advancement of his young country.

The shortcomings of the Confederation were as inevitable as they were unmistakable. A hastily summoned meeting of delegates from the colonies grew, by emergency consent, into the central governing body during a protracted war. Its most essential work was done without benefit of a constitution. The finances were bound to be left in disarray. While interest accrued alarmingly, the morale of Congress and country sank to complaisance in the prospect of repudiation of the domestic debt. Distant from one another by crude means of travel, the states were divergent politically and economically. Untaught by after-events, each clutched its own sovereignty. The war aim continued to invest most minds, not knowing that independence is less than freedom. Indulging jealousy, the states could not rise to joint effort. Time was the cure, and the wonder is that it was so foreshortened. The blessing was a British political heritage. Recently an American visitor who had struggled to grow decent grass around her new suburban home was admiring the sward of one of the Oxford colleges. "How do you get this golf-green perfection?" she asked the gardener. "That's easy," he explained. "You cut, and sprinkle, and roll, and fertilize, and cut and roll and water again. You do this for seven hundred years and you have a lawn like this." The lesson makes for patience with countries while they are trying to raise themselves to competence in a twinkling.

In judging of the Confederation, extenuation is more suitable than defense. Marshal counterclaim as ingeniously as you will, John Fiske was right. The performance from Yorktown to the Constitution was abominable, and alert men of the time knew it. Obstacles to internal and external trade paralyzed the first step toward improvement. Competitive tariffs impoverished all and exacerbated political quarrels. Forebearing to rehearse tragicomic illustrations, it is pleasanter to praise James Madison for his early moves to ameliorate the evils as between Virginia and Maryland. Washington, equally eager, wanted to construct navigation to the interior. From their efforts, by stages, came the Annapolis Commercial Convention in 1786. This is one of the notable historical instances in which failure produced unexpected success. It is almost an argument for irresponsible neglect. Delegates of some states, duly appointed, never set out. Others never arrived. Maryland, the host, sent none. Men from Virginia, Pennsylvania, New Jersey, Delaware, and New York waited impotently for more to come. We may guess at sober reflections in their informal conversations as they cooled their heels. When at length, despairing of their fellows, they sat down in session, all realized that too few states were present to serve the commercial objects. Abraham Clark of New Jersey, which had given her delegates latitude, got quick response when he blurted that the footless meeting should demand political renovation for America.

He must have taken the words out of the mouth of Alexander Hamilton, who drafted the call for a national constitutional convention to assemble the following year in Philadelphia. We are told that the hesitant Governor Edmund Randolph of Virginia reduced the vehemence of the indictment of the Confederation. Hamilton's original paper is lost, maybe burned up by the words he wrote on it. In any event the country rose to his argument and plea, however revised, in sudden common consent. Hamilton's conviction that economic betterment waited on political reorganization was not singular to him, but he held and preached it with peculiar force. The country needed concert and plan; the central authority must be able to regulate interstate and foreign commerce and command national revenue. Sovereignty was a condition precedent to solvency.

This was the mercantilist idea, without reference to particular mercantilist measures. Hamilton promoted its adoption in America some decades after Europe had begun to depreciate the role of government, making private capitalist enterprise the cynosure. Adam Smith's *Wealth of Nations* had been published a decade before, and earlier the French physiocrats had celebrated the wisdom of let-alone. It must be remembered that America was undeveloped, with slender resources in individual hands. Here association, not autonomy of effort, was appropriate. Decision, initiative must be collective before individual, and national before local. The revolt against mercantilism, or against British colonialism, though it accomplished our independence, was premature in the New World. After a brief fling with the minimum of national control we were obliged to "consolidate" our system, put the states in second place, and give central government powers over citizens immediately. Shays's Rebellion in Massachusetts was more than a passing disturbance that persuaded the constitutional fathers to forbid any state to pass laws violating the obligation of contracts. It was a blow to the pretension of the member state to self-sufficiency in a loose confederation. The state did not, could not, preserve order, protect life and property.

As he had been the voice of the Annapolis meeting, if nothing more, Hamilton was naturally chosen by the New York legislature as a delegate to the Constitutional Convention. But Governor Clinton thought to overbalance him by sending along two states'-rights dependables, Robert Yates and John Lansing, Jr. As long as they were present they determined the vote of New York against Hamilton's contentions for a vigorous national government. Steadily at odds with his own colleagues, his credit was diminished in the eyes of the Convention. Fortunately, like Luther Martin of Maryland, convinced that the importance of the states was being sacrificed, Yates and Lansing quit in disgust, thus marching themselves off the page of history. Hamilton was thereafter freer, though New York, with him as single representative, had no vote.

His principal deliverance was in the middle of June, when the Virginia (Madison-Randolph) and New Jersey (Paterson) plans had been offered. The first, enlarging and stiffening the central powers, became the basis of the Constitution as adopted. The second, little improvement over the Articles of Confederation, did not detain the delegates long, but its inhibitions made Hamilton's proposals the more striking, indeed shocking. Hitherto silent, he spoke for the whole day, developing a compact outline of which we have the text. He was not offering a plan which he believed could be approved; he threw in his views for discussion, to test the length to which others would go, and to nudge opinions closer to his ideal of an effective national system. A limited monarchy, like the British, was the best form for such an extensive country as ours, but this he would not urge because America was wedded to republican principles.

As the next best expedient, Hamilton proposed a chief executive chosen practically for life, holding the balance between the excitable body of the people on the one hand, and the minority of citizens of property and position on the other. The democratic lower house was to be elected directly by the people for a short term; the Senators, named by electors chosen by the people, should serve for life. The states, except as convenient administrative units, ought to be erased, but short of this, the way to extinguish their separate sovereignties was to give the President appointment of the Governors, who must have absolute veto on all local laws. The acts of Congress were to be supreme in the land, but with the right of a powerful federal judiciary to declare any national law unconstitutional.

All hearers praised the fire and conviction of his declaration, but none agreed with him. Maybe his bold proposition was the wisest means of influencing the Convention. There was no doubt of his candor. Leading features of his scheme had received partial approval earlier, for example, a President for life. Farthest to the right, he took the curse from the approaches of others. If perverse, he was provocative. Nor did he, later in the sessions, isolate himself by proving dogmatic and stubborn. On the contrary, having beckoned toward a government competent to the crisis, he was indefatigable in composing differences on the floor and in fashioning the best instrument that could be obtained. His detailed constitution, written out later in the sittings when he had been taught by the drift of debate, modified his original conceptions. His efforts, on a visit to New Jersey and New York, for a feasible conclusion to the labors of the Convention were valued by Washington. Hamilton alone, for New York, signed the final document, when members as diverse as Martin and Mason, Randolph and Gerry refused to put their names to it. His exertions, through *The Federalist* papers, for approval by the states and his heroic fight for ratification in New York are better known.

Viewing his part in the Convention, how accurate is the popular belief that Hamilton scorned the discretion of the people and seized the opportunity, so far as in him lay, to construct a new government vesting power in property and privilege? Indeed, that this was the cunning aim of the Convention as a whole is the celebrated proposition of the late Professor Charles A. Beard. Many persons consider that Hamilton was the extreme type of designing aristocrats who, in secret and unworthily, devised a fundamental law to rescue their threatened material claims. Beard's economic interpretation of the Constitution has enjoyed substantial credence for several reasons. Its announcement in 1913 roughly coincided with the arrival in the United States of socialism with its emphasis on class interests, as a familiar, though far from generally accepted, point of view on social development. More narrowly, the historical school of economists was commending itself in this country. Beard examined with pains the security holding and land speculations of members of the Convention, treating these personages no longer as demigods but as men with human frailties like the rest of us. He named names, exposed private concerns of individuals, which, especially when applied to the famous, takes the eye. Reputations mounted in the firmament were brought to earth.

Perhaps Beard's was an overcorrection of our historical astigmatism, so that we have been bent too much at the new angle. Our forefathers were not a different breed of men, but, called on to play a public part in the country's emergency, they summoned their full powers, which were mostly of marked good will. Similar circumstances of national need have produced similar results since, though not, as we see it, in quite that classic form. While it would be fatuous to suppose that material promptings were absent (for we know they were not), one may venture that moral motives were superior in their operation. Particular counter-arguments to Beard's brilliant generalization need not detain us here.[2] As to Alexander Hamilton, unfortunately for the vulgar impression, Beard was obliged to number him among those who had no securities or land claims to burgeon under favorable central governmental authority. Hamilton's prospects were those of gratifying income from arduous practice of his profession of the law, from which now and later he distracted himself *pro bono publico*.

[2] See Robert E. Brown, *Charles Beard and the Constitution* (Princeton University Press, 1956).

True, General Schuyler was wealthy, and Mrs. Hamilton as his daughter might expect one day to inherit a competence—which, in fact, however, did not happen. Hamilton, by taste, marriage, residence in a commercial city, and client connections was drawn to the side of aristocracy and conservatism in the conventional sense. Some, of psychological twist, have conjectured that this preference was compensation for the insecurity of his boyhood, just as they have supposed that his love of military glory would, in his own mind, add height to his slight five feet seven inches. Doubtless these influences figured insensibly. Some was accident, much was nature, more was reason. We must not confuse person and philosophy beyond a certain point. Hamilton was impressed with the necessity of repairs to the country consequent on colonial subordination, costs of war, and confusion in the aftermath of independence. His advocacies could not consist in abstractions, such as the rights of man. His principle of orderly progress in national strength immediately translated itself into concrete policies. These broke down to restored credit, reliable and abundant currency, and varied industry. Such achievements would not be induced by exhortation and would be imperiled by further delay. Therefore a national will must be enabled to reward and punish. This meant economic, social, and political control.

Where was this control to be vested? Surely in the national organs, for wrangling states, pulling and hauling for local advantage, had reduced the country to imbecility. His program demanded for its execution restraint as well as boldness. The central authority must claim "the regular weight . . . it will receive from those who will find it their interest to support a government intended to preserve the peace and happiness of the community of the whole." The segment of the population appropriately devoted to maintaining stability and systematic advance was composed of those of wealth and birth. "Give therefore to [this] class a distinct, permanent share in the government. They will check the unsteadiness," "the imprudence of democracy." But the elite and fortunate were not to have sole sway. They were to hold office by a "responsible" but "temporary or defeasible tenure." We must not forget that to prevent oppression of the people, and denial of individual liberties, the lower house by Hamilton's plan was to be elected directly by the suffrage of all free males aged twenty-one and upward—a more democratic provision than prevailed in most of the states. This was an immediate counterpoise to the lifetime Senate which, in his original proposal, was to be chosen by electors designated by all the voters. In his later scheme he provided that those naming Senatorial electors should have a certain property qualification. The selection of the President was to be three removes from the mass of the people. However, in Hamilton's revised plan, the chief executive had a term of only three years.

We must take Hamilton in his time. He believed that over a period the people, with benefit of a gyroscope to keep the ship of state steady while they came to a deliberate conclusion on the course, would determine right. It was in the short run that they were turbulent and vulnerable to demagogic flattery. He was thus far suspicious of the capacity of the people, at a given juncture, to protect their own interests. Approval of pure democracy was far more limited in America then than since. For convincing illustration, Thomas Jefferson felt that certain governmental officers should be chosen by a prudentially restricted electorate.

So much for constitutional contrivance. The related, but more insistent, question is whether wealth or commonwealth claimed Hamilton's solicitude. The answer is plain in his whole life that he worked for the peace, prosperity, and freedom of the entire community. His client was not a class, but the country. He wanted to employ the privileged class for the general benefit, he did not allow himself to be used by this minority. Superficially dividing the dramatis personae of our early history into "good man" and "bad man," it has seemed to most, though with enthusiastic acknowledgment of his technical skill, that Hamilton belongs with the latter. It is difficult to refute this illusion while standing on one foot. Two signal circumstances may be mentioned. Handling millions for the public, he left the Treasury a poor man. Nearly at the end of his life, to prevent Burr, whom he distrusted as a self-serving potential dictator, from becoming President, he threw his whole influence to his inveterate political enemy, Jefferson. But acquaintance with his thought and actions, in all of the manifestations that we can recapture, illumines his disinterested public service. Lasting renown does not rest on meanness or littleness, no matter how cleverly pursued. Aside from all else, Hamilton was creative in the noble sphere of polity, and the true artist must be idealist.

Much of Hamilton's doctrine found its way into the Constitution, partly because he had early and long urged the general objects, and also because of what he recommended on the floor. His pristine proposals, though known by him to be ineligible as he made them, more than tinctured the prescriptions of others and made for greater strength in the central government than would otherwise have been approved. If to some, of opposite views, he seemed arrogant in the beginning, these must have been drawn to him as he labored manfully in later sessions for the best solution obtainable. This cordial spirit, in no wise egotistical, led him to declare at the end that no man's views were farther from the finished Constitution than his were known to be, but that for the sake of unity and practicality he endorsed it gladly and begged abstaining colleagues to join him. Though self-confident to a remarkable degree, he accepted compromises at many critical points in his public career, and it is for these concessions that he is honored almost as much as for his original contentions.

He next demonstrated to the whole country, had it but known, with what gratitude he could take the half loaf rather than go without bread. Earlier, he had forecast that any improved plan of a constitution ought to be explained and defended by sensible writings in order to secure for it necessary popular support. The Constitution had been arrived at behind closed doors, a procedure which Hamilton approved as the only feasible mode, for the utterances of members, and the changes of utterance, would have been misunderstood, with harmful results, if reported to the country while debates were in progress. Indeed, deliberations might have been widely discredited from the start, for almost of one accord delegates had disregarded their instructions to amend the Articles of Confederation, and had projected a far more consolidated government. Now a finished document was unveiled for ratification by states which found their favorite political pretensions canceled. Accept this, and no longer could states dishonor requests of Congress for revenue, jockey commerce for local benefit, issue paper money, or by less indirect means violate the obligations of debt. Participants in framing the Constitution later referred to it as amounting to a second revolution in the history of the country.

Watching the choice of opponents to sit in the New York convention, Hamilton had abundant reason to prepare for a critical contest over the Constitution in his own state. If the forces of Governor Clinton were to be prevented from swift and sure rejection, the proposed fundamental law must be publicly analyzed to dissipate fears and banish bias with reason. Forthwith Hamilton, Madison (who was in New York attending Congress), and Jay commenced in the newspapers the series of persuasive essays signed with the one signature "Publius." As they began to take effect, the purpose was broadened to win to the Constitution the people of other states as well. Hamilton wrote two thirds of the total number. Probably no such exposition, in American history, ever helped fix so decisive a result. Dashed off in rapid succession, inspired by imminent demand, these "Federalist" papers, as they came to be called, have since been taken as an authoritative interpretation of our scheme of government.

They were far removed from modern methods of mass appeal. They did not rely upon prestige of a personage, for they long remained anonymous. They coined no slogans, diverted passions to no whipping boy. No disarming entertainment to tune the ear for a singing commercial. In these degenerate days we may pause to ask how so literate a performance as *The Federalist* could provoke so solid a response. In the absence of radio, television, picture tabloids, and fetching propaganda techniques, the habit of reading, reflection, and man-to-man discussion was cultivated. By these essays the features of the Constitution were made familiar and grateful, much as, by contrast, not long ago the face of a United States Senator in inquisitorial action was rendered distasteful to millions with surprising consequence.

The earnestness and wisdom with which Hamilton and his colleagues argued in *The Federalist* carried conviction. One of the softer impeachments of Hamilton is that, egotistical and imperious, he lacked popular appeal, the common touch. Superficially, maybe so. But it is to be remembered that he was chief author of this most successful effort to win friends and influence people. Moreover, as in his vote for the Constitution in the Philadelphia Convention, preparation of *The Federalist* was with him an act of compromise, an abrogation of anything like stubborn dogma. The whole procedure of approval of the Constitution, in which he figured so dramatically, was democratic so far as the election laws of the time permitted. In the end the states, in their individual capacities, could take it or leave it, and three of the most important—Massachusetts, Virginia, and New York—almost left it. In this crisis a superb mind, warm heart, and aroused purpose served the turn. Severe critics have charged that all was calculated to enthrone property and privilege under false pretenses. The last humiliation to which too-clever historians will ever be brought is the admission of simple sincerity. Hamilton's actions, when swayed by party as distinct from the public good—and there were such occasions—failed, or, worse than that, invited the opposite result. By contrast, when he ran counter to popular clamor for what he believed to be the general good, he was apt to achieve his aim. His life celebrated the success of moral force, and it is a disservice to truth to tell his story otherwise.

All that we have rehearsed leads up to the finest victory of Hamilton's early manhood. This was in winning New York to the new nation. He proved to be the prophet with honor in his own country. It is proper to compare the ratifying convention at Poughkeepsie with that meeting simultaneously at Richmond and the earlier one at Boston. All three were stressful, but at Poughkeepsie the odds against the Constitution were heaviest. In Massachusetts, Sam Adams was the most celebrated of the oracles who did not find favorable signs in the viscera. He was justly respected, but Massachusetts had recently given the most conspicuous demonstration, in Shays's Rebellion, of the incapacity of a state to maintain law and keep the peace. A farmer—"plough-jogger" he called himself—from the heart of the Shays country, expressed in the Massachusetts convention the sovereign conviction that only the Constitution promised protection against the dismaying disorders that all had witnessed. Moreover, if the new Union was rejected, Massachusetts was the chief of the New England states threatened with being sucked back into British allegiance and incorporation into Canada.

In Virgina the opposition met by Madison and his friends was more powerfully led. It is enough to mention Patrick Henry who had refused to attend the Philadelphia Convention and George Mason who liked so little what he heard there that he refused to sign the Constitution. But the declamation of Henry and the reservations of Mason were more than offset not only by the indefatigable efforts of Madison, Marshall, and others. Governor Randolph had repented of his recalcitrancy, and pled for approval. Washington would surely be President, and was as palpably a member of the convention as had he sat in the midst.

In New York the antagonism was perfectly organized, more massive, and saving elements observable elsewhere were missing. In the beginning only nineteen delegates were for the Constitution, twice as many were for rejection, and these proportions held far into the debates and voting. Governor Clinton, unlike Hancock and Randolph, was the champion of the enemy, with his cohort drilled to protect state autonomy. He had not been a general in the Revolution for nothing. His chosen spokesman on the convention floor was Melancton Smith, as cool and pointed as Patrick Henry was furious and irrelevant. Smith was seconded by John Lansing, Jr., the rising lawyer who with Robert Yates had turned his back on the making of the Constitution in the first place. Clinton, in command of his overwhelming majority, had no doubt of defeating the Constitution outright by an early vote on the whole, by calling for a new convention of the states, or, at worst, by making adherence conditional on alterations in the instrument that would continue the old pernicious anemia.

And yet to have New York join was essential to the operation of the new nation. Otherwise the country would have been cut in two. Remember that the extreme northern and southern portions along the Atlantic strip counted for little. Georgia was only potentially populous and powerful. New Hampshire was a few settlements. Vermont did not exist except in the demands of Green Mountain Boys who were fending off the claims of New Hampshire and New York, at the same time carrying on sporadic but ominous conversation with Canada. Doubts of North Carolina proved well founded. If Virginia did not ratify, as seemed too likely, and New York flung out, that left only Pennsylvania as a distant stepping stone between New England and South Carolina, for New Jersey, Delaware, and Maryland were ancillary. Therefore the battle at Poughkeepsie was more than for New York. It was for a united America.

Governor Clinton was too confident, and as the convention opened let the pro-Constitution fighters get in under his guard. This was by agreeing to the first resolution offered, which was that the document should be debated clause by clause before a vote was taken on the entire instrument. This gave the chance for reason, persuasion, and for delay while Virginia might come in and act as a pry on New York. The manuscript of the brief resolution is preserved with other convention papers in the New-York Historical Society. Significantly, it is in the two hands of Hamilton and his principal colleague, Robert R. Livingston. We can see them putting their heads together for a momentous object. Hamilton had the loyal help of others, including John Jay and James Duane, but throughout he generaled the struggle. He smote in center, darted to the flanks, brought up all reserves he could muster. In his whole life his resources of brain and nerve and feeling were never so completely in play. In contrast to his self-conscious deliverance at Philadelphia, Hamilton forgot himself in his single determination that the convention at Poughkeepsie should never rise until New York was unequivocally in the Union.

Hamilton was fully prepared. Eight years earlier, before Yorktown insured military victory, he had concerted with this same Duane for a new national government that would promise political triumph. Three years along, he and Schuyler had induced New York to prod Congress for a constitutional renovation. At Annapolis he had penned the call for the Philadelphia Convention. Here he had learned more than he taught. His greatest lesson was subordination of himself to a practicable plan to save America. His *Federalist* arguments gave him his own treatise ready to hand. He knew it all by heart, but every utterance at Poughkeepsie was informed with original vigor, was bent to the strategic demands of the moment. He used no tricks, spared no opponent, and was himself not spared, for his extremest sallies at Philadelphia were flung in his face by enemies with good memories.

He had arranged with Sullivan for an express from Portsmouth to announce New Hampshire's adherence. This made the ninth state, and guaranteed the Constitution at least technically. This news took only potential effect in the New York convention, where the ranks of Clinton remained unbroken. Sped by arrangement between Hamilton and Madison, another rider brought the anxiously awaited word that Virginia had come in. As Hamilton proclaimed the dispatch Clinton, in the midst of a speech, lost his hearers.

Perhaps ratification by Virginia, as we look back, turned the tide in New York. At the time chief opponents said not, and for days afterward Hamilton and his friends must hammer away. They rejected any conditional approval, beat off every specious overture. At long last their courage was rewarded when Melancton Smith, with candor that did him honor, acknowledged himself convinced for the Constitution. Lesser men, notably Gilbert Livingston, played their part in breaking away from Clinton, who stood adamant to the end when the huge majority against was turned to the precious majority of three in favor of ratification. Hamilton could afford to agree in recommendations by New York for early amendment. The victory had been won.

New York City, in an elaborate procession of floats led by the federal ship named for Hamilton, had already celebrated the fact of union. When the young champion reached home, fatigued but flushed, the universal gratitude to him was repeated in a new demonstration. The hour was his. That was incidental. It was the practical triumph of the Revolution. It was the birth of the nation as the Declaration of Independence had signaled its conception.

Now remained new tasks in plenty, in which Hamilton would never relax. A fine resolve had been taken. But the piece of paper now endorsed must become a living government, equipped with means to the end. The infant must be nourished, protected, raised to self-command and to stature in the family of mankind. This would produce parental disputes that became determined party differences. Would the lusty youngster, inheritor of a continent, thrive best on liberty to find his own directions, or would he profit by deliberate molding lest inexperience undo his promise?

These two philosophies, equally solicitous, have persisted in our national history. By quirk of fate the political parties espousing them have changed places. The followers of Jefferson, inspired by the liberty of Locke and finding fresh confirmation in early manifestations of the French Revolution, are persuaded that the rights of man are promoted by more instead of less government. On the other hand, devotees of Hamilton, who shared the apprehensions of Hobbes, who lingered in the purlieus of mercantilists, who conceived that wisdom lay in organized control, now plump for individual free will. This, of course, with shadings forced by events and the circumstances of gradual mutation.

The swap of allegiances serves to emphasize the commonplace that the two parties increasingly partake of each other, have grown to be more similar. This commenced early, for doctrine proved less influential than did economic and social development. And it is here that Hamilton's forecast and the result that he worked to bring about is conspicuous. With the exception of a dwindling minority which harbors partial or occasional cause for dissent, the country acknowledges the dominance of the national government, and, correspondingly, contraction of the sphere of the states. This is the fulfillment from Hamilton and his Federalist friends. As population has burgeoned even in proportion to area, as distances have shrunk, as mass production has superseded craftsmanship, the country has become knit and our culture becomes more nearly homogeneous. States' rights, the fences that were erected around local differences, have become increasingly anachronistic.

Hamilton would have brought the states, doubtless too early, to the national heel, making them mere administrative units under an expanding central sovereignty. Indeed, later in life he considered that the larger states should be broken into pieces, further to insure against possible competition with national authority. But the pertinence of Hamilton's project to diminish disparate loyalties in the country is evident all around us. State Governors, formerly lesser presidents in their own domains, now with one voice sue for federal subsidies. States of their own accord join in regional improvements which overlie mere political boundaries. The flow of a river determines the actions of states sharing its valley. In the Great Depression of the thirties states became insolvent, could not put bread and cheese in the mouths of their people. Their vaunted sovereignties then suffered a blow from which they can never recover.

Hamilton hoped to have the national government the magnet, the interests and therefore inclination of all the people assimilated to its strength. When, in the midst of economic collapse, only national power could extend relief, old inhibitions founded on traditions of localism disappeared. Hamilton's prophecies were coming to pass, his purposes were being justified. The way was opened to a new scale of action for

Congress, so different in degree as to be different in kind. If the national legislature could rescue not only millions of the unemployed and the aged, but set up a bread line for business and for the farmers, could it not, must it not, undertake preventive measures as well? The national government became, as Hamilton had wished and foreseen, the planning agency, promoting this sector of the economy, restraining that, coordinating all. The "welfare state" has been used as a term of reproach, approximating to the "slave state." However employed, the phrase contemplates national supremacy. Government responsibility and enterprise is shorn of the imputed evil connotation if we think of it as the democratic organization of our capacities for the common, which includes the individual, benefit.

This is not to say that local and regional divergencies of habit and interest and preference do not exist, or that they should not be consulted, or should not be protected against blanket legislation issuing from Washington. Or that the federal judiciary, so much a dependence of Hamilton's system, should be able to nullify state legislation arbitrarily. This has not happened and is most unlikely ever to happen. As Hamilton remonstrated more than once, we must not, in the heat of argument, "terrify with imaginary dangers." What has gone forward over many years with approval of the American people is the establishment of certain minima judged necessary to the health, prosperity, and safety of the nation. When states, by their incapacity or intransigence, imperil the welfare of the country, they must be aided or commanded to conform to national standards.

The issue at the Poughkeepsie convention was that of state against nation. Governor George Clinton was so proud of his bailiwick that we feel an element of compassion in his defeat. But in antagonizing the Constitution and national unity he would sacrifice the greater to the lesser claim. Though he was overcome by Hamilton, and the Union was made a fact, others, with more pretension to philosophy, sought to qualify national obligation. Kentucky and Virginia resolutions, mutterings at Hartford and nullification in South Carolina, led on to secession and civil war. In our own day we must be treated to rehearsal of this regretful history in the imprecations and threats of Southern states against national authority. That trading ship that tied up to the Jamestown trees and supplied the colonists with slaves brought us a cargo of national sorrow. Not the Negroes, but their status, formed the calamity. Madison knew, even better than Hamilton, that slavery would prove superior to all else in producing dissension in the nation. Is it too harsh to say that afterward, in changing from nationalist to sectionalist, Madison himself fell victim to the evil?

We have come a long way in remedy of wrongs to Negroes, wrongs to whites. Are we to witness now attempted revival of "interposition" by the white South, the state to stand against the patient verdict of the nation? Though he has been dead a century and a half, Alexander Hamilton made this impossible. His dust is valiant. As a Southerner born and bred, with not a Yankee in my acknowledged ancestry on either side, I would say to my defiant brethren below the Potomac: Do not feel that you are made to suffer under compulsion. Hamilton's passion was the expanding prosperity of happiness of the American people. Before we recoil too far at reproof, maybe we can remember to share in his noble hope.

11
F. S. Oliver: A View from England[1]

Measured by years, Hamilton, like Pitt, his contemporary, died young, at the age of forty-seven. It is difficult to picture him as an old man, for the note of his character was youth. It was said of Pitt that "he did not grow, he was cast." At twenty-five he was as good as at forty-five. To a certain extent the same is true of Hamilton, with this difference—that he was cast in the mould of a young man, Pitt in that of an old one. The highest virtue of each was his courage; but Hamilton's courage was eager and impetuous, while the courage of Pitt was remarkable chiefly for its extraordinary endurance. There is in all Hamilton's work—writings and speeches—the intense seriousness of youth. The qualities that made him a great statesman and a terrible combatant were force, lucidity, and conviction. His confidence in himself and in his ideas is amazing, amounting almost to fanaticism. It is possible that the Union of the States would, in one way or another, have achieved itself had he been shot at Yorktown instead of Weehawken, for it was in the order of great events; but the speculative historian would be puzzled to supply the deficiency or explain the method.

If we seek for a complete presentment of the man in what he wrote and spoke we shall not find it. He treats his public ceremoniously and with reserve. An excessive gravity is the rule. Anger is the only passion which is permitted to appear; not a beam of humour or a flash of wit. The whole procedure is stately and tense. This also is in accordance with the nature of youth.

Hamilton has left us no records of his private life from which we can construct a human being. His pen was a sacred weapon which, if it had to write of private affairs, dealt with them as if they had been state papers or a legal précis. The elaborate sprightliness of his correspondence with Gouverneur Morris and Laurens is intimidating. The picture of Hamilton is drawn from the accounts of others. This serious young statesman we gather to have been remarkable in private life chiefly for his high spirits, his good looks, his bright eyes, and his extraordinary vivacity. He loved the society of his fellow-creatures, and shone in it. He loved good wine and good company and beautiful things—even clothes and ruffles of fine lace. He despised slovens and people like Jefferson, who dressed ostentatiously in homespun. He belonged to the age of manners, and silk stock-

[1] From F. S. Oliver, *Alexander Hamilton* (New York: G. P. Putnam's Sons, 1906), pp. 404–7, 410–12, 423–25, 438–39, 444.

ings, and handsome shoe-buckles. In Bagehot's excellent phrase, he was "an enjoying English gentleman"; companionable and loyal, gay and sincere, always masterful and nearly always dignified.

Hamilton would have appeared in all likelihood a more heroic figure in the annals of his country, his memory would have been brighter and more fortunate, his fame more splendid and universal, had his death chanced to coincide with the retirement of Washington instead of falling some eight years later. For he would then have died at the very height of his achievement. Up to this time he had never known defeat. His ideas had prevailed even against the racing tide of popular emotion. He had won a victory not merely against his rivals or over a party. He had fought with the people itself, and had held it till it yielded to his masterful intention. Men knew they had been beaten by him, and as wisdom in due course began to illuminate the confusion of their thoughts, they were satisfied with the issue. They did not love him, for he had treated them rudely, nor ever hesitated to speak his mind; but they feared his great strength, and his unerring sagacity filled them with respect. They felt towards him as one running upon a precipice feels towards a rough deliverer who, catching him by the throat, pitches him on to a heap of rubbish. The escaped victim is at once grateful and indignant; safe, but badly bruised. His dignity is ruffled, and he feels himself to have been a fool. In his heart, perhaps, he thinks that he might have been rescued from his folly with something more of tenderness, and consideration for his feelings.

When the *Farewell Address* and the last of the letters of *Camillus* had been read, and, being read, had worked the revolution in the public mind which their authors intended, the fame of Hamilton was complete. It rested upon a basis of fact, not of opinion. He had arrived at authority and power without incurring popularity, and in a pure democracy it is impossible to conceive any triumph more overwhelming. Up to this time he had been concerned with great events, with the welfare of a nation, in which the exigencies of a party were barely considered. But the party which had grown up and formed itself around his ideas demanded consideration. It had been the instrument of his policy, and after the conclusion of the campaign, like an army which through its conquests has become superfluous, it embarrassed him by its clamours to be exalted from the status of a means to that of an end. Nature had not fitted Hamilton for such a task, and his failure was no great marvel. . . .

The names of Washington and Hamilton, which we honour together, must be honoured in both; for even the spirit of a people is in large measure a tradition with an origin in the effort and suffering of its great men. Washington and Hamilton governed, and directed the policy of the United States when occasion required it against the opinions of the majority. They incurred much hatred in consequence, which even the memory of their services could not keep within bounds. But this bold and uncompromising disregard of opinion is more akin to the special genius of their country, and to the rôle which it has played in the affairs of the world, than the fine discernment, the smooth and pliant dexterity of Jefferson. A man who never disagrees with his countrymen, and who shrinks from unpopularity as the worst of all evils, can never have a share in moulding the traditions of a virile race, though for a time he may make its fashions. Without paradox, we may truly say that Jefferson, in spite of all triumphs, missed every opportunity. He takes rank among the men who succeeded only in success, but had nothing to show for it at the end, save only success. He maintained himself in office and floated gloriously upon a kind of vapour. He built no new defences for his country, and those which he received in custody he barely kept in repair.

Every difficulty which could be postponed was left to a future generation. Every awkward question was adroitly shelved. He was an indulgent and courteous physician, who alleviated the symptoms and soothed the nerves, but lacked both the skill to understand the cause and the courage to treat the root of the disease. His legacy was a lexicon of phrases, a dramatic reputation of homespun equality, and a tangle for posterity to unwind.

The making of the United States owes nothing to Jefferson except a few eccentric fashions, often ungraceful and sometimes absurd. The work of Washington and Hamilton, after a long and dreary interval, passed into worthier hands. Sixty years after the duel at Weehawken the constitution was confirmed. What Hamilton had feared came to pass—a civil war; but what he had given his life for was, as the result of it, secured. The tremendous cost does not lie at his door. To lay so awful a charge against any man is perhaps beyond justice, but as we read of the complacent beatitude of Jefferson, full of years and adulation, our memory calls up a contrasting scene, in which the action is a great rebellion; in which orators of the South invoke not unfairly the protection of his name; in which brave men go into battle with his phrases on their lips; in which the aim of the whole Confederate party, which does him honour, is to destroy the constitution and to break the Union. It is a common event that when a man is dead his name and authority are misused, his words misinterpreted; but Jefferson has to answer a much graver charge than careless sympathy or a mere verbal indiscretion. The Union which he professed to venerate was intrusted to his keeping, and fortune put it in his power to render it secure. He failed even to make the attempt.

The state which Alexander Hamilton had planned and inaugurated Abraham Lincoln completed and confirmed. It is natural to contrast these two men, who in all superficial things were most unlike—in circumstances, manners, age, temper, and appearance. But in the great matter that concerned each of them most nearly they were at one. In many of their qualities they were alike. In both there was the same instinct for reality and contempt for phrases, the same clear judgment and swift decision. Their eyes saw "far and wide," and things appeared to them ever in a splendid and true proportion, rhythmical and harmonious, governed by great laws. In richness of nature they were equals, and equals also in integrity and courage. And in both there was the same rare and consummate mastery of the English tongue, begotten of great thoughts and a fiery sincerity, which not only increases an hundredfold the power of a man in his own day, but continues it as an intimate and living force among generations to whom otherwise he would have been but a remote actor or a great historical shadow. . . .

Hamilton's love for his country was always greater than his love for his countrymen. The emotional side of his nature was stirred by the idea of a nation, rather than by the interests or sufferings of the various masses or classes of which every nation is composed. He was humane, but he was never the philanthropist. At the sight of disorder and injustice he was not swept away by a passionate impatience, but viewed the nature of the evils with a relentless scrutiny. Against the doctrine that some alleviation must immediately be discovered, he was usually found in opposition. His enemies alleged, untruthfully, that his heart was incapable of a generous impulse. What they meant was that he was incapable of acting upon the spur of the moment under no guidance save that of his emotions. His aim was always a complete and permanent cure. He distrusted palliatives and temporary expedients. He would not put forward a remedy for any particular trouble until he had convinced himself that the means proposed would work in harmony with the general principles of his policy.

Hamilton's idea of statesmanship was the faithful stewardship of the estate. His duty was to guard the estate, and, at the same time, to develop its resources. He viewed mankind and natural riches as material to be used, with the greatest possible energy and with the least possible waste, for the attainment of national independence, power, and permanency. A means to this end was certainly the prosperity of the people, but the end itself was the existence of a nation. The emotional spring or motive of his endeavours was not a passionate love or pity for his fellow-creatures, but an overwhelming sense of duty towards his Creator, whose providence had appointed him to the stewardship. This attitude may justly be described as beneficent; but, beyond doubt, it is not the attitude of the philanthropist or of the eighteenth-century Whig.

His foreign policy was dominated by the same principle. The nation had been given into his hands, and the task of keeping it secure was one sufficient for his powers. What happened to other nations was the care and concern of other stewards. He had private sympathies with France and Frenchmen, and to a considerably less extent with England and Englishmen; but these feelings were never allowed to interfere with the performance of what he considered to be his duty as a steward. He judged that the task to which the Almighty had appointed him was, not to put the whole world right, but to keep his own country safe. The view of the philanthropist is widely different. During the ferment of the French Revolution the steadfast refusal of Hamilton to consider anything but the well-being of his own nation was freely judged to be inhuman. The Whig spirit condemned him as a cold and selfish schemer. His enemies had abundant excuse for their attacks, since they believed sincerely that an opportunity had offered itself of changing the whole order of human institutions for the great advantage of the race. Hamilton profoundly disbelieved in this opinion, and held unmoved upon his course. . . .

Hamilton is remarkable among statesmen for the wide extent of his endeavours, and fortunate in having left behind him enough work—done, half done, and attempted—to make us certain of the vision which possessed his mind. A commercial system was an important part of his plan of national policy.

He held no brief for manufactures, merchanting, or agriculture. His aim was a balance, and his idea of the duty of the state was to regulate a just and proportionate development all along the line. He was no advocate of protection for the benefit of any trade or interest unless the advantage of the community as a whole appeared to him to be involved in such a course. If it be true that the tendency of modern American legislation has been to consider the prosperity of certain classes as an end in itself, and to ignore the equal and concurrent development of other branches of industry, his name cannot be invoked. The goal of his policy was a nation supplying the whole of its own needs, which should be independent of foreign countries for its means of subsistence and even for its luxuries. The aim may be open to attack on various grounds; but in view of the variety of soil and climate which is covered by the United States, it cannot be set aside on the ground that it was impracticable. Nor can it be argued against him that individual effort would have been adequate to the task, or that there was any hope of accomplishing it without the intervention of the state.

Like Adam Smith, Hamilton was keenly alive to the advantage of the double bargain. Assuming that in any exchange both parties as a rule are benefited, he considered that it was an advantage to any country if both parties were citizens of that country. If a grower of wheat required a pair of boots, it was better if he bought them from an American cobbler than from a German, for then the profits on both transactions remained in the States.

The wealth of a nation, according to his philosophy, could never be gauged merely by an addition of the private fortunes of its inhabitants. It was necessary to regard the manner in which their capital was employed and invested. From the statesman's point of view a man who had a million sterling fixed in foreign securities, of one kind or another, was a much less valuable asset in computing the wealth of the nation than one who was employing the same sum, or even an immensely smaller sum, in mills or farms in his own country. Even if the income of the former citizen were greater in amount, he was still immeasurably inferior in the imperial balance-sheet. The wealth of a community is to be reckoned mainly by the sums which are fixed within its own borders, giving employment to its own workers. . . .

In putting forward a plea for the respectful consideration of Hamilton's commercial policy, it is necessary to admit that he is in disagreement with the text-books. The national aim was everything in his philosophy. He had not lived long enough to see political economy uplifted into a religion. He took the science for what it was worth, grateful for what he could get out of it. Orthodoxy and heterodoxy in his day were terms of no meaning in this connection. When it served his purpose he made use of the science, but he would have viewed with astonishment any pretensions in it to dictate a course of political action.

12

Cecilia M. Kenyon: Alexander Hamilton: Rousseau of the Right[1]

The thesis of this paper is suggested in the title. It is that Hamilton's political thought was characterized by a heavy emphasis on a concept central to Rousseau's theory, the general will or the public good; that for Hamilton, as for Rousseau, this public good was morally and politically prior to private, individual ends, with which it was occasionally if not frequently in conflict; that the content of this public good as Hamilton visualized it was alien to the prevailing will of the majority of Americans in the early years of the republic; that Hamilton was never able to reconcile his political ideal with his announced view of political reality; and that, as a result, his political theory is confused, contradictory, and basically unrealistic.

It is no light matter to charge Alexander Hamilton with a lack of realism. His writings are filled with references to what has been called the "dark side of humanity"; none of his contemporaries excelled him in constant emphasis on self-interest as man's dominant political motive, or in warnings against the evil passions of man's nature. Every undergraduate knows that Hamilton had a "pessimistic" conception of human nature. Every undergraduate knows, too, that the new government established under the Constitution desperately needed its finances put in order, and that Hamilton accomplished this. How, then, can such a man be called unrealistic? My argument is that Hamilton was not able to accept with equanimity the political facts of life as he saw them, or to relate them successfully to the political ideals he pursued. There remained within his thought an unresolved tension between what he believed man was, and what he believed man ought to be. Such a tension is not of course unusual, but the distance between the *is* and the *ought* in Hamilton's ideas was extreme.

This tension can best be examined by comparing the Hamilton of the Federal Convention with the Hamilton of the Federalist party. They are the same man, but not quite the same thinker.

In his speech of June 18, 1787, Hamilton presented his plan of a political system proper for America. He wanted to do two things: to trans-

[1] From *Political Science Quarterly* 73 (June 1958): 161–78. Reprinted by permission of *Political Science Quarterly* and the author.

fer the attachment of the people from the governments of their separate states to that of the Union; and to construct that government in such a way that it would not be wrecked by the turbulence of democracy and the imprudence of the people.

In the first part of the speech Hamilton analyzed those "great and essential principles necessary for the support of government," [2] and found that all of them then operated in favor of the states rather than of the Union. These principles of political obedience were several—interest, love of power, habit, force, influence. In order to make them support the nation rather than the separate states, Hamilton advocated an almost complete transfer of sovereignty from the latter governments to the former. This proposal is significant because of its apparent assumption that those very passions by which the people were so strongly attached to their state governments might remain sufficiently quiescent to permit the reduction of the states to the position of administrative provinces. It was the most drastic proposal of Hamilton's career and suggests his affinity with the classical tradition of the Legislator as well as his propensity— usually restrained—for Draconian measures.

In the second part of the speech Hamilton defended that part of his plan which provided for a senate and an executive elected for life. These were to serve as checks on the people's will, which would be represented in a popularly elected lower house with limited tenure. The reports of Madison and Yates differ somewhat, and for that reason I shall quote both versions of the crucial passage, beginning with that of Madison.

> In every community where industry is encouraged, there will be a division of it into the few and the many. Hence, separate interests will arise. There will be debtors and creditors, etc. Give all power to the many, they will oppress the few. Give all power to the few, they will oppress the many. Both, therefore, ought to have the power, that each may defend itself against the other. To the want of this check we owe our paper-money instalment laws, etc. To the proper adjustment of it the British owe the excellence of their constitution. Their House of Lords is a most noble institution. Having nothing to hope for by a change, and a sufficient interest, by means of their property, in being faithful to the national interest, they form a permanent barrier against every pernicious innovation whether attempted on the part of the Crown or of the Commons. No temporary Senate will have firmness enough to answer the purpose.[3]

> All communities divide themselves into the few and the many. The first are the rich and well-born, the other the mass of the people. The voice of the people has been said to be the voice of God; and however generally this maxim has been quoted and believed, it is not true in fact. The people are turbulent and changing; they seldom judge or determine

[2] Max Farrand, *Records of the Federal Convention* (New Haven, 1911), I, 365.
[3] *Ibid.*, p. 371.

right. Give, therefore, to the first class a distinct, permanent share in the government. They will check the unsteadiness of the second, and, as they cannot receive any advantage by a change, they therefore will ever maintain good government. Can a democratic Assembly, who annually revolve in the mass of the people, be supposed steadily to pursue the public good? Nothing but a permanent body can check the imprudence of democracy. Their turbulence and uncontrolling disposition requires checks.[4]

I believe these statements constitute the cornerstone of Hamilton's theory. They were made in the course of debates not intended for publication, and in defense of a system which Hamilton should have known had little chance of being adopted. Here Hamilton was his own advocate, not as in *The Federalist,* advocate of a system which he believed to be less than second best. These statements, therefore, require careful explication.

There is, to begin with, the familiar division of men into the few and the many, or the rich and the well born and the mass of the people. There is the further assumption that the interests of these two classes will be different, that they will be in conflict with each other at least part of the time, that the political behavior of each class will be motivated by its interests, and that each class will oppress the other if it gets the chance and has the power to do so. Hamilton does not want this last to happen: "Both, therefore, ought to have the power, that each may defend itself against the other." It was not, then, a class government that Hamilton sought, at least not in the sense of one that had as its end the direct and deliberate promotion of class interests.

Thus far, there is no real difficulty in interpreting Hamilton. But the remainder of the passage, whether as reported by Madison or Yates, is less clear because it is, or appears to be, elliptical. In the second part of the passage, Hamilton suggests that the few will be more reliable in the cause of good government than the many. They, then, should have a share in the governing process, not only to protect their class interests, but in order to secure the national interest. Why will the few be the better guardians of this interest than the many? There seem to be two reasons, though neither is fully expounded.

In both the Madison and Yates versions, Hamilton expresses hostility to change and implies, if he does not explicitly state, that change is inimical to the "national interest" (Madison) or "good government" (Yates). This attitude is accompanied by the assertion that the upper class will be opposed to change. Therefore, the upper class will be the safer guardian of the public interest, not because its members are fundamentally more virtuous than "the people," but because on this particular issue—of change—their separate, class interest coincides with the public interest. It is also suggested (in the Madison but not in the Yates version) that the property of the Lords keeps that body faithful to the national interest in Britain.

4 *Ibid.,* p. 382. Cf. Hamilton's notes prepared for the speech, pp. 387–388.

This is a curious and revealing passage. Consider first the attitude toward change. It seems inconsistent with most of Hamilton's own career, for who among his contemporaries was more constantly in the vanguard of reform than he? He was an ardent Revolutionist; he was wholeheartedly in support of the movement for a new constitution; his proposals as Secretary of the Treasury envisioned a deliberate effort to effect profound changes in the nature of American society; and the very speech in which he expressed this hostility to change was the speech in which he was recommending changes in the existing system far too drastic for his colleagues to accept. In comparison, the fluctuating policies followed by some of the states between 1776 and 1787, and which were so deplored by Hamilton and the other delegates, were the merest piddling. Hamilton was not alone in his quest for stability, but the attitude expressed in this speech, coupled with his own ardent support of sweeping changes, does call for a bit of explaining.

Again, I think, it reveals Hamilton as the modern prototype of the Legislator: take whatever measures are necessary to establish good Laws, and then guard against the undermining forces of future change. It is an attitude which cannot be reconciled with the theory of conservatism expounded by Burke three years later, for not only does it call for radical reconstruction, but it is hostile to the gradual, piecemeal process of adaptation which Burke accepted as characteristic of the natural life of society.

Consider next the assumption implicit in the relationship Hamilton posited between the national interest, the interest of the upper classes, good government, and an inclination or disinclination toward change. He assumes, first, that change is not compatible with good government. He assumes, second, that the upper classes will not be inclined toward change. These two assumptions are explicit. There is a third assumption which is implicit: good government is that which favors or protects the interests of these classes, but not the interests of the many—for it is they who are most likely to advocate change. It is therefore difficult to escape the conclusion that no matter how pure and patriotic Hamilton was in intent, he nevertheless tended to associate good government and the national interest with the interest of the rich, the well born, and the few.

The exact nature of this relationship is difficult to pin down. The national interest is apparently regarded as both different from and separate from that of the many, and different from though not always separate from that of the few. It is, in short, distinct. It is the Hamiltonian counterpart of the Rousseauan general will, that will of the community toward its corporate good, something quite distinct from the will of all, which is the sum of individual and group private, self-interested wills. For Hamilton, this national interest was the primary end of government.

What we are concerned with here, then, is the fundamental question in any political theory: the end of government. It is a question which was not much discussed during the debate over ratification, and its answer was assumed and accepted rather than reached by any genuinely searching analysis even during the Revolutionary debate. This answer was more or less ready-made, and packaged in the doctrine of natural law and natural rights. Now this doctrine is ambivalent in its implications with respect to individuals and social unity. If the emphasis is on natural *law*, as it was during the medieval period, the doctrine tends in the direction of harmony and consensus. But if the emphasis is on *rights*, and especially if happiness is included among the rights, then the doctrine tends toward individualism. It cannot do otherwise, and it was no mere whim which led Rousseau to reject natural-rights doctrine as the basis for his state.

Some political thinkers in America in the eighteenth century realized the ethical implications of their accepted doctrine quite fully, and others did not. Jefferson was among those who did. His poetic passages on the virtues of agrarianism really boil down to a belief that this way of life was the one in which men could most easily fulfill their self-interest without being driven to do so by means which corrupted their integrity or injured their fellows. If Jefferson had an "optimistic" view of human nature, it was because his expectations and hopes were limited not only by a recognition of egoism but by an acceptance of it as ethically legitimate.

Tom Paine, though fully committed to the doctrine of natural rights as a justification for freedom, was not aware of and was not committed to its egoistic ethical implications. Thus his apologia for unicameralism:

> My idea of a single legislature was always founded on a hope, that whatever personal parties might be in the state, they would all unite and agree in the general principles of good government—that these party differences would be dropped at the threshold of the state house, and that the public good, or the good of the whole, would be the governing principle of the legislature within it.
> Party dispute, taken on this ground, would only be, who should have the honor of making the laws; not what the laws should be.[5]

Implicit in this lost hope is the Rousseauan concept of the ideal citizen, he who distinguishes between his private interest and the public good, suppresses the former, and votes wholeheartedly for the latter.

It is my belief that this was also Hamilton's ideal, that he never abandoned it as the standard for judging political behavior, even though he fully realized that it was not in accord with the facts of human nature. This standard, essentially a nonliberal standard, was the springboard of his bitter attacks on the reason and virtue of the people. Thus I would argue that the real difference between Hamilton's and Jefferson's conceptions of human nature and their respective estimates of the people's capacity for self-government lay not in what either believed man actually

[5] Philip S. Foner, ed., *The Complete Writings of Thomas Paine* (New York, 1945), II, 409. From *Dissertations on Government*.

to be, but in what each thought man ought to be and do. As far as politics was concerned, Jefferson thought man should pursue his happiness; Hamilton thought he should seek the national interest. One called for egoistic behavior, the other for altruistic. It was Hamilton who was the greater idealist, Jefferson the greater realist.

Yet Hamilton strove mightily for realism. His method was ambitious, arrogant, and in the great tradition of Plato, Machiavelli and Rousseau. It was the method of the Legislator. The following passages indicate the spirit of Hamilton's belief that man's nature could and should be molded for his own good as well as for that of the state.

> Take mankind in general, they are vicious, their passions may be oper-ated upon. . . . Take mankind as they are, and what are they governed by? Their passions. There may be in every government a few choice spirits, who may act from more worthy motives. One great error is that we sup-pose mankind more honest than they are. Our prevailing passions are ambition and interest; and *it will ever be the duty of a wise government to avail itself of the passions, in order to make them subservient to the public good; for these ever induce us to action.*[6]
>
> The true politician . . . takes human nature (and human society its aggregate) as he finds it, a compound of good and ill qualities, of good and ill tendencies. . . .
>
> With this view of human nature he will not attempt to warp or disturb from its natural direction, he will not attempt to promote its happiness by means to which it is not suited . . . but he will seek to promote his action according to the bias of his nature, to lead him to the development of his energies according to the scope of his passions, and erecting the social organization on this basis he will favor all those institutions and plans which tend to make men happy according to their natural bent, which multiply the sources of individual enjoyment and increase of na-tional resources and strength.[7]

This is the spirit of the Legislator, though, to be sure, infinitely less ruthless than that of Plato or Rousseau. It implies wisdom on the one hand, malleability on the other, and an essentially manipulative relation-ship between the two. In modern times this sort of thing goes by the name of social engineering. Before and during the eighteenth century, it was usually associated with some form of benevolent despotism. Hamilton's problem, like Rousseau's, was to adapt it to republican government. The difficulty for each was the same: the people had the power but not the wisdom, while the leaders had the wisdom but not the power. How, then, could the people be made to follow wisdom? Rousseau's answer was sim-ple: let the Legislator claim for his plans the authority of the gods.

[6] Farrand, *Records,* I, 388–389 (as reported by Yates). Emphasis added.

[7] Richard B. Morris, ed., *Alexander Hamilton and the Founding of the Nation* (New York, 1957), pp. 313–314. Quotation from "Defence of the Funding System," dated 1795–1798 in a hand other than Hamilton's.

Hamilton's answer was not so simple. *The Federalist* papers were an appeal to reason, to self-interest, and to patriotism. Most of his other publicist ventures were similar. In spite of all his diatribes about the weakness of man's reason and the dominance of man's passions, Hamilton never abandoned hope that the better side of man's nature might be reached and might respond. Even the misguided "Caesar" letters, if indeed they were his,* represented an appeal to the people's reason. This was the idealist in Hamilton, relatively pure and certainly indestructible.

His financial program both reveals and represents the other major facet in his answer to the problem of the Legislator. It reflects Hamilton the blundering realist. It is sometimes said that, having failed to secure a permanent share in the structure of government for the upper classes, Hamilton sought to secure their attachment to the new government through his financial program. I believe this is correct. It was a long-term policy and it is succinctly stated in a sentence chosen by Professor Morris to head one of the selections in his excellent anthology. "The only plan that can preserve the currency is one that will make it the *immediate* interest of the moneyed men to cooperate with government in its support." [8] The emphasis on the word *immediate* was Hamilton's. Nearly a decade passed after this was written before he became Secretary of the Treasury, and during that period his fiscal theories were elaborated and matured. But the basic principle remained the same: the private interest of the moneyed class must be made the ally of the national interest. Selfish interest must be made to support the public good. And how? By having the moneyed class's bread buttered by the government. There would, then, be no conflict between its interest and the general welfare. So far, so good. By catering to its self-interest, one class is led to do what is right. This is a fine exercise in political realism.

But what of the other class, the "many" of the June 18 speech in the Convention? In that speech Hamilton implied, though he did not explicitly state, that the interests of the two classes, the few and the many, would be in conflict with each other. Logically, then, any policy which served the interests of the few would injure or at least jeopardize the interests of the many. It is true that Hamilton believed that his fiscal policies would serve the national interest, and it is also true that he believed they would ultimately serve the self-interest of the many. But he *did* emphasize the necessity of attaching the *immediate* interest of the

---

* Professor Kenyon is referring to two letters written under the pseudonym "Caesar" that were published in the New York *Daily Advertiser* on October 1 and 15, 1787. In 1892, the historian Paul Leicester Ford attributed them to Hamilton, and they often have been used to demonstrate that Hamilton favored a dictatorship or monarchy over republican government. For evidence that Hamilton was not the author of these letters see Jacob E. Cooke, "Alexander Hamilton's Authorship of the 'Caesar' Letters," *William and Mary Quarterly*, XVII (January 1960), 78–85 [ed.].

[8] Morris, *Alexander Hamilton*, pp. 335 and 339. From a letter "To a Member of Congress." See Morris' notes for date (probably 1779 or 1780) and addressee.

moneyed class to the government, and he had stated, in *The Federalist,* that men in general were much more likely to act in accordance with what they believed to be their immediate interests than their long-run interests.[9] Logically, therefore, he ought to have expected widespread opposition to the policies he advocated as Secretary of the Treasury, and equally logically he ought to have accepted such opposition with equanimity.

That he did not is well known. His letters and papers of the 1790's are filled with blasts against Jefferson, blasts against the people, blasts against factionalism, and laments about the lack of patriotism in everyone except himself and a few kindred Federalists. Hamilton was genuinely shocked, and he should really not have been. For consider what he had done. In his Convention speech he had posited the existence of two classes, with probably conflicting interests. In the Convention and elsewhere—innumerable times—he had argued that men are dominated by self-interest. He had occasionally, though not consistently, suggested that the upper classes were more likely to be patriotic than the mass of the people.[10] Nevertheless, he had sought the support of this group, not by appealing to their patriotism, altruism, or even long-run interest, but by appealing deliberately to their *immediate* self-interest. It was to them that he held out the carrot. And it was the other class, the many, the mass of the people, upon whom he now called for patriotism, and/or appreciation of long-run self-interest. It was from this class that he now expected and demanded the greater exercise of both reason and virtue. In so doing, he was not logical, he was not realistic, and he led his party straight down the road to extinction.

There were times during the 1790's and early 1800's when he half-realized what he had done and cast about for practical solutions. In 1799 he advocated road-building as a method of courting the people's good will. It was a measure "universally popular." He also advocated the institution of a society with funds for the encouragement of agriculture and the arts. Such a program, he wrote, would "speak powerfully to feelings and interests of those classes of men to whom the benefits derived from the government have been heretofore the last manifest." [11]

Before commenting on this proposal, I should like to place beside it a passage from another attempt by Hamilton to explain his party's failure to win popular support.

> Nothing is more fallacious than to expect to produce any valuable or permanent result in political projects by relying merely on the reason of

[9] Number 6. In the Modern Library edition at p. 30.

[10] H. C. Lodge, ed., *The Works of Alexander Hamilton* (New York, 1885), VII, 241. In the eighth number of his "Examination of Jefferson's Message to Congress of December 7, 1801," Hamilton wrote that the safety of the republic depended, among other things, "on that love of country which will almost invariably be found to be closely connected with birth, education, and family."

[11] From a letter to Jonathan Dayton, 1799, Lodge, *Works,* VIII, 518–519.

men. Men are rather reasoning than reasonable animals, for the most part governed by the impulse of passion. This is a truth well understood by our adversaries, who have practised upon it with no small benefit to their cause; for at the very moment they are eulogizing the reason of men, and professing to appeal only to that faculty, they are courting the strongest and most active passion of the human heart, vanity! It is no less true, that the Federalists seem not to have attended to the fact sufficiently; and that they erred in relying so much on the rectitude and utility of their measures as to have neglected the cultivation of popular favor, by fair and justifiable expedients.[12]

These comments reveal the very deep conflict in Hamilton's thought. In the later one (1802), Hamilton saw his party's error in having relied "so much on the rectitude and utility of their measures as to have neglected the cultivation of popular favor, by fair and justifiable expedients." In the earlier letter, Hamilton admitted that the benefits of the new government had thus far not been "manifest" to certain classes—in the context, the many. In both letters, the two Hamiltons show through: the idealist, sure of the rightness of his policies and regretful that the people were neither rational nor virtuous enough to accept them on their merits; the realist, ever ready to seek support by the enlistment of man's worse (but never worst) nature. He had deliberately done the latter to win the moneyed class over to his side in the early 1790's. Now, at the end of the decade, he proposed to do the same thing for the majority. But it was a classic case of too little, too late. He had, in effect, made a partnership between the national interest and a special class interest. I am not sure whether he intended this partnership to be permanent and exclusive. He did intend it to be universally benevolent; its fruits were meant to trickle down and be enjoyed by everyone. Yet there remains that implicit assumption of the June 18 speech: a desire for change is more likely to exist among the many than the few, because good government will leave the interests of the many unsatisfied. There is an ambivalence in Hamilton's theory which I find it impossible to resolve.

My primary interest is not to decide whether he was or was not a class theorist, however. His political ideas are significant and rewarding because they reflect and illumine a difficult stage in the evolution of liberal democratic thought.

As I have suggested earlier, Hamilton's basic difference from Jefferson, and I think from most Americans of the era, was his rejection of the ethical egoism implicit in natural-rights doctrine. This difference ought not to be exaggerated. No American of the age was an advocate of unrestrained self-interest, and the concept of a general interest which may be separate from and in conflict with private interests was generally present. It was at the root of the Revolutionary generation's distrust of fac-

[12] From a letter to James A. Bayard, April 1802, *ibid.*, p. 597.

tion. Nor, on the other hand, did Hamilton advocate or desire an absolute subjection of the individual to the state. It was rather that Hamilton, like Paine, was more extreme in his condemnation of egoism and in fact represented an older view of the proper end of government.

This older view was preindividualistic, premodern. It was the medieval view that government existed for the good of society, and its end therefore was the common good. One of the things that distinguishes modern theory from medieval is the greater difficulty modern theorists face in defining this concept, the common good. There are a number of reasons for this; among them are the greater unity of medieval society by virtue of Christianity, and the relative roles of legislative and customary law in the governing process. The point is that the existence of a common good was assumed in the earlier period, and its content was easier to define. But introduce into the political system the concept of ethical individualism combined with the practice of legislative determination of policy, and the difficulty of defining the common good is obvious—by hindsight. It was not obvious in the sixteenth century, or the seventeenth. It became increasingly obvious to Americans in the first three quarters of the eighteenth century because they were virtually self-governing communities and met the problem in the everyday conduct of their affairs. Madison's tenth *Federalist* was the culmination of a long and painful process of thought on this subject. Madison, and I think he was here accurately reflecting the dominant opinion of his contemporaries, seems to hover ambivalently between two conceptions: (1) that of an ever elusive public good somehow distinct from the clashing of selfish and private interests; (2) that of the public good as a reconciliation or compromise of these same interests.

Hamilton clung more closely to the former view. One of the reasons may have been his late arrival as a practitioner of republicanism. In this respect he was very like Tom Paine, and I think a comparison of their lives from the time of their arrival in this country will show their fundamental kinship, though one was politically of the Right, the other of the Left. Each devoted himself without reserve to the service of his country. For each of them this entailed a sacrifice of the private interests common to most men—property, or at least greater property for both, and for Hamilton, the welfare of his family. For him, the sacrifice in the end was extreme. Among the documents he wrote before the duel there is one which concludes with a sentence profoundly symbolic of his entire life. After recounting his abhorrence of the practice on religious and ethical grounds, his unwillingness to give grief to his wife and children, his feeling of responsibility to his creditors, his intention of reserving fire on the first and perhaps even the second shot, Hamilton concluded: "The ability to be in future useful, whether in resisting mischief or in effecting good, in those crises of our public affairs which seem likely to happen, would probably be inseparable from a conformity with public prejudice in this particular." [13] He was indeed a patriot.

At every step of his career (except possibly the row with Washington), Hamilton—and Paine—put country first, self second. In a sense this was not sacrifice but fulfillment of their deepest desires. But insofar as it was fulfillment, it marked them off from other men. Each was in essence a political being, intensely so; each realized his nature, his self-interest, in devoting himself to the public good. The personality of each reinforced his conception of this public good as something better than and different from a mere reconciliation of individual and group interests. Neither ever ceased to regard his standard of political behavior as the standard proper for every man. For Paine, this meant an ever recurring optimism punctuated with bitter disillusion. For Hamilton, it meant a steady and self-nourishing pessimism. Both were idealists, and both shared the same ideal: a Rousseauistic community in which men were citizens first and individuals second. Hamilton knew his ideal was incapable of realization, and he sought a substitute which might still achieve the same goal—a government that governed in the national interest. The substitute was an alliance of upper-class interests with the national interests.

Jefferson and Madison opposed him partly because of the nature of the alliance, partly because the content of his conception of the public good was too nationalistic for their tastes. I do not think either he or they ever fully realized the more theoretical, and I think more fundamental, difference between them. The difference was subtle but profound. Jefferson and Madison were committed to the ethical individualism implicit in natural-rights theory: the end of the government as the protection of life, liberty, and the pursuit of happiness. This doctrine recognizes the political legitimacy of egoism. Hamilton was only partly committed to the doctrine. The basic difference between him and most of his contemporaries was that his conception of the public good was the older, corporate one, and theirs was the newer one in which the corporate element, though still present, had given ground to individualism.

The tension between these two concepts, a corporate and an individualistic public good, can be observed throughout the Revolutionary period. It underlay the colonial opposition to the British theory of virtual representation; it was central to the debates in the Federal Convention, and it was a major element in the ratification controversy. During the latter, James Winthrop seemed to be speaking directly to Hamilton when he wrote, "It is vain to tell us that we ought to overlook local interests. It is only by protecting local concerns that the interest of the

[13] Morris, *Alexander Hamilton*, p. 608.

whole is preserved." [14] This was the spirit of the future of American politics: local interests, sectional interests, class interests, group interests, individual interests. The conflict, compromise, or sometimes reconciliation of these interests was to be the main determinant of public policy, not the Hamiltonian ideal of a transcendent national interest, not the Rousseauan ideal of an overriding general will.

Here lay the heart of Hamilton's dilemma. As a genuine patriot of his adopted country, he was loyally committed to the practice of republican government. His grave doubts about the success of the experiment stemmed from his rejection of ethical individualism coupled with his acceptance of egoism as a fact of political life. The real trouble was that his end was incompatible with the means which, as a patriot, he had to accept. Logically, he should have ended up with some sort of philosopher-king theory, and he did have leanings in that direction. Since he was not a closet philosopher, this way out of the dilemma was closed. There was really no way out. The way he chose, an alliance of one special interest group with what he conceived to be the national interest, simply stimulated opposition to the latter because he *had* linked it to the former. So he intensified in both groups the selfishness which was his enemy, and encouraged the growth of factions which he so deplored. That he was regarded by his contemporary opponents as a representative of class interests is perhaps regrettable, but their misunderstanding of him and his motives was no greater than his misunderstanding of them and theirs. They were wrong in believing him to be an oligarch, but they were right in believing that his political ideals were opposed to theirs. His were corporate, theirs individualistic. His end was not logically antirepublican, but, in the context of public opinion at the time, it was bound to make him doubtful that it could be achieved under republicanism. It was unlikely that the people, left to themselves, would faithfully pursue the national interest. They needed a Legislator. Hamilton volunteered for the job.

In this aspect of his thought—means rather than ends—I would again argue that Hamilton's ideas were subtly but profoundly different from those of most of his contemporaries. They all talked a lot about man's passions and emphasized the necessity of taking these into account when constructing a constitution. I think Hamilton had a much more ambitious opinion concerning the extent to which these passions could be actively used—manipulated—by politicians. Consider the benevolent passage quoted above in which he outlined the principles a wise politician must follow if he would lead the people toward the achievement of their happiness and the national interest. Consider his injunction that "it will ever be the duty of a wise government to avail itself of the passions, in order to make them subservient to the public good. . . ." Con-

[14] From the *Agrippa Letters*, P. L. Ford, ed., *Essays on the Constitution of the United States (Brooklyn,* 1892), p. 17.

sider his proposal in the Convention to transfer sovereignty from the state governments to the national government in order to transfer the people's passions from the former to the latter. And consider his tendency during the 1790's to regard the people as dupes who had been led astray by designing politicians. All this adds up to a fairly consistent picture. The people are clay in the hands of the potter, but the potter may be either wise and virtuous, or shrewd and vicious. The former will give them what they ought to have, the latter will pretend to give them what they think they want.

As a Legislator, Hamilton was initially successful. The conditions which existed during and shortly after the inauguration of the new government were congenial for the exercise of his special talents. Afterward, his effectiveness as politician and statesman declined with remarkable rapidity. Both his ends and his means were alien to the ideals and the experience of the people he sought to lead. Their ideals were liberal and individualistic, and their practice of self-government had rendered them impervious to the benevolent molding Hamilton had in mind to impose upon them. They would govern themselves. It was inevitable that he should be rejected.

Though his corporate idealism and manipulative methods be rejected, the central problem for which he offered them as solutions cannot be ignored. That problem is basic: how, in a nation governed by the people, is agreement on the public good to be obtained and put into effect? In this process, what is and should be the relationship between wisdom and public opinion, between private interest and national interest? These were fundamental questions when Hamilton grappled with them, and they still are. We have not yet worked out a satisfactory theory that will tell us precisely when the individual is ethically obligated to sacrifice his interests or when he may legitimately refuse to do so. Hamilton's plea for altruism in politics is relevant and salutary. The pursuit of selfish individual or group interests unrestrained by any sense of the general welfare may produce such bitter and divisive competition as to destroy the unity and consensus which sustain individual freedom as well as national strength.

Yet the Hamiltonian ideal, of each citizen placing the national interest before his own, is not without its dangers. It places an indefinite limitation on the exercise of individual freedom. There must be limits, of course, but this limit is an abstraction, and abstractions, when reified, are powerful forces to set against the solitary right and will of the individual. The national interest, with some exceptions such as sheer survival, will always be an elusive concept, its substance difficult to determine. Therefore there are practical reasons for refusing to concede it a permanently and categorically preferred position in all contests with individual, separate interests.

These practical reasons are merely corollaries of the main one. The main one is the ethical priority of the individual and his welfare as the proper and ultimate end of government. To this end, the national interest is logically and ethically secondary; to this end, the national interest must stand in the relationship of means. At least it must if one still accepts the Declaration of Independence as a statement of the purposes of American government. Hamilton mistook the means for the end, and tipped the scale too far in the direction of the national interest. In so doing he gave it ethical priority over the demands of the individual.

Such a priority seems to necessitate resort to manipulative techniques in order to induce the individual to forego what he conceives to be his own interest. Thus Plato resorted to the persuasion of the myth of the metals, Rousseau to the authority of the gods. In his idealistic moods, Hamilton appealed to reason; in his self-consciously realistic moods, he attempted a calculated alliance between the national interest and selfish class interests. This was bound not only to accentuate conflict between factions, but to obscure the national interest itself. Hamilton's idealism was thus vitiated by a would-be realistic policy which was both shrewd and obtuse at the same time.

The fault lay in the man himself. Hamilton's idealism was genuine and profound. It was also touched with arrogance. His penchant for what he regarded as realism was a fundamental trait of his character; he liked to think of himself as a skillful maneuverer of men's emotions. Thus his realism was likewise touched with arrogance. It may be that this dual arrogance was subjectively justified—Hamilton *was* a superior individual. But in the politics of republican government, such arrogance may operate to blind its possessor to that which he must see and understand if he is to achieve a successful blend of idealism and realism. That is the nature of man, or, more specifically, the motivation and behavior of the voter. It was Hamilton's fortune to serve his country well for a brief and crucial period in its history; it was his fate to be rejected by the countrymen whose ideals he did not share, and whose politics he did not understand.

Afterword:
Hamilton Known and Unknown

Historians, we have already suggested, have begun to display a renewed interest in and appreciation of Alexander Hamilton. His advocacy of realpolitik and of national planning, both currently fashionable, would guarantee as much. Broadus Mitchell's two-volume biography is simply the most ambitious product of this resurgence which includes Clinton Rossiter's impressive pro-Hamiltonian study and John C. Miller's admirable *Alexander Hamilton: Portrait in Paradox,* the most balanced of recent works on the subject.

The subtitle of Miller's work is most suggestive. Today's practitioners of the craft of history see Hamilton and his age as far more complex than filiopietistic historians such as James C. Hamilton or the Federal historians, Hildreth and Lodge chief among them, had realized. It was a time of paradoxes, inconsistencies, divergences. Hamilton, recent scholars are aware, was contradictory and even irrational at times. They see him possessed of some clearcut characteristics and attitudes, to be sure, and these are unwaveringly his: a revolutionist *manqué,* in whom the revolution's pull was strong but never as strong as the pull of property rights or aristocratic notions; a candid champion (at the Federal Constitutional Convention) of strong central government as well as of the "private interests" of the "rich and the well born"; a leader of the "court faction" as well as an anglophile; a marriage broker for the special interests of "moneyed men" and the larger interests of orderly national government; an advocate of a "natural aristocracy" of virtue and talent; a statesman ever fearful of self-interest, mob passions, democratic government, levelling impulses; a party leader singularly lacking in tact and patience; a statesman intent upon an Anglo-American rapprochement as an indispensable foundation for his financial system—so intent, according to Julian Boyd, that he made some very indiscreet admissions to Major George Beckwith in 1789–1790, as he would to George Hammond, the English minister, about four years later.

But even those most hostile to Hamilton now admit to a more generous portrait than painted earlier by a legion of pro-Jeffersonian scholars. Not even his greatest critics—such as Adrienne Koch, Dumas Malone, Cecelia Kenyon—make unequivocally negative commentary. Perhaps, we may speculate, our age is simply too complex and too mature, our scholars too sophisticated, to accept the earlier stark simplicities of portraitists. Perhaps we have come to the disenchanting awareness that all our gods have failed, that all our saints are found to have feet of clay, that only books may be consistent; men are not. After all, Hamilton's great rival—and his most common foil for those sketching simple antinomies—is now found to possess "a darker side"; Jefferson can no longer be drawn as the unflawed libertarian, a fact making the case for Hamilton seem stronger.

There is, then, a "lighter side" for Hamilton. There is the Hamilton who, consciously or not, brought together the discrete elements that came to represent the Federalist Party; there is Hamilton the creator who offered a coherent and intricate program of economic development, the innovator who would stimulate national growth and raise national living standards as well as give benefits to business, the patriot who was at least as concerned with a broad view of the national interest as with the need for immediate political support, the nationalist who was driven by his vision—so fashionable nearly two centuries later—of the United States as a centralized and industrialized world power.

More and more, it seems, historians are seriously asking questions about Hamilton, questions reflecting their doubts about the possibility of rendering ultimate and unambiguous judgments. Did Hamilton advocate *only* government by the affluent? Was the purpose of his program *only* to enrich a class? Did his commentary on the Constitution suggest *only* opposition to republicanism, and is such thought at the taproot of his political economy? How did Hamilton define "democracy" and, equally significant, was he alone among public men in this definition? How important a role must we give to his largely unknown early years?

No reconstruction of Hamilton's political and social thought can fail to deal with such questions or to treat with conflicting theses about the man. But part of the difficulty involved in this reconstruction is that the essential Hamilton was no closet thinker, that he had an athletic rather than a wholly theoretic cast of mind. Partly the difficulty is rooted in the obscurity of Hamilton's childhood which blocks our understanding of the early mix and the shaping factors of his life. Partly, too, the real Hamilton is obscured by time. Posterity creates a heavy price in dehumanization from the great man. "Every hero becomes a bore at last," observed Emerson. But greatness, once it has been seen in works and ideas, demands an approach—however inadequate—to the man himself.

Why, the student may ask, do we need greater understanding of Hamilton? To answer such a question poses others. To what extent, if at all, should government participate in the development of our national economy? What special considerations should government extend to varying economic interests? In promoting economic growth, what should be the roles of central, state, and local governments? In seeking answers to such questions, we see the relevance of Hamilton today. For these questions, so urgently demanding attention and solutions at present, were nearly identical to those with which our first Secretary of the Treasury grappled. They reflect more than his tentative groping about for ways in which a new nation defines its social and economic philosophy; they tell us that the substantive issues remain viable.

Lewis Namier, possibly England's great historian of the last half century, once claimed with as much truth as paradox that men "imagine the past and remember the future." Namier meant that men read the qualities of our own society into the past and draw upon erroneous analogies from history in order to predict the course of events. Such a practice lends itself beautifully to Hamilton, or to phrase it another way, he is heartbreakingly vulnerable to it. Indeed Hamilton more than most in the late eighteenth and early nineteenth centuries lends himself to such a reading of history because, more than most, he prefigured the present; because—refined, resifted, repaired—his lessons are still with us; because he asked the same hard questions confronting us; because, in a way unique among men of his times, Hamilton lived outside of them and, therefore, in seeking to learn how he met challenges, we may face similar ones today and profit from his experience; because with Hamilton as with Gavin Stevens in Faulkner's *Intruder in the Dust,* "the past is never dead. It's not even past."

Bibliographical Note

This assessment of the Hamiltonian literature is very selective, confining itself to the major studies of the man, his life and thought, and to those works that are immediately relevant.

The most useful book is the new and definitive, but still unfinished, collection of Hamilton's own writings, edited by Harold Syrett and Jacob Cooke, *The Papers of Alexander Hamilton* (New York, 1961–   ). Given its degree of completeness and its rigorous scholarly editing, this multivolumed work will eventually surpass in usefulness the earlier collections of Hamilton papers: John C. Hamilton, ed., *The Works of Alexander Hamilton,* 7 vols. (New York, 1851) and, more important for students of Hamilton, Henry Cabot Lodge, ed., *The Works of Alexander Hamilton,* 12 vols. (New York, 1904).

"Alas," observed Merrill Peterson, "it is inescapable": scholars must be forever entrapped by their loyalties to Jefferson or to Hamilton. Such is the case with Broadus Mitchell. His two-volume biography, *Alexander Hamilton* (New York, 1957–1962), is exhaustively researched, highly documented and near-definitive; but marred by a partisan anti-Jeffersonian point of view. John C. Miller's *Alexander Hamilton: Portrait in Paradox* (New York, 1959) is better balanced as well as more analytical in approach, beautifully complementing Mitchell's biography. Nor should Nathan Schachner's *Alexander Hamilton* (New York, 1946) be ignored. It is a gracefully executed account of Hamilton which, until the two later studies appeared, was much relied upon by students of the period. The Jeffersonian historian, Claude Bowers, in his *Jefferson and Hamilton: The Struggle for Democracy in America* (Boston, 1925) again confirms the validity of Peterson's Manichean comments on Jeffersonian and Hamiltonian scholarship. An audacious and colorful evocation of the early national period and the principal actors, it is too journalistic in approach as well as too hostile to Hamilton. Henry Bam-Parkes' *The American Experience* (New York, 1959) agrees with Bowers' judgment and frankly states that Hamilton's financial policies were shaped out of a concern for the interests of a financial aristocracy. Even more severe in his indictment of Hamilton is Joseph Charles who finds, in his provocative study—*The Origins of the Party System* (Williamsburg, 1956)—that Hamilton's plan to strengthen "the moneyed interest" was "flawless." The doyen of anti-Hamiltonians is Henry Adams. His nine-volume, *History of the United States During the Administration of Thomas Jefferson and James Madison* (New York, 1965) is a brilliant but biased work which has long dominated early National Period studies. For example, Adams' account of the famous "great beast" epithet which he claimed, without documentation, Hamilton had applied to the common people has had an enduring impact on the image of the first Secretary of the Treasury.

Hamilton has not lacked in defenders. In addition to J. C. Miller, Broadus Mitchell, and Nathan Schachner, there is Louis Hacker, whose *Alexander Hamilton in the American Tradition* (New York, 1957) pictures Hamilton as an apostle of unity rather than a defender of a limited class interest or English imperial policy. Charles Beard has also called attention to Hamilton's contributions, in his *Economic Origins of Jeffersonian Democracy* (New York, 1915) and *The Idea of National Interest* (New York, 1934), which treats of him as the champion of realpolitik. A more sophisticated appreciation and analysis is offered by Clinton Rossiter, *Alexander Hamilton and the Constitution* (New York, 1964). Finally, it is worth recalling Frederick S. Oliver's *Alexander Hamilton* (London, 1906), since this biography remains a useful introduction to Hamilton. It is a perceptive work, surprisingly so given the conditions of scholarship at the time of publication, and contains some fascinating and instructive ideas about its protagonist.

There are a number of historical studies that cover aspects of Hamilton's life or, in the context of large-scaled treatment, aspects of his contributions. Witness, for instance, Julian Boyd's *Number 7: Alexander Hamilton's Secret Attempts to Control American Foreign Policy* (Princeton, 1964). A fascinating detective story, it is a blow-by-blow account of Hamilton's unauthorized revelations of United States commercial policies in 1789–1790. Manning Dauer, *The Adams Federalists* (Baltimore, 1953) distinguishes the moderate Federalism of John Adams from the more extreme version practiced by Hamilton and his votaries. Hamilton's fiscal and credit policies are presented in a measured yet admiring account by Bray Hammond, in *Banks and Politics in America from the Revolution to the Civil War* (Princeton, 1957), and is indispensable for an understanding of the interlocking character of banking and politics in the National Period. D. R. Dewey, *Financial History of the United States* (New York, 1922), includes a useful summary of Hamilton's financial measures. Clarence L. Ver Steeg, *Robert Morris: Revolutionary Financier* is a very useful supplementary work on the Revolutionary and postRevolutionary financial scene. Nathan Schachner's *The Founding Fathers* (New York, 1954) is useful but unnecessarily detailed. A thoughtful and provocative survey of the National Period is provided by Marcus Cunliffe, in *The Nation Takes Shape* (Chicago, 1959). William Chambers, a political scientist, has written a highly competent political survey, *Political Parties in a New Nation: The American Experience, 1776–1809* (New York, 1963). John C. Miller's contribution to the New American Nation Series, *The Federalist Era, 1789–1801* (New York, 1960) is a carefully researched synthesis and survey. The notable work on Jay's Treaty is Samuel Bemis' *Jay's Treaty: A Study in Commerce and Diplo-*

macy (New York, 1923). Bemis concludes that the treaty might well be "more aptly . . . called Hamilton's treaty." Another historian who possibly overemphasizes Hamilton's influence on National Period diplomacy is Alexander De Conde, *Entangling Alliance: Politics and Diplomacy Under George Washington* (Durham, 1958).

Index